Exploring New Roads

Neil Munro, 1898, by William Kellock Brown (1856–1934)
Photo courtesy of Edinburgh City Arts Centre

Exploring
New Roads

ESSAYS ON NEIL MUNRO

edited by

Ronald W. Renton and Brian D. Osborne

First published by House of Lochar in 2003
This paperback edition published 2007

British Library Cataloguing in Publication Data
A catalogue record of this book is available from the British Library

ISBN 978 1 899863 92 1

The publisher acknowledges support from the Scottish Arts Council
towards publication of this volume

Scottish
Arts Council

Typeset by XL Publishing Services, Tiverton
Printed in Great Britain
by SRP Ltd, Exeter
for House of Lochar
Isle of Colonsay, Argyll PA61 7YR

To the memory of
Annabel Morrison
Head Teacher
Kilmorich and Inveraray
Founder Member of The Neil Munro Society
Clach air a'Charn

Contents

Introduction   ix

1   Neil Munro: Biography   1
    Lesley Lendrum

2   'Place of my people': Neil Munro's Inveraray   12
    Rae MacGregor and Brian Wilkinson

3   Landscape and Scenery in the Writings of Neil Munro   19
    Rennie McOwan

4   Commercial Success and Critical Acclaim   30
    Brian D. Osborne

5   John Splendids and Jaunty Jocks: Neil Munro,
    the Highlands and Scottish Fiction   37
    Douglas Gifford

6   Stories in 'the Highland Manner': *The Lost Pibroch
    and Other Sheiling Stories*   68
    Ronald W. Renton

7   *John Splendid* and Scottish History   79
    Edward J. Cowan

8   Symposium: Mr Neil Munro's *John Splendid*   95
    *Andrew Lang, Fiona Macleod, William Wallace,
    William Sharp*

9   'From so trivial a thing': Tradition and Individual Talent
    in Neil Munro's *Gilian the Dreamer*   104
    Beth Dickson

10 The Post '45 Novels: *Doom Castle, The Shoes of Fortune,
    Children of Tempest*   122
    Ronald W. Renton

11 Some Reflections on Neil Munro's *The Daft Days*   155
    Ronald Armstrong

12 A Shining Book: Mr Neil Munro's *The Daft Days*   163
    A.T. Quiller-Couch

13 Re-reading *The New Road*   166
    Gerard Carruthers

14 Neil Munro's New Romance *(The New Road)*   183
    John Buchan

15 The Humorous Short Fiction of Neil Munro   186
    Brian D. Osborne

16 The Poetry of Neil Munro: An Outline   196
    Bob Preston

17 A Review of Neil Munro's Late Journalism   207
    Beata Kohlbek

18 The Modern Novel   223
    Neil Munro

19 Bibliography   233
    James Beaton

20 Notes on Contributors   241

Introduction

The idea of publishing a collection of essays on the life and work of Neil Munro came from Douglas Gifford, Professor of Scottish Literature in the University of Glasgow, who felt that such a collection would be a very appropriate tribute to the memory of Annabel Morrison, a founder member of The Neil Munro Society, who died suddenly in April 1998. Such a collection would break new ground and promote knowledge and appreciation of an author who is increasingly coming to be recognised as a very significant figure on the Scottish literary scene, but who until recently had failed to attract much scholarly attention.

We are delighted to have been able to bring together such a varied collection of essays which we hope will provide readers with an informed and balanced view of the various aspects of Munro's work. We are deeply grateful to all our contributors for their contributions to this collection, for their enthusiasm for the project and for their individual insights into Munro's writing, career and environment

We would also wish to thank Dr Hermann Völkel for permission to draw on the bibliography in his 1994 thesis *Das literarische Werk Neil Munros* for the bibliography in this volume. Our thanks are also due to Margaret Renton for her considerable secretarial labours in bringing this project to completion. The Committee and the whole membership of The Neil Munro Society have been most supportive of this project since its inception and our thanks go to them for their interest and help.

Ronald W. Renton
Brian D. Osborne

Neil Munro, 1907, from The Bailie

Neil Munro: Biography

LESLEY LENDRUM

'Neil Munro – the very name o' him is grand to hear. A grand name, wi' something baith braw and hamely in it. A name wi' a sniff o' peat reek, the bloom o' the heather, a skirl o' the pipes, an' a glint o' the claymore. A tartaned name, that stirs Scottish blood.' So said a Scottish soldier when Munro visited the front during World War I ... if we are to believe a Canadian obituary. Munro himself would have laughed at the apocryphal rigmarole, yet ruefully, for such 'sentiments' reflect a certain contemporary attitude towards himself and his work.

When he left Inveraray at eighteen his own emotional make-up as a Gaelic-speaking Highlander had something of that conventional romanticism, further fuelled by his homesickness in the Glasgow streets. But he also knew very well the everyday realities of late Victorian Argyll. He felt in his bones that he must leave if he was to develop, and he clung to the idea of development through thick and thin, even unto 'the ruthless deromanticizing of history', to use Francis Russell Hart's description of *The New Road*.[1]

All the same, the Inveraray where Munro was born in 1863 had been a pretty good place to grow up in, half idyllic, and still very 'highland' in the unselfconscious sense that eludes the de-mythologisers. It was small enough to be a community, yet as capital of vast Argyll, with law-courts and lawyers and the Duke in his castle, it had the bustle and importance of a little city-state.

Through his mother and his grandmother, widow of a Glen Aray shepherd, Munro had a direct link back to the old Gaelic-speaking pastoral life in the hinterland of Inveraray. Gaelic was in fact the first language he heard and learned. He was an only child (a twin sister being stillborn) at a time when large families were common, and in addition he had no father. If he knew who his father was, he kept the secret to the end, even from his own children. Such mysteries in such places gather patrician moss.

Of course there were hardships, never chronicled by him, but his lifelong attachment to Inveraray suggests he was happy there on the

1

whole. His mother, who was 33 when he was born, worked as a maidservant to support them and provided an environment that was loving and secure.

Though Munro lacked a father he never lacked benign father figures. One was Henry Dunn Smith, head teacher at the parish school where Munro acquired a sound basic education. He also read whatever he could lay hands on – Smollett, eighteenth-century Gothic romances such as *The Mysteries of Udolpho*, Surtees, 'penny bloods', Grant's *Romance of War* – though somehow no Scott came his way in those days. Many a time he played truant and read in the forest or on the ledge of the prison ramparts, legs dangling over the shore far below. In official free time there was plenty of fun with Charlie Maitland and other chums, joyful possessors of 'the key of the street and the freedom of the seashore and the forest'.[2]

In 1875 his mother married Malcom Thomson, a widower much older than herself, retired governor of Inveraray Jail. His relationship with his new stepson seems to have been straightforward and amicable. About that time also Munro left school, and after an unhappy stint of farmwork was found a place in a solicitor's office. His employer, William Douglas, was a kindly bachelor. After seeing a reporter using shorthand in court one day, Munro sent off for a textbook and taught himself to write shorthand. One of many other ploys was joining the Young Men's Mutual Improvement Society. An essay he wrote on the Inveraray fishing fleet for the Society's magazine was good enough to make a local man ask why he did not go in for journalism. The seed did not fall on stony ground.

The thought of a life of days confined in a law office was beginning to appal Munro. In June 1881 he threw up his job and went to Glasgow on *The Lord of the Isles* with his friend Archie Mackellar. As the steamer passed Kenmore Point and Inveraray receded astern, he comprehended for the first time how dear the old place was to him.[3]

But he had taken an irrevocable step and must now be self-reliant. Once in Glasgow he found work as a clerk with a potato merchant, then as a cashier with an ironmonger. Meanwhile he kept up his shorthand and submitted articles and verse to country newspapers, becoming Glasgow correspondent for the *Oban Times*. Not till 1884 did he obtain a job on a newspaper, the *Greenock Advertiser*, which promptly closed down. He went back to Glasgow and soon found work on the *Glasgow News*, later transmogrified into the *Glasgow Evening News*.

He also found new lodgings in the house of Hugh Adam, a coppersmith from Kilbarchan. In July 1885 he married Jessie, the

Adams' oldest daughter. Though he was only twenty-two, his life was taking the shape it would always retain. Of its four bastions three were already there: Argyll, the *News* and his family.

His journalistic talents were recognised from the start by the editor of the *News*, James Murray Smith, who made him chief reporter in 1888. That was the year of Glasgow's first great International Exhibition which allowed Munro to feel 'devilishly cosmopolitan ... on the verge of the Dumbarton Road.'[4] Mrs. Humphry Ward's novel *Robert Elsmere* was the current best-seller. Munro wrote ironically, long after –

Such lofty heights of literary enterprise scared me stiff. I had dreamt of a literary masterpiece of my own in 1888, but put it off till I had got full value for my season-ticket to the Exhibition.[5]

Earlier literary dreams had been of poetry rather than fiction. In 1887, for instance, he had submitted a poem to *Blackwood's Magazine*, in vain. He still read as much as possible, Meredith, Kipling, Stevenson and (above all) Hardy being favourites. He read a good deal of non-fiction as well, and found interest and delight in Lord Archibald Campbell's *Records of Argyll* and J.F.Campbell's *Popular Tales of the West Highlands*.

After a few years on the *News* Munro was possessed by the notion of moving to the country and making a living by his pen without the daily tyranny of newspaper work. In 1891 he tried his hand at two light-hearted stories, 'Dr. Everton Sharp's Experiment', and 'How the Jeweller of Alnbury was Duped' (1891).[6] Two years later he wrote a 13-episode serial, 'The Afton Moor Mystery' (1893).[7] Cassell's accepted another 'sensational story' and *Black & White*, a new art periodical, took an article. Then *The Globe*, a London paper, took a humorous article, and he supplied them with such 'turnovers' for a good while, this being a recognised literary début.

In the middle of all this, in August 1892 he sent 'a short sketch in a Highland manner, called 'Anapla's Boy'' to *Blackwood's Magazine*. It was a new departure. He tried another in the same vein, 'The Secret of the Heather Ale', and it was accepted by *The Speaker*. In November William Blackwood returned 'Anapla's Boy', but said that if Munro wrote another Highland sketch he would be very pleased to see it. Emboldened, Munro sent him a copy of *The Speaker* with his story in it, for which he had earned £4, more than his weekly *News* salary. However, after two years he had made less than £20 from stories and articles (he had also somehow saved

£75). It might have been enough to risk leaving the *News* if he had been alone in the world.

But the idea was not worth entertaining: his own family meant far too much to him. Their first child, Annie, had died of meningitis, but another daughter was born in 1889, then a son in 1893, and there were four more children. Jessie Munro happened to be both home-loving and practical. With her implicit support he soldiered on.

In the rejected 'Anapla's Boy', he came to think, he had stumbled on his '*Lost Pibroch* manner'. During 1893 he wrote a few more of these tales. Henley published 'Red Hand' in his *National Observer*, then in July William Blackwood accepted 'Shudderman Soldier' for his *Magazine*. Munro replied that he hoped to write enough 'Highland sketches' to make a book. Blackwood, sending a cheque for eight guineas for 'Shudderman Soldier', encouraged Munro to think he might publish such a volume.

Soon after this Munro's commitment to the *News* was reinforced by promotion from being chief reporter to doing 'extra special literary work, reviews, leaders, special articles, interviews, and 'Lorgnette' [gossip column]'. There was even less free time than before. During 1894 he produced only two tales and had none published. One of these, 'The Sgeul of Black Murdo', he sent to Blackwood in September.

Five weary months later a letter from Blackwood arrived. Munro opened it with trepidation and read:

> If you will send me everything you have written beyond what I have accepted for the Magazine, I shall see about publishing the sketches in book form...(26 February 1895)

The title *The Lost Pibroch* and a set of nine tales were agreed upon that autumn, Blackwood going so far as to hope for another volume 'as good'. Munro added two more tales, and in March 1896 his first book was ready. Idiosyncratic in its presentation of Gaeldom, it already marked out the path he would take in his novels. The reviews were mostly excellent, but in its first year it brought him less than £5, the arrangement being that he would be paid half the profits. He could not know that the book would be in print all his life and beyond.

He made a start right away on the novel that was to be *John Splendid*. There was never any question but that it would be a historical romance set in Argyll. But it was hard going in conjunction with his *News* work, the more so as the summer before he had taken over (without any increase in salary) the weekly column 'Views and Reviews', which meant reading a constant queue of books. Longings revived for 'a lodge in some vast wilderness (with a good postal connexion) where one could retire from the fret of city life and write masterpieces'.[8] But his *News* salary was the *sine qua non* of life. The late summer of 1897 was a critical period. At the end of August, before he had sent a single word of his novel to Blackwood, he started a second *News* column, 'The Looker-On'. By 11 September he had sent off fifteen chapters of *John Splendid*. On the 13th he agreed to write a serial (*Gilian the Dreamer*) for the magazine *Good Words*. On the 19th Jessie had her fifth child. On the 25th a telegram and letter came from William Blackwood accepting *John Splendid* as a serial, breaking his own rule anent unfinished manuscripts. On the 27th Munro asked James Murray Smith for two months' leave of absence: he went home that evening having arranged instead to retire from the *News* staff while continuing to write his two columns, his weekly salary being reduced from £4. 10s. to £3. On 28 October Blackwood sent a cheque for £35 for the first instalment of *John Splendid*, to which he gave 'the post of honour' in November's *Maga*.

. Arguably, in Ronald Renton's words, 'the first truly authentic Highland novel'[9], *John Splendid* was published in book form the following September. Before Christmas a fifth impression was needed. Munro's income soared – but he did not give up his two columns, from a variety of motives: loyalty to the *News*, financial prudence, need to be active in worlds beyond his household, sheer enjoyment of his hard won journalistic skills.

By then the Munros had moved south of Glasgow to Waterfoot, a village on the edge of moorland yet only a mile from a railway station. Fortunately Munro found these new surroundings as conducive to work as he had hoped, even though he was not 'in some vast wilderness'. Their two youngest children were born at Waterfoot.

Always gregarious, Munro found his spare time decreasing just when he was meeting new and interesting people. He had made good friends among the artists known as 'the Glasgow Boys' while he was on the *News* staff but there were few distinguished writers then living in Scotland. The pleasure was thus all the keener when he met Joseph Conrad in September 1898. Conrad was in Glasgow looking (in vain) for command of a ship, his first three novels having won critical acclaim but not good sales. Munro, a confirmed admirer of Conrad's work, was also at a critical stage in his career. They hit it off at once, and after leaving their host's house 'foregathered very much', as Conrad wrote to Edward Garnett – so much indeed that Munro missed the last train and had to walk to Waterfoot. Next day they foregathered again at the Art Club, both for lunch and in the evening. They apparently met again only once, quarter of a century later. Later in 1898 Munro got to know R.B.Cunninghame Graham, with whom he also felt great affinity. Again their friendship had to exist without many opportunities to meet.

The four years spent at Waterfoot were probably Munro's most productive period. He wrote *Gilian the Dreamer, Doom Castle* and *The Shoes of Fortune* (his only lowland novel) and made plans for *Children of Tempest*, plans which benefited greatly from a visit to the Isle of Eriskay in summer 1901. But it was a year till William Blackwood got the first chapters of *Children of Tempest*.

Munro, professionally familiar with literary trends, was aware that a Scottish Zola was looked for, who would write a novel of urban realism. It must be conjectured that he knew himself well enough not to try to fill the bill. But he believed that 'literature... is saved periodically from eternal perdition by fresh starts'[10], and had begun to consider a change of direction – away from historical romance – once *Children of Tempest* was completed. While it was still on the stocks, however, *The House with the Green Shutters* by George Douglas Brown was published. He read it with great interest, though without finding it overwhelmingly innovative. In January 1902 Brown came out to Waterfoot to introduce himself. Munro found him 'a nice, genial, unaffected fellow', an admirer of Balzac rather than Zola. They lunched together at the Art Club two days later. Brown died suddenly in August without their having met again. Munro attended his funeral.

But what was his own new direction to be? When *Children of Tempest* was published in 1903 he wrote to William Blackwood, 'I fancy a lighter vein of character and a modern theme.'

By a curious conjunction Munro had invented his droll friend Erchie just after meeting George Douglas Brown. Erchie began essentially as material for the 'Looker On' column but soon took on a life of his own. In 1904 Blackwoods published a book of Erchie sketches for which Munro hastily invented the pen-name 'Hugh Foulis'. He tried henceforth to maintain a distinction between his two identities.

The Munros had been living in Gourock since 1902, for the first time in a house of their own, with a splendid outlook across the Firth of Clyde to the fringes of Argyll. 'I could see Inveraray – if it weren't for the mountains in between,' Munro boasted. Effie and Hugh were old enough to go to Greenock Academy, where Lilian, Moira, Neil junior and Isobel (Bud) followed in due course. 1903 brought more changes. Munro took over the tenancy of a house in the Main Street of Inveraray, and for many years the Munros spent July and August there, travelling by steamer from Gourock. In 1903 also, his mother, now a widow, came to live with them in Gourock.

Children of Tempest had been his sixth book in seven years: it now took him three more even to get to the point of starting another novel. Changing direction was harder than he had imagined, and hindered if anything by knowing that a household of ten relied on his pen. Royalties from Blackwoods, who kept all his fiction in print, continued to trickle in, Erchie being particularly lucrative, and this supplemented his *News* salary.

It was during this interregnum between novels, occurring when his narrative powers were at their strongest, that Munro created Para Handy, again in his 'Looker-On' column. In 1906 Blackwoods published *The 'Vital Spark' and her Queer Crew*, a volume of these 'humoursome Highland character sketches...written solely for the amusement of West of Scotland sea-board folk', as Munro once described them. Para Handy soon cast a spell beyond the West of Scotland, and it is still potent a century later. The BBC has broadcast three television series based on the tales. For the true aficionado nothing beats the printed page, a feast gloriously augmented in 1991 when Brian D. Osborne and Ronald Armstrong included eighteen extra tales, quarried from the old *News* files, in their scholarly 'First Complete Edition'.

Munro's next novel, *The Daft Days*, opened in *Maga* at last, soon after the first Para Handy book. Set in Inveraray c.1900, it carries out his ideas of 'a lighter vein of character and a modern theme', yet with an underlying serious motif of female emancipation. *The Daft Days* sold well, but Munro again found it difficult to get his next novel under way. Meanwhile, after much research, he wrote the text for *The Clyde: River and Firth*, a literary/historical travelogue with beautiful colour illustrations. He also extrapolated Erchie into a successful play, *Macpherson*, for the Glasgow Repertory theatre.

In 1908 Munro received the honorary degree of LL.D. from Glasgow University, and the following year he was given the freedom of Inveraray. Sadly his mother, whom the latter honour would have made so proud, had died in December 1906.

Munro had called their Gourock house 'Carnus' after the

deserted Glen Aray farmtown where he believed his Munro forebears had lived long ago. The choice was good: his own brood of Munros spent uncommonly happy years in their modern Carnus. By the time Isobel, the youngest, started school, Effie was nineteen. Hugh began medicine at Glasgow University in 1910, just after his seventeenth birthday.

By that time *Fancy Farm*, which might be termed a romance of manners and ideas, was running in *Maga*. It airily expounds the problems of a hard-up Edwardian laird and portrays in Norah and Penelope certain traits of the New Womanhood. In book form it sold reasonably well, but after it Munro relinquished contemporary fiction. 'Those tame domestic excursions in the last two books are all very well,' he wrote to William Blackwood in November 1910, 'but I mustn't allow my claymore hand to get stiff.'

Though the idea of his next novel was already in his mind, it was a long time till he set forth on the old road again. The family exchequer revived when *In Highland Harbours with Para Handy* came out in 1911. About that time Jimmy Swan materialised in the pages of the *News*, where Munro still continued with his two columns. In those years too he published here and there most of the tales collected later in *Jaunty Jock*. He also wrote ten short stories to accompany pictures by his friend George Houston, making a handsome quarto volume entitled *Ayrshire Idylls*. In the stories about Burns in particular are fascinating traces of Munro's own thoughts on creativity.

In Highland Harbours includes the tale 'Para Handy and the Navy', in which Macphail the engineer is 'full of patriotic alarm at the state of the British Navy'. He fears the Germans will 'soon hae faur mair Dreadnoughts than we hae ... If ye havena Dreadnoughts ye micht as weel hae dredgers.'

Lighthearted stuff, but Munro, like many another, had long had grave forebodings about war with Germany. In 'Looker-On' as early as 1908 an imaginary Highlander called Macdonald had prophesied that the war was 'pre-destined', and not a war 'to be fought at a comfortable distance from our comfortable semi-detached villas by hired professional soldiers ... a war which will drag my boys, if they're spared, away from the business...'[11]

Having run through the pages of *Maga*, *The New Road* was published in June 1914, eighteen days before the Sarajevo incident. With hindsight it seems apposite that Munro's last completed novel – generally considered his masterpiece – should emerge at that epoch. John Buchan praised 'its masterly construction, its insight into character, its drama, its complete adequacy of style'.[12] And it was of *The New Road* that Francis Russell Hart wrote: 'Historical romance has gone as far as possible in the ruthless deromanticizing of history.'

The 'new road' is Wade's military road, the first road through the Highlands. In the long run it will bring more order and prosperity to the north, but many Highlanders, like Ninian Macgregor Campbell in Munro's novel, saw in the road 'a rut that, once it's hammered deep enough, will be the poor Gael's grave!' – in other words, the Gaelic ethos will be eroded. What with demonstrating the callous rapacity of many chiefs in the early eighteenth century and following the intricate adventures of Ninian and Æneas, Munro had little space for more everyday aspects of Highland life, but these he had dealt with very adequately in earlier fiction.

A few weeks after *The New Road* came out the Munros migrated to Inveraray as usual for the summer. They were there when war was declared on 4 August. On the 6th Hugh, who had been for some time a 2nd lieutenant in the Territorials, marched through Inveraray with A Coy., the 1/8th Argyll & Sutherland Highlanders, before going to train at Bedford. Munro himself rejoined the *News* staff. In October he went to France for a brief period as a war correspondent. In May 1915 Hugh's battalion went to France. At first they were near Béthune, then moved to the Somme. On 22 September Hugh was killed near Aveluy.

In the months after Hugh's death Munro was preoccupied by the thought of getting over to France again as a war correspondent. At last, early in 1917, he was able to spend a month at the British and French fronts and (his true aim) to see Hugh's grave at Millencourt, near Albert. In May he was again in France. It was in those days that he wrote the set of poems he called 'Bagpipe Ballads', published in *Maga*. All this time he was still working at the *News* office, acting as locum Editor. On 17 August 1917 he wrote to George Blackwood that for the first time in his life he felt 'very much under the weather' – nervous, depressed, weak, without apparent physical cause. He made a good recovery, somehow or other, from what was perhaps a form of delayed reaction to Hugh's death compounded by overwork.

With 1918 came a new determination, exemplified by a move across the Firth to Helensburgh and a Georgian house much larger than Carnus. Munro changed its name from 'Rockville' to 'Cromalt'. For their first Christmas there, the first after the Armistice, they had 'a crowded house of young folk most of the time – 18 at table generally.'

Munro was now officially Editor of the *News*. During 1918, at his instigation, Blackwoods began to bring out cheap editions of his books, and also published eleven tales he had been accumulating, under the title *Jaunty Jock*. On 21 September 1918 he told George Blackwood, William's nephew and successor, that he had 'actually begun a Romance (provisionally entitled *The Search*) for you!' Probably most of the ten chapters now extant were written then.

The years slipped past. *Hurricane Jack of the 'Vital Spark'* came out in 1923. In 1924 Munro resigned from his editorship, becoming instead literary editor and director. He now meant to complete *The Search* in short order, but his hopes were unrealistic. He had been persuaded to write for private publication a history of the Royal Bank of Scotland, involving tedious research and not completed till 1927 – 'a tough job, sir – no more hack work for me!' he wrote to George Blackwood on 23 March 1927, yet again proclaiming good intentions as to *The Search*.

Also in 1927 he gave up his *News* columns after a thirty years' stint, having already begun, under the transparent mask of 'Mr. Incognito', a series of 'Random Reminiscences' in the *Daily Record*. These, not *The Search*, were to be his last work, continued into 1930.

Meanwhile the structure of the Munro family had been changing. Effie was married in 1922. In June 1924, while all the rest of the family were in France visiting Hugh's grave, Effie had a daughter – the first grandchild. Neil junior by then had followed his father into journalism. Isobel was married in 1927. The following spring Munro's health broke down, apparently a kind of nervous prostration, and he spent a month with Scottish friends in the south of France. Two years later hypertension and a cardiac irregularity were diagnosed.

When Moira was married in March 1930 her father was not fit enough to walk up the aisle of Glasgow University chapel with her. In August, purely for the sea journey, he went to New York on the *Transylvania*. In the autumn he was made an honorary LL.D. of Edinburgh University.

He died at 'Cromalt', aged 67, just before the Christmas of 1930, and was buried at Kilmalieu, the ancient graveyard of Inveraray.

* * * * *

In Chapter IX of *John Splendid*, young Elrigmore sees his dead mother's spinning wheel 'in the corner, with the thread snapped short in the heck – a hint, I many times thought, at the sundered interests of life'. Neil Munro left a novel unfinished. But others took over his spinning, though no one has had the temerity to complete *The Search*. Within a year of his death a book of his poetry and *The Brave Days* – a selection of his journalism made by George Blake – had been published, also a Para Handy, Erchie & Jimmy Swan omnibus. A second selection by Blake followed in 1933, and in 1935 Blackwoods brought out the Inveraray Edition of Munro's serious fiction, including for the first time the tale 'Jus Primae Noctis' which William Blackwood had thought too 'broad' to include in *The Lost Pibroch*. The Inveraray Edition was re-printed piecemeal after World War II. Thereafter it fell chiefly to Para Handy to keep the flag flying, which he did 'with his least wee bit touch', as Erchie would say, both in print and on the television screen.

In 1996, the centenary of *The Lost Pibroch*, the Neil Munro Society was founded at Inveraray. It flourishes bravely, and is carrying the flag into the new millennium. Just as importantly, many of Munro's books have been re-printed and there have been scholarly theses by Hermann Völkel and Ronald Renton, all of which James Beaton's bibliography in this volume records.

Notes

1 Hart, Francis Russell, *The Scottish Novel: A Critical Survey*, London: John Murray, 1978, p.169
2 Speech of acknowledgement on receiving Freedom of the Royal Burgh of Inveraray, May 1909, *Oban Times*, 29 May 1909
3 *Ibid.*
4 Munro, Neil, *The Brave Days*, ed. George Blake, Edinburgh: Porpoise Press, 1931, p.65
5 *Ibid.*, p.68
6 Munro, Neil, *Newcastle Courant*, 20 June 1891 and 26 December 1891
7 Munro, Neil, *Quips*, 2 November 1893 – 25 January 1894
8 Letter to George Murray of *Falkirk Herald*, 28 September 1896
9 Renton, Ronald, *The Major Fiction of Neil Munro : A Revaluation*, M.Phil. thesis, University of Glasgow, 1997
10 Munro, Neil, 'The Modern Novel', address to Subscribers of Stirling's and Glasgow Public Library, the text being printed as part of a pamphlet by Aird and Coghill, Glasgow, 1906. See page 223 of this volume
11 Munro, Neil, 'The Looker-On', *Glasgow Evening News*, 9 November 1908
12 Buchan, John, *Glasgow Evening News*, 10 June 1914. See page 183 of this volume

'Place of My People':
Neil Munro's Inveraray

RAE MACGREGOR AND BRIAN WILKINSON

> *Here is the shore, and the far wide world's before me,*
> *And the sea says 'Come!' but I would not part from you;*
> *Of gold nor fame would I take for the scent of birches*
> *That hangs around you in the rain or dew.*
> *Place of my people, place of the old brave stories,*
> *Good hearts, stout hearts, keen swords, and their manly glories!*[1]

Given these sentiments it is hardly surprising that Neil Munro centred so many of his stories and novels around the native shores he loved so dearly. In his historical novels, he transposed scenes from the old town to the present town which did not exist in the time in which *John Splendid*, *The New Road* and *Doom Castle* were set. Otherwise, his novels remain by and large historically accurate, and the validity of his observations on the changes overtaking the Highlands and their life and culture remain unaffected.

It is interesting to note, however, that the church bell which calls

12

the people of Inveraray to worship today, is the selfsame bell that rang out over the town when Neil Munro was a boy, and is one of the bells which would have tolled from the church of the old town. The bell bears the burgh coat of arms and the inscription:

Ex benignitate spectatissimi viri Jacobi Campbell de Stonefield: Justitiarii et Vicecomitis Delegati de Argyll. Robertus Maxwell me fecit Edinburgi Anno MDCCXXVII.

The bell is one of two which hung in the steeple of the Kirk in the old town. By the 1720's they were cracked and useless. Campbell of Stonefield, the Duke's Chamberlain, had them recast by Robert Maxwell, the Edinburgh bell-founder. In *The Daft Days*, Munro writes:

Wanton Wully only briefly rang the morning bell, and gingerly, with tight shut lips and deep nose breathings, as if its loud alarm could so be mitigated. Once before he had done it just as delicately – when the Earl was dying, and the bell-ringer, uncertain of his skill to toll, when the time came, with the right half-minute pauses, grieved the town and horrified the Castle by a rehearsal in the middle of a winter's night.[2]

The old Mercat Cross, which once stood in a pulpit before the Kirk in the old town, still dominates the main street of the present town as it did in the days of Munro's youth and there the townsfolk still gather on a summer's evening to set the world to rights in the same manner as did the old soldiers in *Gilian the Dreamer*.

'Is this not a proud day for the town with three generals standing at the cross?' said the Paymaster once, looking with pride at his brother and Turner of Maam and Campbell of Strachur, standing together leaning on their rattans at a market. [3]

Munro's love affair with Inveraray and its environs began in his childhood. He was born in Crombie's Land where a plaque commemorating his birth was placed on the wall in 1986. When his mother married the governor of the jail, the governor's house became his new home.

My earliest impressions of a prison were got, innocently enough, from the inside. A bedroom window looked out on the exercise yard, behind the sea-wall bastions, which were tall, formidable, and forbidding externally, but within were much lower, and more agreeable to the eye, being clothed with ivy toad-flax, which we called 'mother-of-thousands'.[4]

The gaol had been built in 1816 to replace the old Town House and Gaol in Front Street where it had become increasingly difficult to contain the prisoners and escapes were frequent. Even the new gaol was not impregnable and when a prisoner did manage to evade the prison warder Hugh MacIntyre and make a dash for the freedom of the woods surrounding the town, a great hue and cry would erupt which the young Neil took to mean 'Hugh-and-Cry'!

Like most small boys Munro was not averse to playing truant and a favourite hiding place was on the ledge of the sea wall known as The Ramparts which separated the prison yard from the waters of Loch Fyne. There he would spend happy hours devouring the adventure novels borrowed from Miss Macleod's circulating library in the Main Street of the town.

The young Neil attended both Inveraray Grammar School and the old school in Glenaray where John MacArthur, the headmaster, nurtured his love of the hills and the glens which had seen 'old forgotten, far-off things and battles long ago'. And it was those scenes that his fertile imagination peopled with the folks from the old Gaelic tales, heard at his grandmother's knee at the farm of Ladyfield further up the glen where his grandfather had been a herd and which he used as the basis of his partly autobiographical novel *Gilian the Dreamer*. His mission to carry the news of the death of the old wife of Ladyfield weighed heavily on Gilian's shoulders:

> Should it be in Gaelic or in English he should tell them? Their first salutations would be in the speech of the glens; it would be 'Oh Gilian, little hero! fair fellow! there you are! sit down and have town bread and sugar on its butter,' and if he followed the usual custom he would answer in the same tongue. But between '*Tha bean Lecknamban air falbh*' and 'The wife of Ladyfield is gone,' there must be some careful choice. The Gaelic of it was closer on the feelings of the event; the words some way seemed to make plain the emptiness of the farmhouse. When he said them, the people would think all at once of the little brown wrinkled dame, no more to be bustling about the kitchen, of her wheel silent, of her foot no more upon the blue flagstones of the milk-house, of her voice no more in the chamber where they had so often known her hospitality.[5]

It was in the Paymaster's House, above the wide pend in the main street, that Gilian found a home with the three old soldiers and their sister Miss Mary.

In Inveraray School Munro came under the guidance of Henry Dunn Smith, the headmaster, affectionately known as 'Old Skull'. He recognised the boy's talent and encouraged him. The Grammar School he attended was re-built in 1908 and has since been converted into the present Community Hall. He was later to recall his schooldays as:

> Those lovely unperplexed and simple days when I deliberately refused to learn anything and yet in some mysterious way was learning all that was to be of use to me in later life.[6]

During his school years he played about the town with other children of his age, running through the blue-flagged closes and white arches of the buildings which later would figure so prominently in his stories and novels. One of these was the house with the Brass Man's Hand which was home to Munro's first employer Mr. Douglas the lawyer, on whom he modelled Dan Dyce in *The Daft Days*, the story of the little American girl Bud Dyce and the 'mosaic' (mongrel) dog:

> 'I was dre'ffle sleepy in the Mail and the driver wrapped me up and when I came into this town in the dark he said, 'Walk right down there and rap at the first door you see with a brass man's hand for a knocker; that's Mr. Dyce's house.'[7]

In the garden behind this house is the grave of 'Footles' the little dog which belonged to Douglas and on which the 'mosaic' dog was based. Mr. Douglas had his office in the building at the corner of East Main Street and Front Street and which was eventually to become a Temperance Hotel:

> Daniel Dyce had an office up the street at the windy corner facing the cross, with two clerks in it and a boy who docketed letters and ran errands.[8]

Further up the street is the high boundary wall of the Bank of Scotland garden which forms part of the town square and over which Boboon the Tinker found difficulty in resisting the enticement of his family to leave his new found gentility as houseman to Quinten Montgomery the banker and return to his old life:

'Boboon! oh, Boboon! old hero! come and collogue with your children.'...

'And you like it, Boboon?'

'Like it, heroes! But for the honour and ease of it, give me a fir-root fire in Glen Croe and a dinner of *fuarag*. It is not the day so much as the night. Lying in-by there on a posted-bed, I choke for want of air, though the windows and doors are open wide.' [9]

The plumber's shop at the head of Main Street was owned by the Maitland family and where in later years Neil and his great friend Charlie Maitland were often to be found perched on lavatory pedestals exchanging baurs and watching the life of Inveraray pass by. It was here that the ideas for many of the hilarious incidents in his Para Handy tales were born, tales like 'The Malingerer' where to cure The Tar from his lazy ways the puffer crew send for the local joiner – who also doubles as the undertaker!

'Here's MacIntyre the joiner would like to see you, Colin,'...

'What's the joiner wantin' here?' said The Tar with a frightful suspicion.

'Nothing, Colin, nothing – six by two... six by two, six by two...'[10]

The well-known speech which Munro made on being made a Freeman of the Burgh of Inveraray in 1909 includes the words:

The things we love intensely are the things worth writing about. I could never leave Inveraray out of any story of mine and I never will.

How well he kept his promise. His identification of places may be slightly inaccurate, he was often guilty of anachronism, but these sites are still there if one knows where to look though many are ruined and sadly many are covered in the ubiquitous blanket forestry that is the scourge of the country today.

The Doocot which is central to *The New Road* still stands on the banks of the Aray opposite the house of Drimdorran (Tombreck) and the Aray still roars in full spate beside the ruins of the old mill. These places were all familiar to Munro. In his description of the Inveraray of the time of *The New Road* he describes the house of Æneas's uncle as having 'a store beside the quay, below his dwelling-house.'[11] Stand on the quay in the new town of Inveraray today and immediately in front is a house with steps leading to the front door. This was the house built in 1756 for John Richardson (who was later to become provost of Inveraray), and later leased to the exciseman Neil Gillies who utilised its cellars beneath for storage of imports and exports. Munro spent a great deal of his time at the quay listening to the yarns of the old fishermen and town worthies, and watching the puffers loading and unloading their cargoes under the direction of their skippers. Here perhaps he may have found the inspiration for the *Para Handy Tales* and it was from here he left to seek his fortune in Glasgow.

Diagonally across the bay from the quay lies the mouth of Glen Shira.

> Shira Glen, Shira Glen! If I was a bard I'd have songs to sing to it and all I know is one skulduddery verse on a widow that dwelt in Maam! There, at the foot of my father's house, were the winding river, and north and south the brown hills, split asunder by God's goodness, to give a sample of His bounty. Maam, Elrigmore and Elrigbeg, Kilblaan and Ben Bhuidhe – ... to the south, the fresh water we call Dubh Loch... [12]

Glen Shira stretches upwards from the head of Loch Shira into the hills of Benbuidhe and Ben Shian, pointing the way to the Perthshire borders and the lands of Lorne. It was down this glen, on a winter's night in 1644 the ragged hordes of Montrose's army under the guidance of Alistair MacDonald of Colonsay, the young Colkitto, snaked its way toward the castle and stronghold of Gillesbeg Gruamach, Marquis of Argyll, to leave Inveraray a smoking ruin and Argyll on a desperate dash for safety. Two hundred years later Neil Munro was to set his famous historical novel *John Splendid* around these events.

Glen Shira also figures in *Gilian the Dreamer*. From Maam, Gilian and Nan set off on their romantic journey to Lochawe side.

> Soon they were on the summit of the hill range and below them lay the two glens, and the first breath of the morning came behind from Strone, where dawn threw a wan grey flag across the world. They plunged into the caldine trees of Strongara, sped fast across Aray at Three Bridges, and the dawn was on Balantyre, where the farm-touns high and low lay like thatched forts, grey, cold, unwelcoming in the morning, with here and there a stream of peat reek from the *greasach* of the night's fires. [13]

The twin peaks of Dunchuach and Duntorvil stand sentinel at the apex of Glen Shira and Glen Aray. The square tower on top of Dunchuach may only be a folly built at the whim of the 3rd Duke of Argyll but it is not inconceivable that in the dim and distant past this was the site of a lookout and where better to keep watch for an enemy with the wonderful panorama stretching from the glens of the North to the Cowal hills in the South before the eye.

> *'Tis ill to say it, for it's only a boyish softness,*
> *But standing at morning alone on Dunchuach high,*
> *To see all my dear place spread wide around and below me,*
> *Brings the tear that stings to the loving and greedy eye.*
> *The glen and the corrie, the ben and the sounding shore*
> *Have something that searches me in to the deepest core.*
>
> *Oh! here's a cup to my friends and my darling own place!*
> *Glad am I that by fortune my mother she bore me here.*
> *It might have been far on the plains of the Saxon stranger,*
> *With never a hill like Dunchuach or Duntorvil near,*
> *And never a fir with its tassels to toss in the wind,*
> *Salt Fyne of the fish before, and Creag Dubh of the deer behind!*[14]

Notes

1 'Home', *The Poetry of Neil Munro*, ed. John Buchan, Edinburgh and London: William Blackwood & Sons Ltd., 1931, p.17
2 Munro, Neil, *The Daft Days*, Colonsay, Argyll: House of Lochar, 2002, p.78
3 Munro, Neil, *Gilian the Dreamer*, Edinburgh: B&W Publishing, 2000, p.11
4 Munro, Neil, *The Brave Days,* Edinburgh: Porpoise Press, 1931, p.30
5 Munro, Neil, *Gilian the Dreamer,*Edinburgh: B&W Publishing, 2000, p.5
6 From the speech of acknowledgement given by Neil Munro when he received the Freedom of the Royal Burgh of Inveraray, May 1909
7 Munro, Neil, *The Daft Days*, Colonsay, Argyll: House of Lochar, 2002, p.22
8 Munro,Neil, *The Daft Days*, Colonsay, Argyll: House of Lochar, 2002, p.45
9 Munro, Neil, *The Lost Pibroch and other Sheiling Stories*, Colonsay, Argyll: House of Lochar 1996, p.21
10 Munro, Neil, 'The Malingerer', *Para Handy*, Eds. Brian Osborne and Ronald Armstrong, Edinburgh: Birlinn, 1992, p.14
11 Munro, Neil, *The New Road*, Edinburgh: B&W Publishing, 1994, p.16
12 Munro, Neil, *John Splendid*, Edinburgh: B&W Publishing, 1994, p.10
13 Munro, Neil, *Gilian the Dreamer*, Edinburgh: B&W Publishing, 2000, p.243
14 'Home', *The Poetry of Neil Munro*, ed. John Buchan, Edinburgh and London: William Blackwood and Sons Ltd, 1931, p.18–19

Landscape and Scenery in the
Writings of Neil Munro

RENNIE McOWAN

In Neil Munro's novel of the Scottish Wars of the Covenant, *John Splendid*, he has a passage describing the Campbell fugitives fleeing from the shattering defeat at Inverlochy on 2 February 1645. Six of them are pursued by a single mounted trooper and they turn on him once they realise he has become detached from the main body of the Royal army. Munro depicts Colin of Elrigmore and John MacIver of Barbreck (John Splendid) joining the six and Elrigmore recounts:

> Who of that fierce company brought the trooper to his end we never knew, but when M'Iver and I got down to his level he was as dead as knives could make him, and his horse more mad than ever, was disappearing over a mossy moor with a sky-blue lochan in the midst of it. (JS pp.187–8)[1]

There is no need for Munro to mention a sky-blue lochan. It has nothing to do with the incident. The horse does not career into it. The man's corpse is not dumped in the water. His sentence could have finished at 'mossy moor' without detriment to the passage.

It is mentioned for two reasons, I submit, although the second reason is more important than the first. People facing traumatic situations sometimes notice detail of an inconsequential type unrelated to the incident itself. It may well be that this was in Munro's mind. The second and more likely reason is that the sighting of that sky-blue lochan is the kind of vignette which sticks in the mind of a true hillman or woman and Munro has Colin of Elrigmore notice it because that is the way many people's minds 'tick' in the Highlands and outdoors generally.

Any modern stravaiger or hill gangrel who has any soul or capacity for absorbing the beauty of the mountain world has seen such a lochan and can reproduce it in the mind many weeks or months later. It is Munro's ability to capture such nuances which

19

proves him to be a landscape writer of outstanding skill. His sky-blue lochan will strike a responsive chord in many modern hill-goers.

We see the same apparently odd choice of detail in another section of *John Splendid* when the Campbell army is resting for the night in Glen Noe. They are in almost jovial spirits despite leaving a smoking and almost abandoned countryside behind them after the massive assault on Campbell lands by the army of the Marquis of Montrose and Alasdair MacColla, the war leader of Clan Donald. They are bent on revenge. They know their numbers probably outweigh their enemy's and are as yet unaware that their Lowland levies will show no stomach for facing a Highland charge.

The Marquis of Argyll is behaving like a chief of old, chatting with his men, leaving his tent to lie down with the clansmen, cajoling individuals to tell stories or sing songs as they huddle in their plaids in the snow, his ignominious retreat from Inveraray when Montrose's men poured down the glens temporarily forgotten. John Splendid has written an evocative song, 'The Sergeant of Pikes', (JS p.149) which sticks in Elrigmore's mind, and the Marquis's chaplains offer prayers in English for their eventual victory.

Neil Munro could have finished the chapter there. It is a powerful enough scene on its own and it could have ended with John Splendid's comment that despite the prayers and the confident mood of so many in the Campbell ranks he feels a nagging sense of caution as they pursue their enemy into Lochaber. But Munro ends it with:

> And all night long deer belled to deer on the braes of Glen Noe. (JS p.151)

Here is a sentence from the same thought processes as the sky-blue lochan. It is also one which will be recognised by many outdoor folk. This writer has heard deer bell all night in Glen Noe and so, probably, had Neil Munro. That sentence could surely only have been written by someone familiar with such a scene. The nostalgic mood of it, as lodged in the memory of Elrigmore, almost defies analysis. Yet it is so effective, this recalling of a detail of a Highland night in winter linked to familiar landscape that it concludes the sombre chapter in a style which is surely Munro's alone. Despite the recent carnage, despite the jubilation at the thought of soon getting to grips with the enemy once more, despite their numbers and their rejuvenated chief, Elrigmore remembers the deer belling in the night in Glen Noe and it is that kind of detail which makes Munro so memorable as a scenery and landscape writer.

He also has a way of slipping in a little piece of landscape description when it contrasts with some grim event, and by so doing
highlighting the deed's grisly character, as in the duel between
Elrigmore and young MacLachlan in *John Splendid*. Here
Elrigmore, bent on bringing about death or serious injury, has time
to steal a glance at a blackbird singing and the colours of the sunset
(JS p.317). Munro does the same in his short story 'The Secret of
the Heather Ale', when Calum Dubh and his sons are securely
bound by their enemies and facing a terrible death by being hurled
over a cliff:

> With tied arms the father and his sons were taken outside, where
> the air was full of the scents of birch and gall new-washed. The
> glen, clearing fast of mist, lay green and sweet for mile and mile,
> and far at its mouth the fat Blaranbuie woods chuckled in the sun.
> (LP p.17)[2]

There are a number of such examples in the novels and stories.

Of course it goes without saying that Neil Munro is not concen-
trating on outdoor description as such in the historical novels. His
descriptive passages are worked into the plots of the stories and they
are all the more effective for that. He *is* a landscape writer in that
many of his vivid descriptions are remembered and quoted by his
readers and have a clear character of their own. It is not too strong
to say they are unique.

They may well be given in the English language, but they are
Gaelic in style and feel and they bridge two cultures.

It is also, however, important to emphasise what his descriptive
writing is not. He is not writing in the style of the Celtic twilight, and
of these once-popular figures George McDonald and 'Fiona
MacLeod' (William Sharp) who produced so much Celtic myth and
fantasy in their day. Munro is writing from a different standpoint,
from that of long-rooted Gaelic culture, untrammelled by false
emotion. Neil Munro undertook to portray Highlanders and their
world as they truly were.

In Munro's landscape writings he understands the importance of
'place' in the mind and psyche of the Gael and the special way the
landscape is seen, analysed, understood and appreciated. He gives
us that, exquisitely, often starkly, and his language is true and of the
people and of the land. All Munro enthusiasts know how he loved
his native glens which formed his boyhood playground, although

(like many another) he only understood the depth of his feelings when he grew up and had to live elsewhere.

There is much poignant nostalgia of a personal nature in Munro's scenery descriptions. In *John Splendid* he depicts young Elrigmore returning from the foreign wars and exulting in being home:

> Down to Ealan Eagal I went for a plunge in the linn in the old style, and the airs of Shira Glen hung about me like friends and lovers, so well acquaint and jovial. (JS p.9)

Munro's boyhood walking and exploring in the woods, in the glens, on the moors and hills, by the loch-side, had a profound effect on his landscape writings.

Some readers have wondered why he decided to set so many of his books locally with an abundance of place-names from Inveraray and its neighbourhood unlikely to be known by the general reader. In addition to the fact that they enhance the Gaelic atmosphere one reason would certainly be that such a decision was born of love.

His love of 'place' shows itself in his poetry and particularly in 'Home':

> *'Tis ill to say it, for it's only a boyish softness,*
> *But standing at morning alone on Dunchuach high,*
> *To see all my dear place spread wide around and below me,*
> *Brings the tear that stings to the loving and greedy eye.*
> *The glen and the corrie, the ben and the sounding shore*
> *Have something that searches me in to the deepest core!*
>
> *Oh! here's a cup to my friends and my darling own place!*
> *Glad am I that by fortune my mother she bore me here.*
> *It might have been far on the plains of the Saxon stranger,*
> *With never a hill like Dunchuach or Duntorvil near,*
> *And never a fir with its tassels to toss in the wind,*
> *Salt Fyne of the fish before, and Creag Dubh of the deer behind!*
> (PNM p.18–19)[3]

His heart-felt longings and love also show themselves in his poem 'To Exiles':

> *Are you not weary in your distant places,*
> *Far, far from Scotland of the mist and storm...* (PNM p.27)

Only someone with a deep knowledge of the glens, moors, hills, woods and loch shores in all seasons could write (as Munro does in 'The Lost Pibroch'):

> Sometimes in the spring of the year the winds from Lorn have it their own way with the Highlands. They will come tearing furious over the hundred hills, spurred the faster by the prongs of Cruachan and Dunchuach, and the large woods of home toss before them like corn before the hook. Up come the poor roots and over on their broken arms go the tall trees, and in the morning the deer will trot through new lanes cut in the forest. (LP p.8)

There is surely personal experience from Munro's days as a lawyer's clerk in Inveraray in his description in *Doom Castle* of Petullo, the Writer or lawyer sitting in his office 'that smelt most wickedly of mildewed vellum, sealing wax, tape and all that trash that smothers the soul of man – the appurtenances of his craft.' (DC p.99)[4] Sim MacTaggart, the Duke of Argyll's Chamberlain, on entering the office:

> ... felt like thanking God that he had never been compelled to a life like this in a stinking mortuary, with the sun outside on the windows and the clean sea and the singing wood calling in vain. (DC p.99)

There is another important facet of Munro's writings which can seem strange to many people because we are not nowadays accustomed to the idea of beautiful or 'atmospheric' scenery creating feelings of poignant sorrow. Scenery impresses, makes one gasp or exult, moves the heart and mind by its beauty, but nostalgic feelings of near-grief and loss tend to be absent. Munro gives this kind of sorrow a high priority. It is clearly part of the psyche of his characters and of his own. It is difficult for some of us to understand it today and in portraying it for us Munro is again showing that as a descriptive writer he stands out on his own.

When John Splendid and Elrigmore meet up with John Lom, the famous bard of Keppoch, John decides to puncture the bard's vanity by pretending he has never heard of him or his songs, and the bard is aghast and shocked. Elrigmore, who has been a mercenary in the foreign wars, takes pity on him and says:

> 'John Lom, John Lom! I heard a soldier sing your songs in the

ship Archangel of Leith that took us to Elsinore.' (JS p.167)

John Lom glows with pleasure and says:

'Which one did they sing – 'The Harp of the Trees' or 'Macrannul
Og's Lament?' I am sure it would be the Lament: it is touched
with the sorrow of the starless night on a rain-drummed, wailing
sea.' (JS p.167)

Munro returns to this theme several times and also links the
feeling of sorrow with the music of the pipes. In *Doom Castle* the
comic attendant and indifferent piper, Mungo, plays a pibroch
which, heard at a distance by Count Victor, becomes

a pibroch all imbued with passion and with melancholy. The
distance lulled it into something more than human music, into a
harmony with the monotone of the wave that thundered on the
rock; it seemed the voice of choiring mermen; it had the bitter-
ness, the agonised remembrance, of the sea's profound; it was full
of hints of stormy nights and old wars. (DC p.28)

In *Children of Tempest*, Munro writes:

Or it would be in nights of moon, the Islands floating in golden
fire, Hecla and Benmore abrupt and clear against the east, every
rock that jutted from the Sound jet-black. Drifting then at the will
of the gentle wind, they saw dim Barra lit with kelp-fires; the scent
of bracken and peat came from the shores they skirted; in
townships close upon the beach they could hear the bleat of lambs
and sometimes the sound of a pipe lamenting, but sweet, oh!
sweet, beyond words in its very sorrow. (CT p.138)[5]

In *Doom Castle* the Jacobite agent, Count Victor, who has arrived
from France, praises the beauty of the hills, but adds that they seem
to crush his heart. Baron Lamond's daughter, Olivia replies:

'Yes, yes, I understand that ...It is the sorrow of the hills and wood
you mean; ah! do I not know it too?...when I walk the woods or
stand upon the shore and see the hills without a tree or tenant,
when the land is white with the snow and the mist is trailing,
Olivia Lamond is not very cheery. What it is I do not know – that
influence of my country, it is sad, but it is good and wholesome,

24

I can tell you: it is then I think that the bards make songs, and those who are not bards, like poor myself, must just be feeling the songs there are no words for.' (DC p.125)

It is a fact that the sight of a beautiful view can put people into a kind of reverie and quiet pondering of that kind can lead to sad and melancholy thoughts, the sorrows folk are born to (as Munro says in 'The Lost Pibroch'), but he is going beyond that in his references to sorrow being engendered by aspects of the woods, lochs, glens and hills.

There may well be an element of apparently unchanging scenery stirring the viewer's heart and at the same time making him or her realise in the face of apparent timelessness that human beings have a limited time on this planet.

Some of Munro's most memorable writing comes when he is describing one of Scotland's best known wilderness areas, the great Moor of Rannoch, in *John Splendid* and *The New Road* and also when in *John Splendid* he tells of the famous march of the Marquis of Montrose's army over the winter hills in 1645.

Munro's portrait of Rannoch Moor is stark and harsh. He likens its undulating ground to the sea. In *John Splendid* he depicts Elrigmore standing on a little knoll in the night and waiting for the day to show him where he is and how he should continue his fugitive journey to Inveraray:

I stood on the hillock clothed with its stunted saugh-trees and waited for the day that was mustering somewhere to the east, far by the frozen sea of moss and heather tuft. A sea more lonely than any ocean the most wide and distant, where no ship heaves, and no isle lifts beckoning trees above the level of the waves; a sea soundless, with no life below its lamentable surface, no little fish or proud leviathan plunging and romping and flashing from the silver roof of fretted wave dishevelled to the deep profound. The moorfowl does not cry there, the coney has no habitation. It rolled, that sea so sour, so curdled, from my feet away to mounts I knew by day stupendous and not so far, but now in the dark so hid that they were but troubled clouds upon the distant marge. There was a day surely when, lashing up on these hills around, were waters blue and stinging, and some plague-breath blew on them and they shivered and dried and cracked into this parched semblance of what they were in the old days when the galleys sailed over. No galleys now. No white birds calling eagerly in the storm. No silver bead of spray. Only in its season the cannoch tuft, and that itself but sparsely; the very bluebell shuns a track so desolate, the sturdy gall finds no nourishment here. (JS p.261)

Travellers in past times sometimes exaggerated the bleakness and the hostility of the Moor and Munro is no exception. It was once covered with pine trees the roots of which, like skeletons, can still be seen in the peat. The trees withered over the centuries in climatic changes or were cut down for timber or to flush out 'broken men'. Nevertheless Munro's description of Rannoch Moor is one of the best of its kind and many people nowadays who have crossed it, still no easy matter, do find themselves comparing it to a sea and the mountains fringing the Moor do seem like huge waves.

He uses the sea analogy again with great skill in *The New Road* when Æneas and Ninian reach the Kingshouse Inn, at the east end of Glen Coe:

Eastward, where the inn-front looked, the moor stretched flat and naked as a Sound; three days' march from end to end they said were on it – all untracked and desert-melancholy. Its nearer parts were green with boggy grass, on which the cannoch tuft – the cotton-sedge – was strewn like flakes of snow; distantly its hue was sombre – grey like ashes, blackened here and there with holes of peat. The end of it was lost in mist from which there jutted, like a skerry of the sea, Schiehallion. God-forgotten, man-forsworn, wild Rannoch, with the birds above it screaming, was, to Æneas, the oddest thing, the eeriest in nature, he had ever seen. (NR p.89)[6]

In *John Splendid*, Munro depicts Elrigmore and John Splendid being 'taken along' as prisoners in the Marquis of Montrose's army on the march through the hill passes from Fort Augustus (then called Kilchumein) to Inverlochy, now on the fringe of modern Fort William.

Like several other writers of his time Munro initially seems to depict the royal army crossing the hills by way of the Corrieyarick Pass and coming down Glen Nevis whereas nowadays the perceived wisdom is that the army left the line of the Corrieyarick above Culachy and moved west and south into Glen Buck, Glen Turret and down Glen Roy to the River Spean and thence to Leanachan and Kilchonate and on to Inverlochy. The idea of the Glen Nevis route probably arose because McSorleys and Camerons from Glen Nevis joined up with Montrose's main army.

The pass of Corryarick met us with a girning face and white fangs...We had to climb up the shoulder of the hill, now among tremendous rocks, now through water unfrozen, now upon wind-swept ice, but the snow – the snow – the heartless snow was our constant companion. It stood in walls before, it lay in ramparts round us, it wearied the eye to a most numbing pain...We were lost in a wilderness of mountain peaks; the bens started about us on every hand like the horrors of a nightmare, every ben with its death-sheet, menacing us, poor insects, crawling in our pain across the landscape. (JS p.173)

At the head of Glen Roy the MacDonalds, who had lost their bauchles of brogues in the pass, started to a trot, and as the necessity was we had to take up the pace too. Long lank hounds, they took the road like deer, their limbs purple with the cold, their faces pinched to the aspect of the wolf, their targets and muskets clattering about them. (JS p.175)

Every Munro enthusiast will have his or her favourite quotations and the following excerpts are outstanding for their detail and 'feel' for Highland landscape. The first occurs in *The New Road* when Æneas and Ninian are trying to get across Loch Tulla and experience a fine day, not too common in the Highlands.

The corries of the mountains sent a sound of running waters; the red-pine tops, as old as Scotland, bent above them, hushed and dark; the air was heavy with the tang of myrtle and of heath. (NR p.67)

The second occurs in the short story 'The Lost Pibroch' and it has the swing and the hurry of a Highland river in it. Munro describes the tune 'The Macrae's March' as:

The march came fast to the chanter – the old tune, the fine tune that Kintail has heard before, when the wild men in their red tartan came over the hill and moor; the tune with the river in it, the fast river and the courageous that kens not stop nor tarry, that runs round rock and over fall with a good humour, yet in no mood for anything but the way before it. The tune of the heroes, the tune of the pinelands and the broad straths, the tune that the eagles of Loch Duich crack their beaks together when they hear, and the crows of that country-side would as soon listen to as the squeal of their babies. (LP p.4)

The third occurs in *John Splendid*. Sometimes walkers in the hills come across little lochans, some bleak and stark, others quiet and beautiful, and they are often places where people halt to rest or picnic. Munro captures exquisitely the mood of some of these places. He depicts Elrigmore wandering on Rannoch Moor and, although he does not like the black, peaty soil of some of the lochans there, he recalls other, more attractive places elsewhere in the hills:

And then I came on a cluster of lochs – grey, cold, vagrant lochs – still to some degree in the thrall of the frost. Here's one who has ever a fancy for such lochans, that are lost and sobbing, sobbing, even-on among the hills, where the reeds and rushes hiss in the wind, and the fowls with sheeny feather make night and day cheery with their call. (JS p.262)

For me, however, the most memorable treatment of landscape and scenery in the work of Neil Munro is to be found in *John Splendid* in the section beginning 'I know corries in Argile...' (JS pp.223–4). This is a beautiful and moving piece of writing and worthy of a place in any anthology of Scottish and, indeed, British literature.

It speaks of faeries and supernatural beings, the People of Quietness. Munro refers to the shepherd and the hunter as being 'coarse men in life and occupation' (JS p.223). By that he means they are accustomed to the practical world of the croft and the hill farm and to hard reality and, therefore, the fact that special places in the hills put a kind of temporary spell on them is all the more significant and emphasises the strength of atmosphere that surrounds certain locations.

Many modern hill trampers have experienced Munro's 'rapture of the mind and sloeberry bloom of haze' (JS p.224). They have reached some corner of a corrie or glen and stopped, sensing that here is a spot which has a moving, puzzling and evocative character. It is an experience not felt or understood by all, but those who love quiet and often lonely places and who, in the old phrase, listen to the hills, find this much praised passage of Munro's very rewarding.

Some of the terms Munro uses are strange to modern ears. A corrie is, of course, a hollow in the hills. The bog flower can be several plants, including bog asphodel. The cannoch is bog-cotton, a 'magic' plant. The cailzie-cock is the capercaillie and the stag of ten, of course, has ten points to its antlers. Brock is the badger and foumart is the polecat.

The passage is spoken by Elrigmore, a hunted fugitive who can yet muse on the hills he loves. It escapes sounding precious, no easy matter. It is a beautiful piece of writing, surely one of the pinnacles of Munro's descriptive powers. Here is a hard-headed newspaper man who truly loves the culture of Gaeldom, who has imagination, who seeks to tell all Scotland of its richness, who lets us see his heart and soul.

I know corries in Argile that whisper silken to the winds with juicy grasses, corries where the deer love to prance deep in the cool dew, and the beasts of far-off woods come in bands at their seasons and together rejoice. I have seen the hunter in them and the shepherd too, coarse men in life and occupation, come sudden among the blowing rush and whispering reed, among the bog flower and the cannoch, unheeding the moor-hen and the cailzie-cock rising, or the stag of ten at pause, while they stood, passionate adventurers in a rapture of the mind, held as it were by the spirit of such places as they lay in a sloeberry bloom of haze, the spirit of old good songs, the baffling surmise of the piper and the bard. To those corries of my native place will be coming in the yellow moon of brock and foumart – the beasts that dote on the autumn eves – the People of Quietness; have I not seen their lanthorns and heard their laughter in the night? – so that they must be blessed corries, so endowed since the days when the gods dwelt in them without tartan and spear in the years of the peace that had no beginning. (JS pp.223–4)

Notes

1   Munro, Neil, *John Splendid*, Edinburgh: B&W Publishing, 1994 [JS]
2   Munro, Neil, *The Lost Pibroch and Other Sheiling Stories*, Colonsay, Argyll: House of Lochar, 1996 [LP]
3   *The Poetry of Neil Munro*, ed. John Buchan, Edinburgh and London: William Blackwood and Sons, 1931 [PNM]
4   Munro, Neil, *Doom Castle*, Edinburgh: B&W Publishing, 1996 [DC]
5   Munro, Neil, *Children of Tempest*, Edinburgh and London: William Blackwood and Sons, Inveraray Edition,1935 [CT]
6   Munro, Neil, *The New Road*, Edinburgh, B&W Publishing, 1994 [NR]

Neil Munro – Commercial Success and Critical Acclaim

BRIAN D. OSBORNE

The Manuscripts Department of the National Library of Scotland holds Munro's annual royalty statements from his principal British publisher, William Blackwood & Sons, for the years 1899–1951 (MS 26931 and 26932). From these statements it is possible to judge the commercial success of Munro's books and to make some contrasts and comparisons with the critical reception of Munro in his own lifetime and after his death.

There are some complications in working out how well each title did – not least the number of editions that were simultaneously sold on the home market. For example in 1923 *The New Road* was available in the standard 7/6d edition, in the uniform 3/6d edition and in a 2/- cheap edition. Perhaps unsurprisingly only 12 copies of the 7/6d edition were sold but 910 sales of the cheap edition and 1,347 of the uniform edition were recorded. Each edition attracted royalties at a different rate and the returns on cheap editions were very low – the 2/- edition of *The New Road* sold in 1920 only producing £8.8.2. There was also often a 'Colonial Edition' – part of the print run sold at a lower cost into the territories of the British Empire.

Munro's first book for Blackwood, *The Lost Pibroch*, was published in 1896, before this set of royalty statements start, but the 1899 statement shows that 322 copies of the standard edition had been sold and a cheap edition was produced which resulted in about 1,200 sales over the next five years. What is more striking is the success of a 6d. edition reported in the 1903 statement – this had recorded sales of 21,404 copies in its first year – a remarkable figure for a book which the renowned critic Andrew Lang had described in a review of *John Splendid* as 'esoteric' and which he judged 'appealed to the few.'[1]

John Splendid itself really marked Munro's breakthrough. With 5,141 sales in the first year on the home market and over 4,000 copies in colonial editions and US and Canadian editions this was a significantly successful title. It continued to sell reasonably and the publication of the 6d. cheap edition saw the 1904 royalty statement recording sales of over 20,000 copies in this format. After the war *John Splendid,* re-appeared in a two shilling cheap edition and sold almost 10,000 copies in the year of publication.

The commercial success of *John Splendid* was coupled with critical success. Extensive reviews of the novel appeared in all the leading literary journals and *The Bookman*[2] devoted a 'Symposium' feature to it, with contributions by Andrew Lang, William Wallace of the *Glasgow Herald,* William Sharp and his *alter ago* 'Fiona MacLeod.' The equally prestigious journal *The Academy* while concluding that it did not have 'the extraordinary freshness, poetry and savagery of the *Lost Pibroch* volume' did find that it had 'the double charm of a fine swing of style, and of an exquisite atmosphere.'[3]

The Blackwood's royalty statements do not give the whole story of Munro's literary career. For example, he published two novels, *Shoes of Fortune* and *Gilian the Dreamer* with the London firm of Isbister, following their serialisation in *Good Words.* Although these novels later appeared under the Blackwood imprint there are some grounds for believing that this venture away from Blackwood was not entirely successful and there is correspondence between Munro and Blackwood in 1904 and 1905 about the acquisition of rights and stock of the Isbister titles.

The largest print run ever undertaken for one of Munro's books was the astonishing 107,000 copies of *Erchie, My Droll Friend* (1904). This title was heavily advertised and promoted and very large sales outside Scotland must have been anticipated to have warranted this level of print run. William Blackwood wrote to Munro in remarkably positive terms in July 1904:

> We are determined that if the book does not attain to the widest popularity it will not be for the want of effort on our part ... We should I think send a copy of the book to every editor and reviewer in the country, and enclose with it a sheet of extracts giving some characteristic passages likely to attract attention and be quoted. We should also send out a good blaze of advertisements at the very outset... [4]

This bullish enthusiasm explains the hugely optimistic print run but this seems to have been a major miscalculation on the part of the

publisher. Although the first year sales were indeed very satisfactory
– 47,818, with royalties of £474.16.9 (or about £24,000 at current
values) coming to Munro – the sales then virtually stopped with only
240 copies going in the next two years. Almost 60,000 copies left
sitting in Blackwood's warehouse must have been a considerable
embarrassment to the company. *Erchie* was re-launched as a 6d.
cheap edition and 54,147 copies were sold in the first year after re-
launch – but Munro's royalty on these was the negligible sum of
£17.17.7. 3,500 copies were sold in a Colonial Edition and the print
run was exhausted by 1911. *Erchie* was never reprinted until the
collected edition of the 'Hugh Foulis' short stories appeared after
Munro's death.

William Blackwood wrote to Munro in September 1904 that sales
of Erchie had been very disappointing. One factor in this must have
been the difficulties of language for an English readership. When, in
October 1905, Munro wrote to William Blackwood suggesting a
volume of Para Handy stories, which had commenced publication
in the *Glasgow Evening News* in January of that year, he stressed that:

> The dialect, for one thing, is reduced to a minimum and the
> articles are quite within the comprehension of the English reader
> without any glossary.[5]

This linguistic distinction between the Para Handy and Erchie
stories has doubtless had an influence on the much greater, long-
term and posthumous commercial success of the Para Handy tales.

The *Erchie* experience presumably influenced Blackwoods in
determining the print run for the first collection of Para Handy
stories, *The Vital Spark,* in 1906. This was, like *Erchie,* produced as
a 1/- paperback but the first print run was a cautious 19,800
(although a reprint of 10,900 was called for within a month). The
first year sales of Para Handy stories were a very healthy 21,866
(with royalties of £175.7.9) and this volume continued to sell in
respectable but not enormous quantities – running at anywhere from
300 to 1,800 a year. The second Para Handy anthology, *In Highland
Harbours* did somewhat less well and the third, *Hurricane Jack of the
Vital Spark* only recorded 5,574 sales in its first year. It does seem
reasonable to assume that a higher initial level of sales of the Para
Handy stories, bearing in mind their greater acceptability on the UK
market, could have been achieved had they been promoted as ener-
getically as the Erchie stories.

The real success of the 'Hugh Foulis' stories only came with the publication of the omnibus edition after Munro's death and it is interesting to note from the royalty statements in the 1930s and 40s how the proportion of income derived from *Para Handy and Other Tales* came to greatly outstrip the income from all the novels in the collected 'Inveraray' edition. In 1938 *Para Handy* earned £64.6.9 of royalties while the novels in the Inveraray Edition earned £64.7.3. By 1943 *Para Handy* (with sales of 6,005 copies) produced royalties of £423.14.9 while the Inveraray Edition only returned £55.7.7.

One of the more surprising facts to emerge from a study of these papers is the popularity of what is often described as one of Munro's least successful novels – *Daft Days*. In its first year *Daft Days* sold 5,861 copies in the 6/- edition and a further 1,838 copies in a colonial edition. A cheap edition followed and this sold a remark-able 41,118 copies between 1911 and 1918, becoming in this period Munro's best-selling novel. Another of Munro's ventures into the contemporary world, *Fancy Farm*, was, again despite modern critical reservations, surprisingly successful – with 23,911 copies being sold between 1913 and 1918. *Daft Days* was taken up for publication in the United States by Harpers, under the title of *Bud*, and later even appeared in a Finnish translation.

What we now think of as Munro's masterpiece, *The New Road*, failed to show sales figures to match its place in contemporary and later critical esteem. Whereas *Daft Days* in its first eight years on the home market had sold over 40,000 copies *The New Road*, in the same length of time only totalled 27,025 copies, although the influence of the war on sales, paper stocks and availability should not be overlooked.

As an alternative way of presenting this somewhat unexpected fact one might compare sales over the five years 1914–19 following the publication of *The New Road*, when all these last mentioned titles were available. These figures include both full price and cheap editions.

Daft Days	25,236
Fancy Farm	10,686
The New Road	23,729

The New Road did however produce Munro's largest single royalty payment – £492.1.4 – received for the home and colonial edition sales in 1914 – narrowly beating his payment for the first year sales of *Erchie*.

The critical reception of *The New Road* was all that any author could have wished. The *Glasgow Herald* considered that it was 'the best novel Mr Munro has yet given us' and concluded by saying that he was to be congratulated on 'the production of the most suggestive Celtic novel by a Celt, that has yet appeared in the English language'.[6] Munro's own paper, without his knowledge, had John Buchan write a signed review of the book – a relatively uncommon occurrence in a period when unsigned reviews were the norm. Buchan's enthusiasm was evident from the very opening of his review:

> It is a privilege to be allowed to express my humble admiration of what seems to me one of the finest romances written in our time. Mr Neil Munro is beyond question the foremost of living Scottish novelists, both in regard to the scope and variety of his work and its rare quality.[7]

Munro, obviously touched by this praise, wrote to Buchan on 15 June 1914:

> I appreciated your characteristically generous tribute to my book in the *Glasgow News*. It was happy inspiration of the Editor to ask you to do the notice, and the more gratifying to me since I dared not suggest it myself though there is no man's approval of my stuff I would rather have than yours.[8]

Of course, not every title was equally successful. Some, like *Children of Tempest*, while selling a very respectable 4,734 copies in its year of publication, never made it into the volume market of a cheap edition. These cheap editions, while they were only modestly profitable for Munro, certainly brought his work before a wider audience.

There were two standard uniform editions of Munro's novels – a 3/6d edition with green dust jacket and the Inveraray Edition, produced in the 1930s, after Munro's death. These uniform editions sold alongside cheap and full-price editions and their performance is an interesting reflection on the changing demand for Munro's work. Some titles went out of print in the uniform edition during the First World War, problems of paper-rationing being a major factor, and by the early 1920s sales of the 3/6d edition were down to 300 or 400 a year. The early 20s were rather a lean time for Munro's literary earnings with no new novels coming out and only modest profits from cheap editions and the uniform edition.

The uniform edition was re-launched with all the titles again available and in 1923 11,748 volumes were sold. Sales gradually tailed off to about 2,500 a year by the end of Munro's life but his death in December 1930 caused a predictable upsurge in interest and in 1931 sales had increased to 9,439 copies of works in the uniform edition. Sales thereafter declined but in 1935 the effect of the change to the more attractively produced Inveraray Edition were seen with sales climbing to 9,265 copies.

The impression given by the royalty statements is of a remarkably successful literary career. In addition to the earnings shown in these statements it should be remembered that for most of his books Munro also had a very significant income from the serialisation in *Blackwood's Magazine* or *Good Words* which preceded book publication. *Gilian the Dreamer* earned £250 from *Good Words* and Blackwood's serialisation of *Daft Days* earned Munro £400 from serialisation, as well as £371.4.0 from sales of the 6/- edition and £13.15.9 from sales of the 'Colonial Edition' in the first year – a total of £785 (or perhaps about £40,000 in present day values). *Daft Days* might have been a remarkable popular success but even a more 'difficult' novel, such as *Children of Tempest* with 4,734 copies in the year of publication had sales which would certainly delight a modern 'literary' novelist.

This impression of commercial success is confirmed by Munro's habit of noting his annual earnings in his diary. These end of year statements presumably included both his royalties and his journalistic income and give a very clear impression of a developing career, fully justifying his decision to leave full-time newspaper work in 1897.[9]

Year	Earnings noted in Diary
1898	£679
1899	£852
1900	£586
1901	£1,243
1902	£781
1903	£795
1904	£822
1905	£933
1906	£606
1907	£1,108
1908	£1,343
1909	£865

1910	£1,167
1911	£992
1912	£678
1913	£1,046
1914	£720

There is an inevitable problem in translating these earnings into present day values but multiplication of these sums by 50 would not be too far wide of the mark.

An alternative way of looking at Munro's income, which while suffering the inevitable fluctuations associated with a literary career was never less than comfortable, is to reflect that in 1902 he bought a house in Gourock, 'Westview' (which he later re-named 'Carnus') for the sum of £875. This substantial house had 3 public rooms and 5 bedrooms – but its cost only represented one average year's income for Munro. Munro's literary work and his continuing journalistic work enabled him to live a very comfortable middle-class life style – a life style that extended to sending his daughter Effie to finishing school in Switzerland in 1907/8.

Notes

1 *The Bookman*, October 1898
2 *Ibid*. For the complete text of the Symposium see p.95 of this volume.
3 *The Academy*, 1 October 1898
4 National Library of Scotland (NLS) MS 30392 f.50
5 NLS MS 30116
6 *Glasgow Herald*, 10 June 1914
7 *Glasgow Evening News*, 10 June 1914. For the whole review see p.183 of this volume
8 NLS Acc 7214
9 NLS MS 26925

John Splendids and Jaunty Jocks: Neil Munro, The Highlands and Scottish Fiction

DOUGLAS GIFFORD

This chapter will claim that for too long we have mis-read a major strand of Scottish fiction, and that major Scottish novelists from Walter Scott to Neil Gunn have consistently recognised the difficulty of integrating the Highlands historically, culturally and imaginatively with Lowland Scotland, and treated the Highlands and Highlanders with far less romantic reverence than is usually supposed. It will also argue that in his interrogation of Highland culture and values through historical fiction (but also through other fictional genres) Neil Munro is a major novelist and a crucial link between the nineteenth-century novelists and those of the Scottish Renaissance of the inter-war years. His fiction, for far too long read as entertaining Highland escapism, stands next only to the fiction of Walter Scott (rather than Stevenson) both in terms of its quality as historical fiction and in terms of its satirical and deeply critical revaluation of what Highland social culture had become in the eighteenth and nineteenth centuries. Munro was very much a child of Inveraray and Argyll, yet in his adult life, as arguably Scotland's best known journalist, and based in Glasgow, he was inevitably dissociated from it. Munro has both a Highland and Lowland perspective on the culture and territory from which he came. Yet far from associating himself with romanticising and escapist tendencies in Scottish culture of his time, such as those movements in fiction, poetry, and drama termed 'Kailyard' or 'Celtic Twilight', in his best work (*The Lost Pibroch* (1896), *John Splendid* (1898), *Gilian the Dreamer* (1899) and *The New Road* (1914)) he explored questions of Highland identity and values with subtlety and sympathy, yet with often bitter and acute satire analysing fundamental weaknesses in his Argyllshire Highlanders' perception of themselves. Earlier poetical and fictional views of Highland history and culture, from James Macpherson's

Ossian poem-cycles, Thomas Campbell, (and in his poetry) Walter Scott, to later writers like James Grant, William Black and Celtic Twilight writers like 'Fiona Mcleod' were seriously flawed in their romanticised and distorted portrayals of Highland and Celtic society and culture. Munro has for too long been associated with this falsifying tradition when in fact he is the precursor of the twentieth-century Scottish Renaissance's profound revaluation of Scottish history, culture and identity, and its analysis of the predicament of the Scottish writer. It is time now for the rediscovery of an unjustly neglected writer of crucial importance in understanding the history, culture and psychology of the Scottish Highlands, as well as in understanding the emerging and revisionary ideologies of some of Scotland's – and Britain's – greatest novelists and poets, such as Neil Gunn, Lewis Grassic Gibbon, and Naomi Mitchison.

Highland history and culture had been distorted in its represen-tations by prejudiced and inaccurate outsiders long before Macpherson and Scott. For example, Lowland Scotland in the middle ages viewed the Highlands as living in a state of barbarism; later, political antipathy to the Lordship of the Isles simultaneously insisted on maintaining this stereotypical demonisation with a para-doxical positive evaluation of Highland heritage in order to find an ancient and noble lineage for an essentially Lowland Scottish kingship. The eighteenth century philosophers of the Enlightenment and the Common-sense School needed to find primitive nobility among our Celtic ancestors to back up their theories of civilisation and improvement, and they were conveniently supplied with this in the distorted pictures of heroic Celticism of the poems of Ossian. The achievement of James Macpherson's reconstructions was to distance his present Highlands from a long-gone Golden Age of Celtic heroes whose simple nobility had been lost as history moved on, thus safely legitimizing the activities of improvers like Sir John Sinclair. And the consequences of this improvement were of course the controversial Clearances and large-scale forced emigration, urbanisation, and regimentation of the Highlanders.

From the fifteenth to the nineteenth century the Highlands emerge as a territory which was as much a construct of mind as a loosely defined geographical topography. With hindsight we can realise that they were never so much of a concrete threat to Lowland peace and prosperity as a convenient site for ideological appropria-tion by the Lowlands, and a timeless and convenient raiding-ground for British politicians and social leaders in the formation of expedi-ential politics and social theory – with the ultimate distortion surely to be found in Queen Victoria's re-creation of Highlands and Highlanders as Britain's Shangri-la, and home of some of Britain's hardiest and most loyal servants of Empire.

It would be fair to say that literary misrepresentation of the Highlands really took off in the eighteenth century with Macpherson's success in claiming that his poetic presentations of heroic warriors and tragic heroines were authentic translations and reproductions of the poems of Ossian, the ancient Celtic bard. It was arguably Macpherson's poems rather than Scott's novels which established the more distorted view of the Highlands in popular consciousness. Scott's Highland-based novels are too often wrongly accused of false romanticisation, when they were remarkably under-standing of Highland society and culture for their time. But Scott – like Munro after him – would be read not for his satiric and decon-structive view of the Highlands, and his underlying plea for understanding and tolerance of a dying and anachronistic Celtic way of life, but for his surface colour and exotic settings, and it cannot be denied that his work opened up a huge territory for exploitation by European and American writers, painters, musicians.

The nineteenth century was confused in its attitudes towards Highlands and Highlanders. For all Prime Minister Pitt's brilliant pragmatic eighteenth-century redefinition of potential Highland rebels as front-line soldiers of Empire, and for all the illustrious role of Highland regiments in Napoleonic wars and Imperial battles, Lowland Scottish and British opinions of the Highlands in the years around the great potato famines in Ireland and Scotland in the 1840s reveal just how changeable nineteenth century Lowland Scottish – and British – views of the Highlands could be. Within a year or two, sympathy for the plight of a simple people could turn into contempt for their feckless irresponsibility (mirroring contem-porary attitudes to Ireland) – and back again. Clearance and Famine could thus be deplored or condoned, according to bias and perspec-tive. While William Grant's best selling Victorian novel *The Romance of War; or The Highlanders in Spain* (1845) glorified the robust, hard-drinking yet noble kilted regiments in the Napoleonic wars, *The Scotsman* could blame the improvidence of Highlanders for their appalling troubles during famine. That said, writers and artists usually exploited the Highlands to provide romance, vivid landscape, and escape from an increasingly industrialised and commercial Britain. By 1878 novelist William Black ('the darling of the lending libraries') could present his fashionable but confused Victorian stereotypes of the Highland Chief, outstandingly in

Macleod of Dare in which he cast a romantic aura of noble savagery around his young Mull Chieftain of Macleod, whose curious mixture of barbarity and breeding temporarily captivates a famous London actress. She plays with her fashionable toy princeling for a while, then drops him when the social season ends – a mistake, this, since he carries her off from London in his yacht, and, since she won't be persuaded, sinks the yacht in a storm and drowns them both, appropriately enough, off the West coast of Mull. What a confusion of values is here – trivial London (but essential to maintain readers' interest and very much the needed foil for romantic Highlands); noble Macleod (but ultimately tiresome in his obsessive and anachronistic pride of race); dark undercurrents to superficially socialised natives (so don't play around with primitives!).

Kailyard fiction and poetry of the second half of the nineteenth century delighted in celebrating the figure of the Highland soldier. Queen Victoria's Scottish chaplain, Norman Macleod, turned out several of the most successful of these useful Empire-endorsing fictions. The Highlander was not always seen, however, in this glamorous light. More insidiously, 'Fiona Mcleod', the essential feminine Celtic spirit discovered inside himself by Surrey-based journalist William Sharp, ended Victoria's century with her/his Celtic Twilight pseudo-celebrations of the Gaels and their culture, in novels like *Pharais: A Romance of the Isles* (1894), and *The Mountain Lovers* (1895), portraying them as doomed children of the mist, last remnants of an ancient poetic race, now brain-fevered and dying into their Western oceans. Romantic though this might appear, it has perhaps a more sinister political subtext, as it can be seen as effectively condoning a political attitude of *laissez-faire* towards the by now all too moribund Highlands, taken over as they were by absentee landlords of great hunting estates, landscape painters, and an educational system which outlawed the speaking of Gaelic in Schools. To add to the confusion of views, at the same time Ernest Renan, Matthew Arnold, and Grant Allan paid glorious lip-service to Celtic achievement in the world. Two contrasting quotations here from Holbrook Jackson's chapter on 'The Discovery of the Celt' in his classic study of 1913, *The Eighteen-Nineties*, illustrate some of the worst excesses of pseudo-Celtic enthusiasm. The first is 'Fiona Macleod', indulging her poetic sensibility in lament for the glory that was the Gael's – and implying that the Gaels should accept their destiny...

Strange reversals, strange fulfilments, may lie on the lap of the gods, but we have no knowledge of these, and hear neither the laughter nor the far voices. But we front a possible because a spiritual destiny greater than the height of imperial fortunes, and have that which may send our voices further than the trumpets of East and West. Through ages of slow westering, till now we face the sundown seas, we have learned in continual vicissitude that there are secret ways whereon armies cannot march. And this has been given to us, a more ardent longing, a more apt passion in the things of outward beauty and in the things of spiritual beauty. Nor it seems to me is there any sadness, or only the serene sadness of a great day's end, that, to others, we reveal in our best the genius of a race whose farewell is in a tragic lighting of torches of beauty around its grave...[1]

It is striking that in both the Ossian poems of Macpherson and in the work of 'Fiona Macleod' there is the same dark view of noble savagery declining into racial decadence. Yet, if Macleod typically exemplifies a view of the Gael which, for all its apparent dignifying of its subject, could be read as supporting political and social neglect of Gaelic economy and culture, other southern commentators presented a diametrically opposed but equally overblown rhetoric. Jackson quotes Grant Allen, who had in 1891 in *The Fortnightly Review* claimed an astonishingly ubiquitous Celtic influence over all things English (by which he meant, of course, British). In his grotesquely inflated claim – which to many readers must collapse under the weight of its own pretentious exaggeration – Allen found that Celtic influence had brought about almost every significant achievement and development in late Victorian Britain, including Home Rule, Land Nationalisation, Socialism, Radicalism, the Tithes War, the Crofter Question; it had introduced to political life 'the eloquent young Irishman, the perfervid Highland Scot, the enthusiastic Welshman, the hard-headed Cornish miner', as well as Methodism, Catholicism, the Hebrides, the Scotland Division of Liverpool, and a host of Irish-Scottish Celtic writers.

> The Celt in Britain, like Mr Burne-Jones's enchanted princess, has lain silent for ages in enforced long sleep; but the spirit of the century, pushing aside the weeds and briars of privilege and caste, has set free the sleeper at last...[2]

Celtic Twilight proved to be a literary dawn in Ireland; but its counterpart in Scotland never emerged out of the gloaming. For a decade or so, under Patrick Geddes and his journal of the new Scottish Celticism, *The Evergreen* magazine, with 'Fiona Mcleod' and other painters and poets (and with Rennie Mackintosh its most interesting by-product at the vogue's end), the Lowlands flirted with this latest fashion in Highland appropriation. Munro's work owes something to both the Irish Revival of Yeats and that of Geddes in Scotland; but its achievement goes beyond that of both revivals in its analysis of Highland and Celtic culture, drawing more deeply on an older and darker tradition of Scottish fiction.

Nineteenth-century Scottish culture did not always distort the realities of Lowland and Highland society and culture. Some Scottish fiction tried, amongst its other aims, to see both Highlands and Lowlands with far greater realism and understanding. This tradition began early in the century with Scott, Ferrier, Hogg, and Galt and and their fictional juxtaposing of past and present, disorder and order, romance and realism, in novels like *Waverley* (1814), *Old Mortality* (1816) *Rob Roy* (1818), *Redgauntlet* (1824), Ferrier's *Marriage* (1818), Hogg's *The Justified Sinner* (1824), and Galt's *The Entail* (1823). These novels established the symbols and patternings of opposites which would become characteristics of Scottish fiction thereafter. In this earlier period, as writers struggled to articulate their deepest responses to their divided Scotlands, the fundamental oppositions were those of older Scotland in tension with the new, especially when linked with civil wars of religion and Jacobitism – and more often than not the central figures of their novels, far from being conventionally heroic, were flawed protagonists, even anti-heroes, illustrative of the broken societies and divided cultures in which they acted. Munro's best fiction should be read as working within this tradition. *Waverley* and *Rob Roy* are of course the classic Scott representations of the Highlands; read eagerly for their apparent romance, less often read as subtle in their irony and satire on their trapped heroes and anachronistic and often morally and ideologically suspect Highlanders, and their recurrent patterning, in which a doomed past is set against a prosaic present and future, and colourful disorder set against mundane order. Underneath the glorious landscape settings of *Waverley* lie a complex web of Highland treacheries and betrayals; Edward Waverley, the remarkably un-heroic and trapped English observer, will learn a sadder and wiser view of Highlands and romance. Rob Roy, surprisingly, turns out to be the most decent and noble figure in Scott's novel; yet history forces him to represent outlaw Scotland set against mercantile Scotland, he and his clan against his cousin, Bailie Nicol Jarvie and the new and flourishing mercantile Glasgow and its trade with America. What emerges recurrently and strongly in all these novels are central figures torn in conscience and loyalty, Scott's 'men in the middle', trapped in uncertainty between contending claims of conscience in politics and religion. And the same theme of divided claims and allegiances is found in the other major novels of the period. Hogg's Sinner is torn between the claims of fanatical religion and of his 'common sense' conscience and nature's voice; Galt's tormented fanatic in *Ringan Gilhaize* (1823) is driven beyond his essential decency by the atrocities of an intolerant government towards his family and community to the point where he himself becomes a fanatical 'justified sinner'. Brutal authority, often expressed in father-figures (who can be of the establishment or of the anti-establishment) is recurrently seen as repressing moderation and sensitivity, this side of the polarisation often being symbolically represented in rebellious sons; and this central patterning is found thereafter in the work of Stevenson, Munro, and Douglas Brown, and Buchan.

What is striking is how so much of this major fiction concerns itself with the Highlands and the reduction of its apparently romantic and exotic character and history, to the extent that its heroes and causes are seen to be far more deeply flawed and anachronistic than conventional and popular culture would believe. The reason for this focus on the Highlands is perhaps that the major writers find in the prevailing popular and romantic iconography the biggest obstacle to their attempt to bring imaginative perceptions of Scotland closer to historical actuality, and what they perceive to be the less romantic and more mundanely tragic realities of Scottish character and psyche. The later work in this serious tradition of fiction which deals with the Highlands, such as George Mac-Donald's *Malcolm* (1875), *The Marquis of Lossie* (1877), and Margaret Oliphants's *Kirsteen* (1896) moves away from locating these family divisions within history, focusing more closely on the psychological antagonisms within self and family. It is true that *Kidnapped* (1886) and *Catriona* (1893) are set within historical periods reminiscent of Scott, but the emphasis is on the psychological contrast in the opposing qualities of David Balfour and Alan Breck, Lowlander and Highlander, just as in *The Master of Ballantrae* (1888) the emphasis is on the two fundamentally different kinds of Scot to be found in stay-at-home account-watching Henry Durie and his earth-wandering and demonic brother James. This opposition is represented in many Scottish novels set around the turn of the century, becoming the clash between an authoritarian father-figure and his hyper-sensitive son, in such as *Weir of Hermiston, The House with the Green Shutters, Gillespie* – and, subtly re-arranged, in Munro's *Gilian the Dreamer*. This opposition between family figures inextricably linked yet diametrically opposed, are to Stevenson and his successors representative of a Scotland divided between realism and romance, rational prudence and imaginative release, and unable to reconcile its artistic and creative energies with its economic and commercial ambitions.

Munro was thus not alone in later nineteenth-century decon-struction of romanticised notions of Scottish culture. And as the century neared its end the Kailyard and Celtic Twilight movements were increasingly attacked by many poets and novelists who had grown heart-sick of their use of false mythologies and time-serving icons of nineteenth-century Scotland – the chieftains, the stags at bay, the minister and dominie serving simple worthy peasants in bens and glens, the lads of intellectual and high moral parts from simple schools and straths, the Scottish soldier, the Highland Lass – as well as all the cohorts of Lowland and the Heaven-taught farmer-and-weaver poets. Writers of the period – Munro, Douglas Brown, the Findlater sisters, John Davidson John MacDougall Hay, Violet Jacob, John Buchan, and, surprisingly, even James Barrie in fiction, and James Young Geddes, Robert Buchanan, James Thomson and John Davidson in poetry – can all be read as part of this decon-struction, working through parody and satire.

Their work marks the point where old expediential prejudices of Lowlands against Highlands begin at last to change. MacDiarmid, Gunn, Gibbon, Mitchison and others of the so-called 'Scottish Renaissance' are usually credited with this revaluation; but this destruction of the abundant distortions in Scottish cultural and historical representation was just as much the work of Neil Munro and his neglected contemporaries. Munro especially was working against the romantic idealisations of proud Highland culture in the fiction of popular novelists like James Grant, Norman Macleod, William Black, and 'Fiona Mcleod'. They represented the Highlander as the heir to a simple communality, as *primus inter pares*, a chief amongst equals – but they failed to explore more deeply, to find the underlying paradox in a culture which exalted the valour and status of the clan chief, to whom the individual Highlander was deeply subservient. It was this central inconsistency which would be identified by writers like Munro as the fatal flaw in Highland ideas of valour and kinship, leading to a fatalistic acceptance of Clearance and imperial militarisation. Munro's work anticipates the dark and sceptical novels of Lowland and Highland realism and despair of the 1920s, in Lowland novels like Gibbon's *Sunset Song* (1932), A.J. Cronin's *Hatter's Castle* (1931) and James Barke's *The Land of the Leal* (1939); while the Highlands were similarly re-visioned in the work of Neil Gunn, Ian Macpherson and 'Fionn MacColla' (Thomas Douglas Macdonald).[3]

These are some contexts for Munro's achievement. As one of the most prolific and internationally influential writers about the Western Highlands, his work going into ten editions by the first world war, with another eleven by 1940, and new editions of his work regularly appearing now, where does Munro stand in relation to the nineteenth century's Highland image-making, and to the later 'Scottish Renaissance' which claimed revision of all previous portrayals of the Highlands?

Neil Munro was born in Inveraray in 1863, the illegitimate son of a kitchen-maid in the castle. Rumours continue to the present that he was the unacknowledged son of one of the noblest of the house of Argyll. Whether he was or not, the equivocal nature of his birth pervasively influenced his fiction. On one hand Munro identified with the great House of Argyll, Inveraray, and the West Highlands as representative of the best of Gaeldom, and leading it from barbarism to a new future in which it would bond with the Lowlands. But Munro also recognised the limitations of clan inheritance, leading to a portrayal in story after story of a series of Argyll father-chieftains and Campbell aristocrats as apparently noble, but deeply flawed – sometimes bombastic, sometimes duplicitously charming and pretentious, recurrently anachronistic and representative of the failure of the Highlands to come to terms with a new world order where clan military and mercenary values were outmoded and irrelevant What makes this the more complex in his work is Munro's tension between, on one hand, instinctive loyalty to his people's past, with its age-old reverence for martial Gaeldom, which leads to Munro's vivid evocation of scenes of clan battle, such as Montrose's devastation of Argyll in 1644 – and, on the other, his compassionate distaste for such wanton slaughter, which comes out in his sensitivity to the aftermath of such destruction, in the descriptions of smoking ruins and families destroyed. Munro understood traditional Highland ferocity; the reader of his war-poems for 1914 like 'Hey, Jock, are ye glad ye 'listed?' and 'Wild Rover Lads' could be forgiven for thinking that Munro celebrates the continuity of the

Highland warrior tradition. In the light of Munro's recurrent fictional deconstruction of the warrior ethos of chieftain and clan, it is arguable, I believe, that just as in his presentations of Highland characters like John Splendid and Sim McTaggart of *Doom Castle*, where he seems to celebrate but in fact slyly parodies and ultimately exposes the falsity of their values, similarly in these poems he is parodically speaking not for himself, but in the voice of a timeless Highland *persona* representing the traditional blood-instinct for war of his forebears, as found so often in his historical novels. Fierce sentiments like 'Come awa, Jock, and kill your man!' can be misunderstood as representing an uglier side of Munro, when arguably they were not essentially his own feelings, but anachronistic Highland sentiments. (Munro himself described how he deliberately tried to capture the 'braggadocio' of older Highland war-feelings in his poetry.)[4] The 'Jaunty Jock' of this poem can be read as merely one of many dubious heroes following what the poem calls 'your daddy's trade', and the images and values of cocked bonnets and swagger are very much those attacked most ferociously by Munro in his short story 'War', discussed below. Taken with Munro's work as a whole, the poems are part of his lifelong and complex exposure of what he perceived as the historical weaknesses of Highland character and ancient warlike clan attitudes, a lifelong preoccupation which in 1914 would culminate in his greatest attack on Highland military anachronism, his last novel, *The New Road*, in which General Wade's opening up of the old Highlands with the side effect of stimulating trade with the Lowlands is triumphantly endorsed, most of all for its destruction of the selfish, sinister and manipulative Chieftains at the centre of webs of anachronistic corruption, such as the strutting, double-dealing Highland blackmailer Barisdale or the treacherous Mafia-style Highland chieftain 'MacShimi', Simon Lord Lovat, symbol of all that Munro sees as the endless betrayals and treacheries of the Northern clans.

Significantly, Munro did not stay past childhood and adolescence in his Western Highlands. At eighteen he left Inveraray for Lowland Glasgow, shortly to begin an illustrious career in journalism – and initiating a Highland-Lowland ambivalence of perspective which would come to characterise all his work. He would become one of Scotland's outstanding newspaper editors and critics with the *Glasgow Evening News*. (The bulk of Munro's huge body of journalism has never been published in book form, although his close friend, the novelist George Blake, published two collections, *The Brave Days* (1931) and *The Looker-On* (1933) showing the richness and range of his commentaries on the new twentieth-century Scotland.)[5] Munro never returned to live permanently in Inveraray, but his successive homes in Glasgow, Eaglesham, Gourock and Helensburgh perhaps reveal an underlying desire to accommodate both Highlands and Lowlands. The maps which Munro chose to accompany his study of *The Clyde* (1907) and the Highland novel *The New Road* (1914), reflect Munro's interlocking and overlapping territories. The reader who surveys their coverage of both Lowland and Highland territory begins to understand how this writer, vastly influential in his time, was so important in developing a new phase in Scottish cultural awareness, where Lowland perceptions of the Highlands as the romantic other, the wild zone beyond the Clyde and the barrier mountains of Perth, begin to disintegrate, with the Scottish regions becoming, in popular consciousness and in the minds of Renaissance writers, intertwined and part of an emerging meta-identity for Scotland. After the Great War others like MacDiarmid followed, if they did not always acknowledge, Munro's inspiration (C.M.Grieve's choice of pseudonym is, after all, homage to the master-tribe of Diarmid, Munro's oldest, pre-clan Campbell forebears, suggesting an underlying ideological link). The work of Gunn, Gibbon, Linklater and Mitchison would follow his lead in developing a synthesis of Highland and Lowland folk tradition, legend and myth.

Munro is profoundly important for this later reorientation. Hostile to the Kailyard and Celtic Twilight movements from the beginning, his first desire was to interpret the Highlands from the inside, since he felt that all previous literary evocations had been Lowland distortions. The result was the pioneering collection of short stories, *The Lost Pibroch* of 1896, in the same year as Barrie's satire on Scotland's repression of imagination and art, *Sentimental Tommy*, and in the period of the most ferocious of anti-kailyarders – and anti-Scots! – of the time, John Davidson, whose fiction and poetry marks another savage break with a romanticised past. Subtly exploiting and parodying the nostalgic self-indulgence and pseudo-Celtic mannerisms of 'Fiona Macleod', these poetic stories are essentially tragic, elegiac, and satiric. They draw in style from the great collections of oral tradition by J.F. Campbell, *Popular Tales of the West Highlands* (1860–2), but they consciously underweave a dark sub-text which can easily be missed, given the strength of their narratives, their cruel and often shocking twists of fate, and their seemingly sincere but deceptively mannered Celticism. The title story tells of a haunting and ancient pipe tune which must not be played. If it is played – and of course it is played, such is the vanity of the rival pipers – a blight will descend on the dear green places of the Highlands, and villages will lose their young men to emigration and war, following a nameless yearning. Munro never explicitly answers the implied question as to why an ancient pipe tune played by a blind piper should contain a curse of such power; but there is already the suggestion that something dark in the Gaelic inheritance, a 'feyness' or fatedness, has entered Highland culture, together with an excessive vanity and jealousy of loyalties which forces endless and unnecessary challenges of blood and vendetta. Story after story has this sly sub-text. A jealous second wife slashes the piping hand of her stepson, who threatens to outplay his father, a son kills his unknown father as a result of a pointless, long-drawn blood feud, jealous brothers drive a French lover from their enchanted sister, and again and again tragedy results when neighbouring communities and clans are mutually distrustful and ready to find the insult that leads to bloodshed. Romance is a deceit, the traditional artist an anachronism, – blind, crippled, or pushed outside community to wander. The lost – and last – pibroch has been played.

Three stories outstandingly represent Munro's attack on what he felt had become the weakened heart of his Highlands; 'Boboon's Children', 'Castle Dark', and 'War'. The first tells of how John Fine Macdonald, leader of an ancient nomadic tribe, at one with season and landscape, portrayed as a kind of *ur*-Highlander, is 'civilised' by the Campbell Captain of Inveraray. The Captain (at this stage so much humbler than the later Argyll nobility) is seen as a pseudo-father who aims to destroy these original and natural Highlanders, by literally enclosing their leader's ancient and nomadic simplicity of spirit within the confines of his town house. Boboon hears his tribe calling at night to him from outside the garden wall, and eventually succumbs to their outlaw temptations of salmon and deer and freedom – but he leaves his daughter to die as the captain's prisoner-wife. 'Castle Dark' is even more revealing of Munro's sense that something ancient and good in Highland tradition has been corrupted by dominance of ideas of castle power and male assertions of the values of war. In this, the closing story of the collection, a fable of Highland history and culture, the blind piper Paruig Dall – he whose piping of the Lost Pibroch sent Highlanders wandering the earth, and whose story opened the volume – opens with his description of Castle Dark, which seems to be an archetype of all great Highland houses and clans. 'Once upon a time', Paruig tells us, 'Castle Dark was a place of gentility and stirring days...now it is like a deer's skull in Wood Mamore, empty, eyeless, sounding to the whistling wind, but blackened instead of bleached in the threshing rains'. To find this quintessential and *ur*-Castle of all the Highlands, the traveller must journey twice on the Blue Barge, the *birlinn ghorm*, the timeless and mythic galley of Fairy Lorne; thus Munro deepens the idea that the journey is one of spirit and imagination rather than actuality. Paruig tells us how an Adventurer made the two trips; Munro, behind him, setting out his dark vision of the three phases of Highland decline. On his first trip:

When the Adventurer reached the bridge, it was before the time of war, and the country from end to end sat quiet, free, and honest. Our folks lived the clean out-by life of shepherds and early risers. Round these hills the woods – the big green woods – were trembling with bird and beast, and the two glens were crowded with warm homes – every door open, and the cattle untethered on the hill. Summer found the folks like ourselves here, far up on the sappy levels among the hills, but their sheilings more their own than ours are, with never a reiver nor a broken clan in all the land. Good stout roads and dry went down the passes from Castle Dark from all airts of Albainn – roads for knight and horse, but free and safe for the gentlest girl ever so lonely. By sea came gabberts of far France with wine and drink; by land the carriers brought rich cloths, spices and Italian swords....[6]

But the harmony of these ancient days is not to last. Even as the Adventurer marvels at the tranquillity and beauty of the land, he realises how the Highlands are changing, as he overhears the young chief of Castle Dark taking farewell of his lover. Echoing the first story of the volume, he tells her 'I am for the road tomorrow'. 'For yon silly cause again?' she sighs.

'For the old cause', said he; 'my father's, my dead brother's, my clan's, ours for a hundred years. Do not lightly the cause, my dear; it may be your children's yet.'[7]

And, with the false promises of 'War', the chief goes off to the endless clan feuds, battles, and wars so beloved of romance, but which Munro sees as terminally destructive for his Highlands. The second trip on the blue Barge reveals the extent of the tragedy.

'Twas a summer's end when he [the Adventurer] went on the next

49

jaunt, a hot night and hung with dripping stars. The loch crawled in from a black waste of sorrow and strange hills...and swished on the shore trailing among the wreck with the hiss of fingers through ribbons of silk.[8]

Suddenly, with savage and surreal reversal, it is winter, despite Paruig's beginning the jaunt with summer. 'Winter I said, and winter it was' – and morning too, emphasizes Paruig, deliberately contradicting himself to emphasize that the times are out of joint:

It was the middle and bloodiest time of all our wars. The glens were harried, and their cattle were bellowing in strange fields. Widows grat on the brae-sides and starved their bairns for the bere and oat that were burned. But Adventurer found a castle full of company, the rich scum of water-side lairds and Lowland gentry, dicing and drinking in the best hall of Castle Dark. Their lands were black, their homes levelled, or their way out of the country – if they were Lowland –was barred by jealous clans.... [9]

Munro's nightmare picture of what Argyll and the Highlands have become after internecine wars and Jacobite rebellions is prolonged with drunken cardplaying and slumbering wrecks of revellers littering the castle. The extent of degradation is represented in the self-hatred of George Mor, a mercenary 'namely for women and wine and gentlemanly sword-play'. That 'gentlemanly' is deeply ironic; George Mor is one of the first of a long line of 'Jaunty Jocks' and John Splendids, raffish adventurers twisted by Highland feud and war-culture into a deformation of older Highland values. The story's climax comes with the return of Castle Dark's young chief, embittered and yet again disillusioned to find that George Mor would appear to have taken his place with his lady; they fight, and George is killed. The story – and the collection – ends as it began, with desolation, the end of Castle Dark, the young chief yet again for the road that leads to the furthest ends of the world, as a Highland soldier of fortune.

Munro's satiric vision of his Highlands can be seen developing in these tales. Broadly, he sees his Highland culture and history as existing in three distinct periods – firstly, a golden age, the world of the nomadic Boboon and his children, his very name suggesting his prehistoric antiquity (this vision anticipating key ideas of later Renaissance writers such as Gunn, Gibbon, and Muir); secondly, the descent into clan rivalry and bloodthirsty wars of so-called honour; and thirdly, an inevitable move of Highlanders out into the big world, in trade and commerce, yet too often as exiles or mercenaries, and leaving behind the nostalgic wasteland of half-pay retired soldiers and empty boasters mulling over their war memories, so vividly represented in the novel *Gilian the Dreamer*. Increasingly Munro's work identifies the archetypal Highlander as unreliable, deceitful and flattering, too often a braggart who represents the tragic flaw at the heart of the degeneration of a once-noble clanship. These not-so-splendid and spuriously Jaunty Johns and Jocks (and Paruigs, and Paras?) thrive parasitically in a world of clan feuding and approved despoliation, a social system which finds its ultimate value in stealing cattle and killing women and children in the name of tribal honour, and in which the traditional equality of blood kinship (found with Boboon and his children) has been replaced by the hierarchical claims of the clan chief in his new and Anglicised guise of Captain, Earl, Marquis or Duke.

Munro was never more scathing about this male-dominated and hierarchical swaggering than in 'War', one of the starkest and most effective of his many tragedies. Rob Donn follows Duke John to Culloden and the complacent and boastful killing of fellow-Highlanders, leaving his wife with no money, but with pretentious promises of his returning glory. Months pass; the restless soldier squanders the money he took from his wife; glutted with killing, he returns just as his wife, her own milk long dry, in last extremity of famine drawing off blood from her cow for her baby, hears the child's death-cry. The closing passages, with their evocation of the swagger of the Campbells as they boast of their defeat of Charles at Culloden, convey the depth of Munro's hatred and disgust at warlike male swaggering, as Rob Donn returns home with the cockade of the seventh man he has killed as a gift for the child he has left to starvation and death:

... Rob Donn left the company as it passed near his own door.
    'Faith, 'tis a poor enough home-coming, without wife or bairn to meet one', said he as he pushed in the door.
    'Wife! wife!' he cried ben among the peat-reek, 'there's never a stot, but here's the cockade for the little one!'[10]

Here, with George Mor of 'Castle Dark', is the prototype for the Jaunty Jocks, the 'John Hielanmen' – and ultimately the Campbell chieftains themselves, who are merely their swaggering clan unreliables writ large. In later stories Munro will play cunningly with many variations of the type – and the name – of Highland Jock. A kindlier and later mood – yet, I will argue, still parodic and satiric, and occasionally as savage as anything earlier, as in his final and arguably most subtle presentation of his recurrent John Splendid/Jaunty Jock figure in Hurricane Jack – will see Munro reshape them into the crew of *The Vital Spark*, slipping in and out of Highland and Lowland ports with all the unreliability and shiftiness of their forebears, generally avoiding any claims of duty and responsibility, and covering their tracks with the relics of older self-inflating importance. But in 1898, with *John Splendid*, Munro was out to change Lowland perceptions of the Highlands with a subtle but deadly undermining of the House of Argyll from within.

For this is the strangest of historical romances – indeed, it is closer to the anti-romance of Lowlander James Hogg in his *Tales of the Wars of Montrose*, and particularly the parody of historical romance of *An Edinburgh Bailie* (1835); and it clearly shows the influence of Stevenson's ambiguities and psychological subtleties in *The Master of Ballantrae*, published ten years earlier. The two 'heroes', ex-soldiers of European fortune, John McIver (John Splendid, so called because of his vain but charismatic demeanour, and perhaps influenced by Stevenson's Alan Breck, or the more complex and ambiguous figure of James Durie in *The Master of Ballantrae*) and 'sobersides' Colin Elrigmore, are amongst the Marquis of Argyll's right-hand men. The events are those of the Wars of Lorne, when in 1644 Montrose and Macdonald ravaged Argyllshire, with the consequent pursuit of Montrose by Argyll, in which the hunter became the hunted. However, after his legendary mountain march Montrose surprised and destroyed Argyll's army at Inverlochy, and – for the second time – Argyll fled from him, leaving his men to death and disgrace.

Argyll's double shame hangs over the entire story and most of its characters. There is throughout a sense of anti-climax; for John and Colin achieve nothing for their side, apart from saving their own – and some of their friends'– skins. As far as battle goes, they are strangely ineffective, getting caught by their enemies as they carelessly dispute Highland poetry with the cranky Bard of Keppoch, John Lom Macdonald, before the battle of Inverlochy. They are on the run constantly; slouching like thieves, begging from poor women in lonely cottages, lost on Rannoch moor, inglorious in their company and their cause. This is a parodic extension of Scott's ambiguous presentation of complex protagonists such as Edward Waverley or Redgauntlet, a presentation continued by Stevenson in

Kidnapped, with its apparently similar but essentially different Breck-Balfour relationship. Munro is working here with the Scottish novel's traditional use of sly dramatic monologue, found so strikingly in the work of Galt and Hogg down to *The Master of Ballantrae*, in which the suspect teller of the tale reveals more about his limitations than he knows. Here the teller of the tale, Colin Elrigmore, is the unreliable narrator in his guileless simplicity, in his obtuse unawareness throughout the novel that his sweetheart Betty, the Provost's daughter, loves, and is being wooed by, his apparent boon companion John Splendid. Little is as it claims to be in this novel; Highland honour is exposed as sham bragging, shallow loyalty, and male egocentricity, as John wheedles, struts, manipulates, up to the edge of murder, with Colin as his deliberately-drawn rather dull Sancho Panza.

These nasty 'little wars of Lorn', with their rival leaders Montrose and Argyll seen as hardly in control of their bloodthirsty armies, are strangely detached from what is going on in the bigger British world. Munro deliberately leaves out any account of what Argyll is up to in the bigger world, and nothing of how he plays his much greater game with Covenanters, King Charles, and Westminster parliamentarians. The Highlanders are simply not interested in the larger picture, and Munro thus shows their limited and disconnected mindset. And nowhere is Munro's point about reductive Highland insularity made more clear than in the treatment by his Campbell adherents of Archibald the Grim, Gillespie Gruamach, Marquis of Argyll. Their failure to understand his new-world vision, and their insistence on fawning upon his least wish, is summed up in his relationship with John Splendid. Here is the key to Munro's psychological analysis of the destructive mindset of Gaeldom, and it is a critical assessment the more trenchant because it comes from within, from the heart of Inveraray – or at least from Munro as an Inveraray exile, seeing his Highlands from a Lowland perspective, and moved by love – and profound disillusion.

If this novel, with its central symbolic figure of John Splendid, represents the second phase in Munro's account of the decline of the Highlands, encapsulating its excessive chief-worship, love of war, pride in appearance over reality, and inability to see beyond the clan, it also suggests the movement into the third and final phase. For all his apparent failings, Argyll can be read as representing the movement of the Highlands into modernity as predicted and half-welcomed, half-deplored by Munro; namely, a move away from clan identification and ethos to acceptance of the values of a bigger world. Argyll plays his part – whatever his failings – in this bigger world; it will lead him to execution in Edinburgh ten years after Montrose. John Splendid will have none of Argyll's bookish and civilising tendencies – freedom to war, at home against Macdonalds or the Athole men, or abroad as mercenary, never judging the morality of the cause, is John the Hielanman's way, as long as he cuts a good figure, and fair speech is given to friends. As the novel develops, however, John is shown as the anachronism, and – pointing forward to John MacDougall Hay's *Gillespie* of sixteen years later, with its portrait of close-by Tarbert developing its fishing industry and links with the Lowlands – Munro shows the Lowlands changing Inveraray. The new shopkeepers, the vessels from Glasgow and Ayr, and the new 'English' church with its dour minister Gordon seem to sleepy Colin at first an intrusion, but by the end of the book he accepts the need for Lowland influence and change, and even decides – to Splendid's discomfiture – that the most courageous soldier and the best man throughout the sorry wars of Lorn has been the minister Gordon, the dour and inflexible Lowlander, the only man to speak plain and honest, without Highland flattery and face-saving and boasting – especially to Argyll. The most impressive part of this strange treatment of what could so easily be the subject for romance lies at the end, when Argyll lies sick in his castle after Inverlochy. John Splendid and Argyll's leaders had at the beginning advised him to quit Inveraray – and then again Inverlochy – to lead the clan another day. Their subservient and face-saving advice has brought about the spiritual demoralisation of the Campbells. Now at last Argyll begs his cousin McIver, John Splendid, to speak true and to tell him what he thinks of his chief, maintaining that he has been the victim of the smooth-tongued 'Highland liar'. And at last John seems to speak out honestly – although even now it will appear afterwards that his apparent final frankness has been calculated role-playing, and his dramatic declaration to abandon Argyll for European wars was for effect only:

'What do I think?' echoed McIver. 'Well, now – '
    'On your honour now', cried Argile, clutching him by the shoulder.
    At this McIver's countenance changed: he threw off his soft complacence, and cruelty and temper stiffened his jaw.
    'I'll soon give you that, my Lord of Argile', said he. 'I can lie like a Dutch major for convenience sake, but put me on honour and you'll get the truth if it cost me my life. Purgatory's your

portion, Argile, for a Sunday's work that makes our name a mock today across the envious world. Take to your books and your preachers, sir –you're for the cloister and not for the field: and if I live a hundred years, I'll deny I went with you to Inverlochy....Tomorrow the old big wars for me...and I'll find no swithering captains among the Cavaliers in France.'[11]

This is a subtle novel, and a superficial reading will miss the fact that both Argyll and McIver are being satirised, the one for accepting corrupt and hierarchical flattery, the other for giving it, and failing to see that the day of the old barbaric Highlands is over. Yet even in McIver's retraction we realise that he is equivocating; as he admits to Elrigmore, 'I could scarcely say myself when a passion of mine is real or fancied'; while Elrigmore, while still seeing him as his friend, can describe him in these closing stages as 'a most wicked, cunning, cruel fellow'. Such ambivalences and qualifications are Munro's way of expressing his love and hate for the way the essential early and natural goodness of Highland culture has been warped into time-serving deceit and arrogance. John must not be read solely as Highland deceiver; he has much of the old virtues – the skills of a scout, the loyalty to immediate comrades, an instinctive protectiveness to women and children. He may deceive Colin Elrigmore in love, but he relinquishes his chances for love to the younger man, and does indeed go off to Europe – leaving as the end of the novel the realisation by Betty that she has lost the man she really loves through misunderstanding, and the possible realisation – for he *is* dense! – by Colin that the woman he will marry will always love another – hardly the conventional romantic finale.

If *John Splendid* is important as Munro's fusion and summation into the two main figures of John Splendid and Argyll of all he deprecates and values in a period of Highland culture which has lost its way, then his next novel, *Gilian the Dreamer* (1899) changes its focus. Now Munro moves from the seventeenth-century figure of the showy clansman to the nineteenth-century figure of the lost child, symbol of Highland wasted potential and cultural decline, the long-term consequence of excessive patriarchal and martial values. This is a penetrating and deeply negative assessment of the nineteenth-century Highlands at the tail-end of the Napoleonic wars, when innumerable half-pay colonels ('Cornals' in Inveraray) and major-generals returned from the wars to rot in Inveraray and the small Highland towns, their only consolation their glorious and bloody memories of their part in the foreign wars of Empire. It is the era of an even more illustrious and by now remote London grandee Duke John, McCailean Mor, and these washed-up soldiers are the heirs of John Splendid. Munro mercilessly anatomizes them, and their repressive and malign influence on a burgh struggling to enter modernity. Casual reading will miss the deadliness of Munro's satire on these pensioned-off relics, boorish to their women, utterly self-centred, and nurturing old feuds. Munro was never more acidic than in his picture of the three Campbells of Keil – the old general Dugald, virtually dead apart from his memories in his dull room in a dark tenement; his brothers, Cornal John and the bull-necked Paymaster Captain John Campbell, another version of Jaunty Jock, and perhaps the least attractive. His is a portrayal of colossal male egotism which was be developed in Douglas Brown's Ayrshire merchant-tyrant Gourlay in *The House With the Green Shutters* two years later, and in the Highland merchant-tyrant Gillespie in Hay's novel of 1914. Munro's half-pay officers are in varying degrees bullies, philistines, anachronisms, unquestioning killers for empire. Munro allows some of them – like the decent general, John Turner – respectability and a place to fulfil in the world; but in the main this town has become a place of drunken ex-soldiers roistering in its taverns while their women-folk do the work.

But Munro has even deeper issues to explore – and now he artic-ulates a crucial Scottish predicament, which illustrates how he transcends Highland limitations to speak, like Neil Gunn after him, for Scottish culture and its failings. Gilian – the name a mocking echo of Gilian-of-the-Axe, one of the great Celtic folk heroes – is a fatherless boy of twelve whose grandmother has died. From the start we realise he is an unusual and perhaps not entirely healthy child; utterly alone at her death in Ladyfield, a small farm outside Inveraray, he rehearses in his imagination how he will tell his sad news in the town – suddenly, for maximum impact? Leading up slowly, for other, more complex effect? Gilian plays with his grief, genuine enough, but dearer still to him for its imaginative and emotional effects. His is a fine natural sensibility and creative awareness – but, left as marginalised, without any encouragement, indeed sneered at and mocked for its irrelevance to its distorted society, it is in danger of turning in upon itself, unhealthily pre-occupied with its own imaginings and hyper-sensitivities, just like the wasted creativity of Barrie's Tommie Sandys in *Sentimental Tommy* (1896) and *Tommy and Grizel* (1900), or of Douglas Brown's talented but unfocused young John Gourlay. Clearly these writers are concerned to explore what they see as a singularly Scottish social and cultural deficiency. It is significant that this presentation of the dangers of creative imagination dissociated from any supportive cultural tradition is frequently found in Scottish fiction, from as early as Scott's analysis of the imaginative delusions of young Edward Waverley in *Waverley* (1814), through the period of Stevenson, Munro and Brown, to be found persisting in the modern Scottish novel, in novels like Eric Linklater's *Magnus Merriman* (1934), Robin Jenkins's *Fergus Lamont* (1979) and Alasdair Gray's *Lanark* (1981). Such recurrent diagnoses of the same failure over generations of imaginative creativity in finding a society and culture to nurture it surely speaks for their authors' feelings of alienation from their own communities.

Munro's novel is central to Scottish fiction's sense of its country's cultural fragmentation and waste. For this boy is in his way a genius, with an imagination which cannot be fulfilled in this repressive burgh, with its lack of any aesthetic nourishment. It is important to realise that this novel is not just about the loss of ancient bardic involvement in Highland community. Munro's perception of the Highlands is beginning to merge with a more general perception of the overall problems of Scottish culture, including problems of Anglicisation, neglect of native language and genius, and a hardening of philistine attitudes towards local talent and subject-matter.

Gilian is no John Splendid. Indeed, he is closer to Munro himself, and this novel is arguably a working out of Munro's own troubled awareness of Campbell fatherhood as well as his recognition that Inveraray could never be an imaginatively nourishing home to him. We never learn who Gilian's father is; – is he the Paymaster, who owns Ladyfield, where Gilian's mother worked? Why else does he reluctantly assume responsibility for the boy? Gilian is a misfit who will fail in the eyes of all but the very few who love him or see his buried qualities. To his adoptive Campbells he's a playacting fool; to his contemporaries at school a wild and unpredictable solitary; to his friend Nan, merely a foil to her love interests elsewhere. Yet again Munro introduces parody of the conventional love narrative of romance, as Gilian woos Nan Turner – only to lose her to the genuine boy of action, young Islay Campbell, who saves her from shipwreck when, like the wayward hero of Joseph Conrad's *Lord Jim* (1900), he is frozen at the moment of truth into thinking too precisely on the event. Imagination is divorced from action, argues Munro, seeing Gilian's predicament as symptomatic of a sickness at the heart of Highland culture. (Intriguingly Munro knew and liked

Conrad, having met him in Glasgow in 1898, when Conrad was seeking a ship's command; one is tempted to speculate as to whether they shared thoughts on their mutual preoccupation with the dangers of disablingly excessive imagination.) Casual reading will miss the parody of romance, as Gilian, utterly at home with birds, animals and all nature, finds himself trapped between what Munro portrays as the ancient and natural Highland landscape and its traditions, the world of Boboon's Children, and this ugly, contradictory and deeply unsatisfying modern world which has no respect for Art, whether it be legendary tale or traditional song – a Highland world, but now very like its Lowland counterparts, in its absorption into Empire and Britain.

A chapter such as this cannot do justice to the entire and neglected output of this writer. Other Highland – and island – novels, such as *Doom Castle* (1901) and *Children of Tempest* (1903) followed, together with Lowland work like *The Shoes of Fortune* (1901) and of course the *Para Handy*, *Jimmy Swan* and *Erchie* stories running from 1904 into the 'twenties. Always the dark undercurrents remained, together with the sense of a writer seeking new, parodic ways of handling old romances or humorous yet deceptively realistic stories of the new, urban Scotland. And again and again the John Splendid figure recurs, in different guises – as the magnificently handsome and duplicitous villain Sim McTaggart, Argyll's factor, in *Doom Castle*, a spy on the Jacobites in France who has fled home from his betrayals, but a charmer whose flute playing hypnotises the reader throughout the novel into disbelief that he can be such an evil sham. In *The Shoes of Fortune*, Lowlander Paul Grieg, exiled from Scotland, falls in with Highland intrigue in France with Prince Charles and Clementina Walkinshaw. He discovers that the lady is formidable, if decent, while the prince – the ultimate John Splendid? – and his adherents are utterly vain and corrupt. This novel leads directly to Violet Jacob's historical deconstruction of Jacobitism in her novel *Flemington* (1911),[12] while *Children of Tempest* helped inspire Gunn to *The Grey Coast* and *The Lost Glen* in the 'twenties. And then there are two experimental and highly theoretical novels set in what is virtually the modern Scotland of the turn of the century, which, if not as successful as these others, break entirely new ground in their speculations regarding future Highland development. *The Daft Days* (1907) shocks the sleepy backwater of Inveraray with a girl-version (but now successful) of Gilian, the thoroughly modern and irrepressible American child Bud, whose fresh thinking sweeps cobwebs out of the old town. Indeed, in this novel

Bud's progressive aunt Ailie said that she loved Americans 'because they beat that stupid old King George and laughed at dynasties'. *Fancy Farm* (1910) unsuccessfully tried to recreate a Highlander of the old natural order in the unbelievable reformer Sir Andrew Schaw – but this strange novel's intention may be to show how he, in trying to re-live ancient values, is bound to fail. The novel by contrast more successfully presents a symbolic picture of its New Woman heroine Pen (Penelope Colquhoun) ruthlessly sweeping out Highland failings and prejudice. Clearly Munro was trying to envisage a fourth phase of development for his Highlands; and his efforts here are innovative and unusual in their emphasis on the regenerative and affirmative role he allows his New Women, who can be seen as pointing towards the new perspectives of the Renaissance of the 1920s, particularly in the work of writers like Catherine Carswell, with her taboo-challenging protagonist Joanna Bannerman in *Open the Door!* (1920), and Nan Shepherd in *The Quarry Wood* (1928) and Willa Muir in *Imagined Corners* (1931).

Munro was writing now as the successful and influential Lowland and Glasgow editor. His perspectives had greatly changed. He was now the sophisticated art critic, whose discussions of the paintings of Whistler, French impressionism and Rennie Mackintosh richly deserve republication, as do the dozen or so unpublished volumes of rich commentary on war, on the changing and shipbuilding Clyde, on the fascinating new technologies of the Empire exhibitions and twentieth-century Glasgow. Munro would certainly have laughed at MacDiarmid's ideas that Glasgow, at any rate, needed a renaissance, since he believed that Scottish culture around the turn of the century was already in revival, with his Glasgow and Lowland life a rich mixture of art and commerce. But for all this, he was still developing his final view of the Highlands, which found articulation in 1914 in his last and greatest historical novel, *The New Road*, of what he saw as the most significant transition in Highland culture, that of the period between the 'fifteen and the 'forty-five Jacobite rebellions, when Wade's roads would drain away what he now clearly saw as the poison at the heart of the Highlands.

At the same time he was also trying out other ways of expressing this sense of the flawed Highland inheritance than in his final masterpiece. Osborne and Armstrong's recent and richly annotated editions of Munro's later comic stories of Para Handy and the crew of *The Vital Spark* suggest that we have not always realised the depth of social and satiric comment in Munro's presentation of his Highland sailors.[13] I would argue that Munro's aims here are only partially comic and entertaining, and that these stories, albeit in an apparently more light-hearted way, are nevertheless critical, derogatory and ironic portrayals which continue into the modern period Munro's portrayal of Highland cultural malaise. Yes, there is a sense in which Munro suggests that somewhere in the activities of this anachronistic bunch of misfits and their elusive adventures in out-of-the-way Highland ports lies a lost and essential vitality, an ability to take life as it comes, in an increasingly bureaucratic world. It is also true, however, that these anachronistic misfits – and especially the charismatic but utterly selfish, manipulative, and amoral Hurricane Jack – are the heirs of John Splendid, latter-day Jaunty Jocks who cannot adapt to modern realities.

The hilarity of Para's hilarious escapades should not blind us to two deeper, if typically ambivalent messages. The first of these sub-texts is that the crew are a feckless, squabbling lot, who will neither work nor want, who slip in and out of Highland and Lowland harbours with equal disrespect, who would literally sell each other down the river. And their idol, Hurricane Jack – the arch-schemer, is the most dubious and clay-footed Jaunty Jock of them all. Readers could well re-visit his exploits; they will discover the most manipulative and ruthlessly selfish of all Munro's Highlanders, cunningly disguised by Munro through the adulation of the crew as a colourful scamp.

The second sub-text is less satirically damaging. The subversive, the lowlife and the bawdily irreverent have been celebrated in our literature from the Makars to Ramsay, Fergusson, and the Jolly Beggars of Burns. Are the crew not the descendants of Burns's motley misfits, as they mock the pretentious, refuse to be located in any system, and generally ape their betters with their parodic and pompous philosophising? In any event, they are the heirs of the mixed qualities of John Splendid; and Munro's deceptively genial re-location of them into a territory neither sea nor land, neither ocean nor river, neither Highland or Lowland, marks their author's re-visioning of Scottish literature and culture as having become a single entity, where no part of the whole can any longer claim separate vitality, and where the Highlands are seen as having to accept this inevitable commercial and cultural change.

All of Munro's development to this point goes into his last and historical novel, clearly separated from the earlier Highland work by ten years. *The New Road* has all his old irony on the Highlands, but now it is a more detached irony which runs alongside a more generous and affectionate recognition of a lingering but doomed survival of that original and natural spirit of the Highlands. This survival is exemplified in his vivid and affirmative picture of Ninian MacGregor Campbell, who takes his place between Scott's Rob Roy, and John Splendid at his best. Inveraray and the House of Argyll are now seen as a bridge between old Highlands and new Lowlands, fulfilling Gillespie Gruamach's dream. It is a novel in the grand tradition of Scott and Scottish mythic regeneration in fiction, taking its place in the tradition of Scott, Gunn, and Mitchison.

It begins in 1733. Æneas Macmaster is a tutor in Drimdorran house to the daughter of Black Sandy Duncanson, agent supreme of London and Edinburgh based Duke Red John. Æneas's father Paul, who rashly went out on the Jacobite side in the little-remembered Glenshiel rising of 1719, is presumed drowned, and Black Sandy has taken over his forfeited estate. Fears are growing of another rebellion; arms are being smuggled from Holland, and the feared Chief of Clan Fraser, the dreaded *McShimi*, Simon Lovat, is spinning his latest web of intrigue and self-aggrandisement in his fastness beyond Inverness. Against this movement into typical Highland unrest, however, is The Road; Wade's regiments are toiling without cease to drive the first-ever passage for troops and commerce through the glens.

These two counter-movements are echoed in subtle patterns of juxtaposition throughout he novel. And here the debt of Munro to Scott must be acknowledged, for Munro is once again reworking an earlier fiction – this time that most misunderstood of Scott novels, *Rob Roy*. Scott's great oppositions of past and present, disorder and order, Highland and Lowland, are reworked here to bring Scott's predictions of the triumph of order to fulfilment. The oppositions are rich; here is the Inveraray Bailie Alan Iain Alain Og Macmaster, reformed Highlander, the modern Baillie Nicol Jarvie who relishes the impact that the Road will have on his wild countrymen; and set beside him, his friend – a subtle joke here – a cousin of Rob Roy's in the form of *Iain Beachdair,* John the Scout, Ninian Macgregor Campbell, who can be seen almost as a Rob Roy himself, if more socially acceptable, since he is in the Duke's service as his Messenger-at-Arms, and since he has all Rob's cunning and natural skills. The connection with John Splendid through his nickname is also intentional; for, if the Bailie is the future, third phase of Highland integration with the Lowlands, then Ninian is a descendant of Boboon, the original captain of the children of the mist (a motif which runs through the novel), chanter of ancient and pagan prayers and absolutely at home in wild nature.

As in Scott's novel, this pairing of opposites is symbolic. Ancient and modern will destroy the corruption which came with the Clans – of McShimi, of all the petty chieftains, and of Black Sandy, who turns out not to be serving his Duke, but to be the murderer of Æneas's father and in league with McShimi and his treacherous chieftains. And with another unlikely pairing, Munro returns to exploit *Kidnapped* again, this time by setting Æneas on a journey with Ninian, with two aims. Æneas is to learn the new trading skills, while Ninian is to seek out the arms smugglers and the plotters of rebellion. The journey will finally destroy all Æneas's romantic notions of the Highlands; he finds the apparently impressive and romantic giant Highland brigand Col Barisdale to be a hollow drum, a huge bullying bubbly-jock; he finds in Inverness the Chiefs haggling like fishwives over salmon and salt and pickled beef; he finds the lairds planning to cut down woods to feed their new furnaces. He vows never to wear the kilt again, and, says Munro, 'his dream dispelled of a poetic world surviving in the hills, he got malicious and secret joy from stripping every rag of false heroics from such gentry' – summarising Munro's own longer journey of highland re-valuation.

At the heart of the novel lie potent symbols. Munro places in opposition two kinds of Highland power-brokers – on the one hand, the black Highland spider, McShimi, rotten to the core, with his kidnappings, his flattery of his fawning clansmen with the old lie of equality, his lust for total power; on the other, Duke John, accepted now as a force for improvement – but never allowed the dignity and status given to Duncan Forbes of Culloden as the real new peace-maker of the Highlands. And, most powerful symbol of all, the Road; a nightmare construction for Wade's men, threatened by winter, flood and attack by the clans, who see all too well what it spells for them. Its epic, steady movement north is brilliantly evoked by Munro, a vision of the future Scotland, its internal boundaries broken down. Munro has regrets; Ninian will lament the loss of open landscape and freedom, and the decline of the Gael's sinewy athleticism – but, as in Scott's ambivalent treatments of Scottish history, his reason sees these losses as secondary to necessary progress and national integration.

The treatment of boundaries is one of the most intriguing features of this novel. Æneas may at times feel Inveraray a Gaelic-speaking, Highland place; but frequently its status as a gateway to the Lowlands is emphasized, and roads south from it are main routes, stripped to the rock by passing commerce. And, conversely, as Æneas and Ninian move north, they encounter boundaries as real to them as any separating Inveraray from the Lowlands. Several times Ninian will indicate to Æneas that they are crossing another boundary – at Glenorchy, at Kingshouse near Glencoe and Rannoch Moor, and – most of all – as they approach Inverness, where Ninian warns Æneas of 'The Wicked Bounds' – the boundaries of McShimi's power. Isn't Munro making a fundamental point? That boundaries aren't fixed in nature, but man-made? That Highland-Lowland separations mean as little as these internal Highland separations of greed and violence?

Duncan Forbes, the great peace-maker after Culloden, is one of Munro's heroes in this novel, and he is allowed to have the last word. For all his even-handedness, he too is a Highlander; and 'half-mocking and half-sad', he sums up the great changes that Wade's new roads will make. Sympathising with Ninian's regrets for the passing of the best of the old Highlands, he surely speaks for Munro's ambivalent mixture of criticism and love of his original country and culture:

> The hearts of all of us are sometimes in the wilds. It's not so very long since we left them. But the end of that sort of thing's at hand. The man who is going to put an end to it – to you, and Lovat, and to me – yes, yes, to me! Or the like of me, half fond of plot and strife and savagery, is Wade…Ye saw the Road? That Road's the end of us! The Romans didna manage it; Edward didna manage it; but there it is at last, through to our vitals, and it's up wi' the ellwand, down the sword…It may seem a queer thing for a law officer of the crown to say, Mr. Campbell, but I never was greatly taken wi'the ell-wand, and man, I liked the sword![14]

Munro had continued to write short stories based on his two beloved territories, north and south of the Clyde, in *Ayrshire Idylls* (1912) and *Jaunty Jock* (1918), though in these later years he was by now more than anything else the war correspondent, the editor, the commentator on Scotland as a whole, who has said goodbye to his ancient, pre-clan Highlands. *Ayrshire Idylls* shows his involvement with lowland history and culture; here is a writer who has well digested his Burns and Galt, who recreates Ayrshire in sympathetic stories of its Covenanting heroes, Peden and Cameron, of Boswell and Burns, with irony on Lowland religious excess and acute psychological analysis which follows that of Scott, Galt and Hogg.

That said, these Lowland stories lack the unifying and haunting *motifs* of *The Lost Pibroch*; lacking the deepest personal involvement in this new territory, the stories read more as exercises in exploring a new culture.

In contrast, the stories of *Jaunty Jock* starkly re-inforce our awareness of Munro's ambivalent love-hate relationship-in-exile with his Highlands. At their kindest, as in 'A Return to Nature', a hilarious tale of a modern man's ridiculously romantic dream of returning to the old ways, the underlying serious point still remains; Munro stresses that we cannot return to the world of Boboon and Ninian. But most of the stories are much darker, like 'Young Pennymore', filled with atmospheric gloom and the incestuous tragedy of the Highlands after Culloden, or 'Isle of Illusion', which even more strongly suggests that behind the apparent beauty and innocence of the Highlands and islands lies a poisonous evil.

Three stories particularly focus on the figure of the sham Highlander. The title story tells of Macdonald cousins in eighteenth-century Edinburgh; one is ugly but decent, but 'a dismal Dan' in contrast to his swaggering, handsome braggart cousin, Jaunty Jock himself – who, it turns out is Barrisdale[15], the bubbly-jock of *The New Road*. Once again Munro exposes the pathetic reality behind the highland bluster, as Jaunty Jock, 'every shred of his manhood gone', flees unheroically from the Edinburgh fire as his braver cousin emerges as the real hero. The twist in the tale is that the real hero has been pretending to be Barrisdale; he saves the heroine, allows the real Barrisdale to take the credit, upon which Jaunty Jock excels himself in unmannerly ingratitude. The theme of pretended virtue is repeated in 'The Scottish Pompadour', a story of modern Paris, with once again a central figure who is not quite the Admirable Crichton he seems – although this time the protagonist is playing someone else's game, and is revealed as essentially decent. The most powerful story in this vein is the last – and can almost be read as a Munro's final echo of *John Splendid*, since the story is set at the same time and in the same place as the novel, when Montrose and Macdonald ravaged Argyll. Alan and Ealasaid are lovers; but their love is blighted by Alan's relationship with Red John. Munro tells us of the Argyll saying, 'Every man his boon companion, every man his maid', thus indicating that this is yet again a comment on Argyll culture and society – and in the curious hollow male camaraderie of Alan and John, based on tavern drinking and boasting, the tragedy is rooted, as the Boon Companion turns out to have feet of clay, in an enigmatic ending which suggests that Red John recognises his own shallowness. Fleeing from Madonald's ravaging troops, Red John seems at first to save Alan and Ealasaid, hiding them in a cliff-cave. 'Here's a cunning and notable end to the botched life', John says to himself, as he then makes his final stand against the hunters. But his apparent heroism is undone by the fact that he has cut the rope which Alan and Ealasaid need to escape from their cave. His actions, like his life, have been full of sound and fury, but all they finally achieve is a slow death for the trapped lovers.

This last story sums up Munro's ironic and ambivalent attitude towards his Highlands. He would continue to write stories of Para Handy and non-fiction journalism, but his exploration of Highland character and culture was over. The rest was for the Scottish Renaissance to take up from him, and Sorley Maclean, Gunn, McColla, Mitchison, Macpherson (and Linklater for the non-Gaelic Orkneys) continued his deconstructions. Many later twentieth century writers, like Crichton Smith and Jessie Kesson in fiction, and Norman MacCaig in poetry (and Mackay Brown with the Orkneys), modified romantic perceptions to the point of recognition of the paradoxical relationship in Highland (and island) territories with their underlying tragedies, in which ironic awareness of cultural disintegration accompanies profound love of landscape and tradition. The process continues: in Lewis and the Western isles, in the work of writers like James Shaw Grant, Calum Macdonald, and Anne McLeod; in Orkney, Shetland and the northern isles, in the work of writers like John Graham, Gregor Lamb and Margaret Elphinstone.[16] Most recently some of the more bizarre effects of modernisation of the Highlands have been anatomised in the work of writers like Alan Warner, Duncan McLean, and Bess Ross. Criticism, whether through fiction or non-fiction, has however not yet recognised the crucial role of Neil Munro in his radical revisioning of both Lowland and Highland perceptions of Highland society and culture, a revisioning which has enabled contemporary perception to see clearly the complex and often sinister reasons for the decline of an ancient people, their language, and their ways of life.[17]

Notes

1 Jackson, Holbrook, *The Eighteen-Nineties*, London: Grant Richards, 1913. Quotations from Pelican Edition 1939, p.147
2 *Ibid.*, pp.147–8

3 For examples of Gunn's reassessment of Highland history culture and character see *Sun Circle* (1933), *Butcher's Broom* (1934), *Highland River* (1937), (Edinburgh: The Porpoise Press); and *The Silver Darlings* (London: Faber, 1941). Virtually all of Gunn's works of fiction and non-fiction contribute to this revaluation; most of his work is available in recent editions. For typical work of Ian Macpherson and 'Fionn MacColla' see Mcpherson's *Shepherd's Calendar* (1931), *Land of Our Fathers* (1933), *Pride in the Valley* (1936) (London: Cape) and MacColla's *The Albannach* (London: John Heritage, 1932), *And the Cock Crew* (Glasgow: Maclellan, 1945) and *The Ministers* (London: Souvenir Press, 1999)

4 The line is from Munro's apparently bellicose poem 'Hey, Jock are ye glad ye 'listed?'. Munro intended a collection of his poetry; this was unpublished in his lifetime but appeared in 1931 with an introduction by John Buchan as *The Poetry of Neil Munro* (Edinburgh: Blackwood, 1931; Stevenage: SPA Books, 1987). In an early draft of a prefatory note Munro explains that some of his war poems …'take on that spirit of braggadocio which comes so naturally to youth … and to races like the Gaels who loiter so much in their past …' p.5

5 As 'Mr Incognito', for the last three years of his life (1927–30) Munro produced a series of 'Random Reminiscences' for Glasgow's *The Daily Mail and Record*. A selection by George Blake appeared as *The Brave Days: A Chronicle from the North* (Edinburgh: The Porpoise Press 1931). Blake's second selection, from Munro's huge number of articles for the *Glasgow Evening News*, spanning almost forty years' contributions, appeared as *The Looker-On* (Edinburgh : The Porpoise Press, 1933)

6 'Castle Dark', *The Lost Pibroch and other Sheiling Stories*, Eds. Renton, McOwan and MacGregor, Colonsay, Argyll: House of Lochar, 1996, pp.77–8

7 *Ibid.*, pp.78–9

8 *Ibid.*, pp.79–80

9 *Ibid.*, p.80

10 *Ibid.*, p.71

11 *John Splendid* Edinburgh: B&W Publishing, 1994, pp.283–4

12 Jacob, Violet, *Flemington*, ed. Anderson, Carol, Aberdeen: Association for Scottish Literary Studies, 1994

13 Munro, Neil, *Para Handy: First Complete Edition*, Eds. Osborne, Brian D. and Armstrong, Ronald, Edinburgh: Birlinn, 1992. See also Munro, Neil, *Erchie and Jimmy Swan: First Complete Edition*, eds. Osborne, Brian D. and Armstrong, Ronald, Edinburgh: Birlinn, 1993

14 Munro, Neil, *The New Road*, Edinburgh: B&W Publishing, 1994, p.200

15 Munro uses the spelling 'Barisdale' in *The New Road* but the spelling 'Barrisdale' in the story 'Jaunty Jock'

16 A selection from some of the newer fiction on Highlands and islands includes (For the Hebrides) Iain Crichton Smith, *Consider the Lilies*, London: Gollancz, 1968 (and many other novels, stories and poems) ; James Shaw Grant, *Their Children Will See, London: Hale, 1979* ; Charles McLeod, *Devil in the Wind*, Edinburgh: Gordon Wright, 1976; Norman Macdonald, *Calum Tod*, Inverness: Club Leabhar, 1976 and *Portrona*, Edinburgh: Birlinn, 2000; Anne McLeod, *The Dark Ship*, Glasgow: Neil Wilson, 2000: (for Orkney, Shetland and the Northern Isles) George Mackay Brown, *Greenvoe*, London: Hogarth, 1972 (and many other novels, stories and poems); John Graham, *Shadowed Valley*, Shetland: Shetland Publishing Co., 1987 and *Strife in the Valley*, Shetland:

Shetland Publishing Co., 1992; Gregor Lamb, *Langskaill*, Orkney: Byrgisey, 1998; Margaret Elphinstone, *Islanders*, Edinburgh: Polygon, 1994 and *The Sea Road*, Edinburgh: Canongate, 2000. The dubious effects of Highland modernisation are satirised in the work of writers like Lorn Macintyre, *Cruel in the Shadow*, London: Collins, 1979 and *The Blind Ben*, London: Collins, 1981 and *Empty Footsteps*, Duns: Black Ace, 1996; Alan Warner, *Morvern Callar*, London: Jonathan Cape, 1995 and *These Demented Lands*, London: Jonathan Cape, 1997 and *The Sopranos*, London: Jonathan Cape, 1998; Duncan McLean, *Blackden*, London: Secker and Warburg, 1994 and *Bunkerman*, London: Jonathan Cape 1995; Bess Ross, *A Bit of Crack and Car Culture*, Nairn: Balnain, 1990, *Those Other Times*, Nairn: Balnain, 1991, *Dangerous Gifts*, Nairn, Balnain, 1994 and *Strath*, Edinburgh: Canongate, 1997

17 Editions of Munro's novels have recently been appearing from B&W Publishers, Edinburgh. They include *John Splendid*, 1994, *The New Road*, 1994 and *Doom Castle*, 1996 all with introductions by Brian D. Osborne, and *Gilian the Dreamer*, (2000). This chapter is an expanded version of my introduction to the 2000 edition of *Gilian*. Readers interested in following up writing and writers discussed can find extensive treatment in *Scottish Literature in English and Scots*, Eds. *Gifford, Dunnigan and MacGillivray*, Edinburgh: Edinburgh University Press, 2002

Stories in 'the Highland manner':
The Lost Pibroch and Other Sheiling Stories

RONALD W. RENTON

Neil Munro's appointment as reporter to *The Greenock Advertiser* in 1884 marked the beginning of his career as one of Scotland's most distinguished journalists. Evidence that he was also to become a distinguished writer of prose fiction began to appear with the publication of the short stories 'How the Jeweller of Alnbury Was Duped' and 'Dr Everton Sharp's Experiment' (1891) and a 40,000 word thriller called *The Afton Moor Mystery* which was serialised in a short-lived periodical called *Quips* (1893–4).[1] He also submitted 'turnovers' to the *Globe* newspaper at this time. But in 1892 he also began experimenting with Highland subject matter and we find that he had a short story, 'The Secret of the Heather Ale,' (a re-working of Stevenson's poem of the same name) published in W.E. Henley's magazine, *The Speaker*, in the November of that year and in 1893 a further short story 'The Red Hand' was also published by Henley in *The National Observer*. By 1893 he had completed two further stories which were accepted by Blackwood, the Edinburgh publisher – 'Shudderman Soldier' and 'The Lost Pibroch'[2].

These Highland stories indicate the road that Munro was to take for the greater part of his career as a writer. He hoped to have them published along with some others in book form by Blackwood and in a letter of 26 February 1894 to Blackwood concerning such a project we gain considerable insight into his ideas about current literary practice and the future direction of his writing:

> ... I shall be only too glad to lay before you at some early date, for your consideration, such a number of the West Highland stories as might make a volume. I am not the most impartial judge, perhaps, but I have a strong belief, amounting almost to a certainty, that my sketches have something of the stuff of popu-

larity in them. They strike upon a field absolutely untouched for one thing, being purely Celtic in their treatment of the Highland Celt and Highland scenery whereas all the men who have dealt with the romance of the Highlands hitherto have been Lowlanders, writing from the outside. The Barrie-Crockett-McLaren 'boom' has confined itself to the Lowlands; the stuff they deal with is becoming attenuated, and run to seed. Here – or I am a Dutchman! – is a new vein, rich and untried. It should appeal to English readers even more than the Lowland Scots stories for it dispenses almost entirely with dialect. At all events a glossary is unnecessary. We are having a Scots revival in literature and now or never is, I recognise, the chance for anyone who would expound the genuine Highland character and direct attention to the illimitable stories of romance and poetry still lying in the old glens. I wish I could, if it never brought me a penny![3]

From this it is clear that Munro was well aware of the current state of Scottish writing. To take the latter part first, it is clear that he was well aware of the limitations of the Lowland 'Kailyard' writing represented by the early work of Barrie and Crocket and, particularly, by the stories in *Beside the Bonnie Briar Bush* (1894) of 'Ian MacLaren' (Rev. John Watson).[4] He had no intention of imitating their sentimental style. And further proof of his desire not to be identified with Kailyard writing can be seen in his retrospective look over his life from his retirement when he tells us in 'Random Reminiscences' for the *Daily Record and Mail* how at the very beginning of his career he used to submit 'turnovers' to the *Globe*, a London paper, in 1890:

> the traditional first step in literature. Every established novelist had done it, and 'my turnovers' put Scotland on the map for this London paper's readers.[5]

In these he wrote (as he thought) humorous sketches which involved portrayals of naive Scotsmen in kilts complete with whisky and haggis – but to his horror the humour went undetected:

> Finding myself in danger of being regarded as an earnest adherent of the Kailyard School, I switched off.[6]

Secondly, the letter draws attention to the fact that all previous writers who had dealt with 'the romance of the Highlands' had no real feel for the subject. They had been 'Lowlanders, writing from the outside', the creators of the Celtic Twilight, like William Black[7] and especially the mystical 'Fiona Macleod', the pen-name of the Paisley novelist William Sharp. Like Ireland, Scotland was experiencing a 'Celtic Revival'. In 1888 'The Glasgow Boys' Hornel and Henry had painted a Celtic picture, 'The Druids', of which Munro was later to comment acerbically :

> Its aim was not information of any kind but sumptuous decoration...Fiona MacLeodish in its Celticism.[8]

This 'Celtic Revival' took a much more structured shape in Edinburgh largely under the inspiration of Professor Patrick Geddes, especially with his periodical the *Evergreen* (1895–6). It sought to revive Celtic styles of art and literature (and did, indeed, have a major influence on the architect Charles Rennie Mackintosh and his artist wife Margaret), but Munro was highly sceptical of a Celtic movement which had no knowledge of Gaelic:

> This so-called Celtic Revival in Edinburgh is rather a curious thing. It is engineered very largely by people of no Celtic pedigree, and perhaps the only Celtic scholar in it is Mr. Alexander Carmichael, whose knowledge of Gaelic, of Hebridean folklore and hymnology, is greater than that of any living.[9]

As far as the literary output of the Edinburgh movement was concerned, its sole creative writer was 'Fiona Macleod' (William Sharp) whose grasp of Gaelic was slight and whose stories were written in standard English. Munro clearly thought very little of his extravagantly mystical and superficial interpretation of the Highland people:

> To paint the Scottish Gael as if he were eternally listening to the wail of Ossianic ghosts, looking out for corp-lights, and strumming his Clarsach to plaintive numbers is to misrepresent a very varied and interesting people. Besides his musings on the hill, he had and has his noisy nights in the change-house, and his laugh and song at the ceilidh fire; when he was harrying the adjacent glens there was about him a fine loveable zest for adventure; his songs are often of love and roaming, but rarely of death and ghosts. The Gael Miss Macleod knows, in short, is the Gael who has been made by the Free Kirk.[10]

As a native Gael Munro felt he could redress the balance.

It is from this background that Neil Munro, a fluent Gaelic speaker familiar with Highland literature and tradition, pioneers this 'new vein, rich and untried' of Scottish literature as he seeks to give a more genuine and unsentimental account of the Highlands and the Highlander in his first collection of short stories *The Lost Pibroch and Other Sheiling Stories* in 1896.[11]

A major feature in his attempt to represent the Gael more accurately is his special use of language. In this he differs from Fiona Macleod's standard English, from William Black's naïve attempt at Highland accent and, indeed, from the older parodic and mocking Highland English used by Lowlanders from the fifteenth century Richard Holland's *Buke of the Howlat* to Scott and Hogg, as the following illustrate:

> Na, na, Hughie Morrison is no the man fo pargains – ye maun come to some Highland body like Robin Oig hersell for the like of these – put I maun pe wishing you goot night...[12]

or even more exaggeratedly,

> I wat pe te mhotter with te prave shentleman' in te oter rhoom? Hu! she pe cot into creat pig tarnnation twarvel with her own self. She pe eiter trunk or horn mat.[13]

Munro rejects all this. Instead he moves towards a much more authentic Gaelic-English, influenced by the translations of *Popular Tales of the West Highlands* (1860–2) by the polymath and scholar, John Francis Campbell of Islay (known in Gaelic as Iain Og Ile),[14] whom he had admired from his youth:

> Campbell collected and translated his folklore and heroic tales into an English which is steeped in Gaelic sentiment, and is in truth a distinctive variety of English worth the study of the philologist and the artist in words.[15]

Among other things Campbell sought to retain the Gaelic syntax and idiom in his English translations and this was the model on which Munro based the language of his stories – except of course that they were not translations but fresh creations. Obviously it would be impossible to write whole paragraphs in this way but he does it sufficiently often to give a strong flavour of Gaelic idiom and syntax e.g.

it's lame he'll be all his days anyway ('Black Murdo' p.38)

reflects modern Gaelic idiom and can be rendered thus:

is ann crubach a bhios e fad a laithean co-dhiù.

In this approach to language he anticipates J.M. Synge's pioneering use of Irish-English speech in his play *The Shadow of the Glen* which was written in 1902 and in his later plays *The Playboy of the Western World* (1907) and *Deirdre of the Sorrows* (1910). W.B. Yeats, the father of the Irish Celtic revival, used standard English for his poetry.

In addition he frequently incorporates specific Gaelic idioms e.g. 'the mouth of the night' literally translates *beul na h-oidhche* and means 'twilight'; 'squint mouth' translates *cam beul* from which the name Campbell is derived; and throughout the text there is a gentle spattering of actual Gaelic words though not so many as to hold up the reader's progress e.g. *caman* (shinty stick), *iolair* (eagle), etc. He also incorporates an abundance of Gaelic place names and accurate local references. Other not strictly linguistic features such as the use of often genuine proverbs or *seanfhaclan* (literally: 'old words'), the names of well known pipe tunes and vivid descriptions of nature in the tradition of the great Gaelic eighteenth century nature poets Alasdair MacDonald and Duncan Ban MacIntyre also enhance the Gaelic atmosphere. Furthermore, and a point not often noted, Munro includes a remarkably wide range of Scots words and idioms – which would, of course, have infiltrated the Highland speech of Inveraray and its environs long before standard English.

The effect of all this is to create the illusion for the reader of initiation into the language and culture of the characters in much the same way that Lewis Grassic Gibbon's 'Speak of the Mearns' takes us into the world of his East Coast region. Munro's task, however, is more difficult since he has a completely separate language to represent as opposed to a dialect of Scots. It has to be said, however, that he is not always successful and an early review complained of the need to keep consulting the appended glossary of Gaelic words[16] and there are times when the attempt at transposition of idiom can be too awkward and clumsy e.g.

'There's dignity in yon craft, or less than red-shirts was the wearing of the scamps who row her. ('Castle Dark' p.77)

Nonetheless, as his work developed he became more adept at handling this technique and by the time he comes to write *The New Road* (1914) he has it to a fine art.

The Lost Pibroch and Other Sheiling Stories consists of twelve stories. Superficially they have the appearance of the tales of oral tradition and it was almost inevitable that Munro chose the folk tale model since it was the dominant prose genre in the Gaelic literature of the time, the modern short story not yet having been developed (except for the homiletic and rather Kailyardish stories of Rev Norman MacLeod).[17] There was, however, considerable vogue for publishing the products of the oral tradition: songs, proverbs (e.g. Alexander Nicolson's *A Collection of Gaelic Proverbs and Familiar Phrases* (1881)) and folk tales, especially, of course, John Francis Campbell's *Popular Tales of the West Highlands* in four volumes (1860–2) which became extremely well-known and many of which had been gathered around Inveraray by Campbell's assistants. On closer inspection, however, it can be seen that in terms of general technique (apart, of course, from the language issue already dealt with) *The Lost Pibroch and Other Sheiling Stories* mainly owe only their one dimensional characters to the influence of the traditional tale. In terms of structure, like their Lowland counterparts Scott's 'Wandering Willie's Tale' and Stevenson's 'Thrawn Janet', they have only the appearance of folk tales; closer examination reveals a much tauter structure than that found in a genuine oral piece and almost all are shot through and held together by bitter irony. The setting (again unlike the traditional tale) is highly localised and almost every one of these stories is set in the area adjacent to Inveraray, especially Glen Aray.

'The Lost Pibroch' itself is a mysterious story told in highly poetic language. It is set in Half Town, in the environs of Inveraray. (Half Town or *Leth-Bhaile* is quite a common name for a village or small settlement in Gaelic and has echoes of the song '*Rosan an Leth-Bhaile*' ('Rosey of the Half Town') by Eoghan McColl (1808–98), the bard from Kenmore just outside Inveraray.) A piping competition takes place between two travelling pipers who arrive in the village and Paruig Dall (Blind Peter). Eventually Paruig Dall plays the tune 'The Lost Pibroch' and this has a tremendously unsettling effect at first on the other two pipers and then on the men of the village and eventually on Paruig himself. All grow restless and depart, even the animals, and the women and children are left behind to fend for themselves in a derelict economy.

Although the story has a vague historical setting of about 1750 just after Culloden, it is possible to see the whole piece as an allegory of the history of the Highlands, depicting the dereliction of the Highland way of life (although ironically the story is set in the anti-Jacobite Campbell area) after Culloden, the Clearances and the years of emigration to the lowland cities, to Canada and elsewhere.

The story is rich in allusion to authentic pipe tunes and the speaking animals owe something to oral tradition. It is ironic, however, that beautiful music which, for example in Shakespeare's last plays, is a symbol of healing and reconciliation should here be the means of destruction and dislocation. Munro appears to be hinting that the break up of the old Highland way of life with its language and culture is inevitable – a theme which persists throughout almost all of his Highland romances.

With the exception of 'Jus Primae Noctis' ('The Right of First Night') a humorous story of mistaken identity which was rejected by Blackwood for the first edition (judiciously, as its tone was too risqué to be consonant with the other stories of the collection) and 'Boboon's Children' which demonstrates the power of nature over nurture, the remaining nine stories are dark and bitter pieces – the antithesis of the sentimentality of the Kailyard and Celtic Twilight. 'The Fell Sergeant', 'The Sea-Fairy of French Foreland', 'Shudderman Soldier' and the fantasy 'Castle Dark' deal in various ways with love thwarted or unrequited. 'Red Hand', 'The Secret of the Heather-Ale', 'Black Murdo', 'War', and 'A Fine Pair of Shoes' show how far people will go to protect pride of family or clan.

Of the stories of thwarted love 'The Fell Sergeant' is a particularly poignant example. It is the tale of Aoirig, an old Mull woman, who is dying in Glen Aray. She tells how long ago she was courted in Mull by a man from Glen Aray called Macnicol who brought her blue flowers, 'cuckoo brogues', all the way from Argyll. As her end draws near the wright (who performed the duties of undertaker) is sent for – none other than Macnicol himself, although no longer young and handsome. Aoirig dies and the wright enters the room with the stretching board. Suddenly Aoirig sits up for a moment, clearly recognising him, 'and then she fell back on the bed with her face stiffening.' (p109) This irony is compounded by Macnicol's innocent remark:

'I once knew a woman who was terribly like yon, and she came from Mull.' (p.109)

The tragic atmosphere saves the ending from falling into bathos and leaves us to savour the grim humour of the situation. Cohesion and pathos are added to the story by the references to the blue flowers which Aoirig could see from her bed and which Macnicol had given her in youth.

Of the stories which deal with pride of clan and family 'Black Murdo' and 'War' come very near to true tragedy in the Aristotelian sense: the *hubris* (pride) of the two protagonists brings appalling results.

In 'Black Murdo' the springboard for the story is an 'old word' (proverb): 'a stolen bitch will never throw clean pups'. The hero, Murdo, a Macarthur, sets out from his home in Stronbuie across Glen Aray to Inneraora (Inveraray) in order to get a midwife for his Campbell wife Silis. He has had a *taibhs* (vision) suggesting that she will die in childbirth. On the way he is challenged by Campbells, the bitter enemies of the MacArthurs, and gives them his dirk and shield as payment for safe passage. He collects the midwife and begins the return journey. He is again challenged and this time his assailant demands his sword for safe passage. Murdo's pride can stand it no longer and he agrees to fight. In the heat of the struggle he has a further *taibhs* which tells him the baby has been born and his wife needs the midwife. He redoubles his efforts and wounds his assailant so severely that he will have a severe limp for the rest of his days. He then proceeds on his way but this delay to defend his pride causes his wife's death for, by the time they reach Stronbuie, it is twenty minutes too late for the midwife to be of assistance.

The cruel irony does not cease there, however, for Murdo naturally assumes that Silis's red haired baby, who survived the ordeal, is his own son and he brings him up to hate, as the murderer of his mother, the man who challenged him for his sword in Glen Aray on that fateful day. When Rory, the boy, is old enough Murdo takes him to Inneraora to challenge his lame enemy. The cripple is loathe to hurt the boy but is eventually wounded by his slashing blows. The boy then, urged on by his father, stabs his victim to death. Just after this the midwife appears to reveal that the lame man is, in fact, the boy's father. The boy had killed his own father and both 'fathers' had killed Silis by the delay caused by their duel. The proverb is fulfilled: Silis was 'the stolen bitch', the Campbell girl who had been abducted from her own clan but had given birth to a Campbell child, an unclean pup.

Whilst 'Black Murdo' deals with the elemental emotion of tribal pride which one associates with Scott's Robin Oig in 'The Two Drovers' or Fergus Mac-Ivor in *Waverley*, 'War' is a grim story which deals with the fierce *hubris* of a woman, Jean, who will not show a sympathetic world her poverty, thus causing the death of her child.

Jean's husband, an irresponsible, thoughtless fellow called Rob Donn, an early version of John Splendid, in order to earn twenty pounds has gone with the Campbells to fight the forces of Bonnie Prince Charlie. He leaves none of the money to his needy wife who is too proud to ask him for any and yet, while he is on the march, he gives some to another needy woman. After this he gambles away the rest of his cash.

At the news of Culloden the townspeople rejoice and prosperity returns, but all the time Jean's poverty is growing more acute, yet her pride will not permit her to ask for help. Indeed, she gives away what little she has to protect her reputation. All the time her child grows more and more weak, but the mother pins their hopes on Rob returning with money and animals as he had boasted he would. Finally the child dies at the very moment the soldiers return. But, to add to that irony, even if Rob had been a little earlier it is doubtful if he could have helped since he had no money. All he had brought home for the child was a captured white cockade!

The Lost Pibroch and Other Sheiling Stories was enthusiastically received when it was issued in 1896 and there is no doubt that these stories in which the emphasis is most frequently on action show a high level of craftsmanship and skill. All are beautifully structured and they are often marvellously ironic. Furthermore, they are a breakthrough in the depiction of the Gael and Gaeldom in non-Gaelic Scottish Literature. Nonetheless, they are early work and they do, understandably, show certain teething troubles; Munro had after all embarked on a completely new literary experiment. As has been shown above he was reacting against the sentimentality of the Kailyard and wanted to paint a more authentic picture of the Gael than the Lowland purveyors of Celtic Twilight had done. In his enthusiasm to do so he anticipates George Douglas Brown's criticism of his own book *The House with the Green Shutters*, that 'There is too much black for the white in it.'[18] Certainly the grimness and savageness of 'Red Hand', 'Black Murdo', and even 'The Secret of the Heather Ale' are too black to be 'natural'. And, indeed, if George Douglas Brown's and John Macdougall Hay's black novels *The House with the Green Shutters* (1901) and *Gillespie* (1914) are the first major counterblasts to the sentimental malaise which had befallen *fin de siècle* Scottish writing, then *The Lost Pibroch and Other Sheiling Stories* must be recognised as their forerunner. Also, from the point of view of style they are somewhat overwritten for modern taste and the author in his endeavour to enrich his descriptions of nature makes overuse of the pathetic fallacy. The stories are often set in a past that has no clear historical context and this sometimes has the effect of producing vague, elemental and semi-Ossianic characters whose world lacks historical credibility. That said, the freshness of Neil Munro's approach with his detailed knowledge of the Highland way of life and his interesting experimentation with Gaelic-English constitutes a breakthrough in the representation of the Gael in mainstream Scottish literature. *The Lost Pibroch* collection prepares the way for Munro's well-judged and carefully researched historical novel *John Splendid* which was to be published the following year, for his other fine historical romances, especially *The New Road* (1914), and for the Highland fiction of the Scottish Renaissance writers Fionn MacColla and Neil Gunn.

Notes

1 'How the Jeweller of Alnbury was Duped' and 'Dr Everton Sharp's Experiment' appeared in newspaper *The Newcastle Courant* in 1891. *The Afton Moor Mystery* was serialised in 14 episodes in *Quips* from November 1893 to February 1894. Intriguingly, it was published under the pseudonym 'George Gaunt' although it had been trailed in Quips the week before publication as 'A serial story of thrilling interest by Neil Munro.' See Brian D. Osborne, *ParaGraphs* 6 p.14, and *ParaGraphs* 7 p.16

2 Munro also submitted a Highland short story called 'Anapla's Boy' to *Blackwood's Magazine* in November, 1892. In a letter of 17 November 1892, although he rejected the story for publication William Blackwood encouraged Munro to continue in this style. (See Hermann Völkel, *Das literarische Werk Neil Munros*, Frankfurt: Peter Lang, p.121.) The manuscript, commonly believed to have been destroyed, is in the National Library of Scotland MS26915 f109–132

3 Letter from Neil Munro to William Blackwood, 26th February, 1894, National Library of Scotland MS 4621

4 A clear indication of Munro's view of *The Bonnie Briar Bush* can be seen in his devastating parody of Maclaren's lad o'pairts in 'The Student Lodger', *Erchie and Jimmy Swan*, Eds Brian D. Osborne and Ronald Armstrong, Edinburgh: Birlinn, 1993 pp. 66–76

5 Munro, Neil, *The Brave Days,* ed. George Blake, Edinburgh: The Porpoise Press, 1931, p.145

6 Blake, *op. cit.*, p.146

7 Black, William (1841–98) was a prolific novelist who was born in Glasgow and moved to London. He made his name with popular novels with Hebridean settings in the Celtic revival style. The best known of these are *A Daughter of Heth* (1871), *A Princess of Thule* (1874), *Macleod of Dare* (1878), *In Far Lochaber* (1888), *Donald Ross of Heimra* (1891)

8 Blake, *op. cit.*, p.268

9 Munro, Neil, 'Views and Reviews', *Glasgow Evening News*, 5 March 1896

10 *Ibid.*

77

11 The edition referred to in this essay is Munro, Neil, *The Lost Pibroch and Other Sheiling Stories*, Eds R. Renton, R McOwan and R. McGregor, Colonsay, Argyll: House of Lochar,1996

12 Scott, Sir Walter, 'The Two Drovers', *Scottish Short Stories 1800–1900*, ed. Douglas Gifford, London: Calder and Boyers, 1971, p.31

13 Hogg , James, 'The Strange Letter of a Lunatic', *The Short Stories of James Hogg*, ed. Douglas Mack, Edinburgh: Scottish Academic Press, 1982, p.167

14 Campbell, John Francis, *Popular Tales of the West Highlands*, Edinburgh: Birlinn,1994

15 Munro, Neil, 'Views and Reviews', *Glasgow Evening News*, 29th August, 1895

16 Review of *The Lost Pibroch and Other Sheiling Stories*, *The Bookman*, London, May,1896

17 Macleod, Rev. Norman (1783–1862), known even today in Gaelic circles as Caraid nan Gaidheal (friend of the Gaels) was a major figure in Gaelic society. He did much to relieve poverty and to promote education. Among his many writings were stories intended to edify and instruct his readers. A selection of his prose writings is contained in Rev. Norman Macleod, *Caraid nan Gaidheal*, ed. Archibald Clerk, Glasgow, 1876

18 Brown, George Douglas, letter to Ernest Barker, 24th October,1901. Quoted in Ian Campbell, *Kailyard* , Edinburgh: The Ramsay Head Press,1981, p.7

J.F. Campbell of Islay
Iain Og Ile

John Splendid and Scottish History

EDWARD J. COWAN

Neil Munro contributed an article commemorating the life and work of Robert Louis Stevenson to a special issue of *Bookman* in 1913 wherein he described Stevenson as 'the culminating figure in one epoch of romance now temporarily somewhat in eclipse'. In his enthusiastic yet critical review he alluded to RLS's comfortable personal circumstances – 'Fate never drove him to the necessity of banking down his fires periodically to boil a domestic pot. His artistic reputation was carefully fostered by his friends'. In a stunning sentence he wrote that Walter Scott's limp 'had never spoiled his stride across the mountains'. Having thus made the transition from Stevenson to Scott he included a few remarks on the Wizard of the North. 'Rob Roy, in almost every manifestation, is a Borderer without one drop of mountain blood.' He thought that Stevenson had a quicker ear than Scott for alien idioms and turns of utterance and 'had evidently read [J.F.] Campbell's *Tales of the West Highlands* with profit to his manipulations of the thought and speech of persons like Alan Breck and Catriona'. The only blundering chapter in *Kidnapped* he opined, was the piping contest in Balquhidder.

Munro's article reinforces an important point for anyone interested in his art and his output, namely that in tackling his historical novels he was self-consciously taking on both Scott and Stevenson. Presumably he was attempting to demonstrate how best to handle the genre. When Stevenson first hit on the idea of writing what would become his beloved *David Balfour*, later published as *Kidnapped* and *Catriona*, he requested two books about Rob Roy which had been mentioned in Scott's introduction to the novel. RLS was picking up where Scott had left off both chronologically and artistically.[1] In contriving the inheritance of the Scott/Stevenson mantle Munro was to take the process one step further. A major source of his inspiration in writing *John Splendid* was Scott's *A Legend of the Wars of Montrose* but, like Stevenson, he did not believe that Scott truly understood the Gàidhealtachd. RLS once observed

79

that Scott 'never knew, never saw the highlands: he was always a borderer. He missed that whole long strange pathetic history of our savages.' While Munro obviously agreed with him he personally eschewed the rather simplistic device of personifying Whig and Jacobite in the characters, say, of David Balfour and Alan Breck Stewart, in favour of exploring one of Scottish History's greatest conundra. He would investigate the personal dilemma of a man who was both leader of the covenanting movement and at the same time the greatest clan chief in all of the Highlands – Archibald Campbell, 8th Earl, First (and only) Marquis of Argyll, known in Gaelic as both MacCailein Mór, the title reserved for all chiefs of Clan Campbell, and Gilleasbuig Gruamach, or Archibald the Grim, a designation originally applied to his father. Scott had already placed Argyll at the heart of his *Legend*, but in his rational heart of hearts, he despised both Covenanters and Gaels, both the victims of History whose inevitable demise, in his view, was far from unwelcome.

The immediate context of Munro's tale was the invasion of Argyll in the winter of 1644 by the royalist army of James Graham, Marquis of Montrose, and Alasdair mac Cholla Ciotaich MacDonald, known to fearful Lowlanders as Colkitto, an event also central to *Legend*. Inveraray, along with the surrounding countryside, was brutally ravaged and 900 Campbells slain in an extraordinary episode which, however bitter the experience, was to be outdone by the subsequent defeat of the Campbells at the Battle of Inverlochy, 2 February 1645. So it was that in 1898 Neil Munro dedicated his *John Splendid The Tale of a Poor Gentlemen and the Little Wars of Lorn* to his son who, he hoped, would read the tale 'without any association of its incidents with the old respectable chronicles of the Historians':

> I give you this book, dear Hugh, not for History, though a true tale – a sad old tale – is behind it, but for a picture of times and manners, of a country that is dear to us in every rock and valley, of a people we know whose blood is ours.

The story is told by the poor gentleman, Colin Campbell of Elrigmore, who is returning from the Thirty Years' War. A clue to the man's character is given in the first words of the novel. 'Many a time in college or camp I had planned the style of my home-coming.' This man is a dreamer who after all his adventures and experiences is still dreaming at the end of the story. In his honest, plodding, rather unaware attitudes and behaviour he is related to David Balfour. Indeed, in flight from Inverlochy he would cover some of exactly the same territory as David and Allan Breck. At his return from Europe Inveraray is crawling with covenanters imported by Argyll, 'to teach his clans the arts of peace and merchandise' (p.11).[2]

The way in which Munro introduces his readers to Argyll contrasts sharply with that of Sir Walter and immediately signals the essential difference in tone between the two novels. Already by page eight Scott is poisoning minds against Campbell as 'a man rather of political enterprise than personal courage' adding rather unfairly and incongruously that he was 'better calculated to manage an intrigue of state, than to controul the tribes of hostile mountaineers'. Later the author reluctantly allows that he was 'possessed of very considerable abilities and very great power' but that these were outweighed by great 'failings' which included fanatical devotion to the covenant, insatiable ambition, a lack of generosity, and – or so it is hinted – cowardice (p.8, p.55).[3] On the other hand although Elrigmore's first glint of the marquis revealed one of the dourest and sourest faces he had ever beheld first impressions were soon forgotten as Argyll humorously chatted with those around him – 'He might have been a plain cottar on Glen Aora side rather than King of the Highlands for all the airs he assumed' (p.12).

Argyll speaks St Andrews English – he was a graduate of that university where, like his great rival Montrose, he won the silver arrow for archery. He was always a man who disdained to converse much in Erse (p.14), a point presumably made for artistic effect and one which can be easily challenged for MacCailein was undoubtedly quite at home in the language. The MacEwan bards and others cele-brated him in Gaelic poetry as the descendant of King Arthur, ruler of the Hebrides, and for sheer nobility unequalled in the whole of Britain:

> The kin of Arthur, the great son of Ambrose, many a king has been crowned therefrom; its counterpart is not in Scotland, a blood with greater share of noble blood... Since thou art the noblest of British blood, history has exalted thee beyond the due men pay to earls; to match another with thee is unmeet: no man has a right to do it...
>
> From the bounds of Lewis to the coast of Banbha there is no region that pays not tribute due to thee; in the whole kingdom no kingship matches thine; thou art the noblest of every land and lord.[4]

Argyll and his wife took pains to ensure that their son and heir, young Archie the future ninth earl, should acquire the Gaelic tongue. When in 1639 it was recommended that a new tutor be found for the boy it was deemed essential that the appointee should be 'sume discreite man that is ane scoller and that cane speike bothe Inglis and Erisse'. Archie was not, apparently, either a keen or an apt pupil, as his unhappy mother discovered: 'I heare my sone begines to wearye of the Irishe langwadge...Since he hes bestowett so long tyme and paines in the getting of itt I sould be sory he lost itt now, with leasiness (laziness) in not speaking of itt'.[5] There has long been a notion that as the Campbells increasingly involved themselves in the processes of government the less Gaelic they somehow became, a view not borne out by the evidence. Argyll was clearly just as comfortable in the medium of English but it would be difficult to justify the view that he disdained the language of the Garden of Eden.

John Mair in his *Historia* published in 1521 remarked that in Argyll people swore 'by the hand of MacCallum Mor', a custom still observed in John Splendid's time. The author's reports of Inveraray Kirk Session come straight out of the records (not published so far as I know in his lifetime) and Alexander Gordon really was the minister of the parish. From what we know of Gordon he was perfectly capable of a statement such as 'in the heart of man there is hell smouldering, always ready to leap out in flames of sharpened steel (p.50). It was he who reported, according to Robert Wodrow, that Argyll when at home remained at his devotions from 5 until 8 a.m. as well as having prayers with his wife and family morning and evening, that he never left Inveraray without taking with him his bible and Newman's concordance, and that as a lay elder he often wrote the sermon (p.239).

And so one could go on. There is very little in Munro's novel that actually contradicts, or jars with, the main historical sources. He must have used some oral tradition but he also read a great deal. It must be stressed that there was no biography of Argyll until 1903, nor has there been one since. There was no history of Clan Campbell that he could usefully consult. He had read, as had Elrigmore, the 'fabulous Wishart' (p.56),[6] that is to say, George Wishart, Montrose's chaplain and author of a flattering Latin life of his hero. When Montrose was executed in 1650 a copy of Wishart's Latin *Life* was tied around his neck.

The Covenanting Revolution represented one of the most profound upheavals in all of Scottish history. The National

Covenant, subscribed in February 1638 had come about, in part, because of Charles I's determination to anglicise the Scottish Church. It fell into three parts, the first a total abjuration of catholicism, the second comprising a long list of statutes safeguarding the protestant establishment. But the third part, truly the crux of the covenant, committed signatories to the defence of both Kirk and King, an idea which would rapidly prove impossible of fulfilment due to the hopeless incompatibility of the two constituents. A point too often overlooked, however, is that throughout protestant Europe the covenant was a concept to which frequent appeal was made, but which was nonetheless an abstraction, whereas in Scotland it was an actual tangible document which people physically signed. A covenant was a contract entered into with God for eternity; the first such was the covenant which God gave Noah after the Flood, promising that never again would such a calamity engulf the Earth. It is not actually clear whether anyone asked God if He was willing to covenant with a section of the Scottish population in 1638 but since He was omniscient He presumably did not require a written list of names to remind Him of who had subscribed. There was, of course another dimension to all of this, a highly secular motive which has been buried beneath all of the pious claptrap written about the subject by unimaginative presbyterian divines during the last 350 years. The covenant was also about the reformation of society, about politics, about the legitimacy of resistance to Stewart tyranny, about the extent to which monarchs were answerable to their subjects, and about a new sense of civic responsibility. Hence the need for signatures. People must be seen to be responsible for their actions, must be willing to stand up and be counted.

The Solemn League and Covenant of 1643, in the drafting of which Argyll was much involved, was a covenant with England which sought to impose religious conformity upon both countries at the dictate of the covenanters who, in return, would provide the English parliamentarians with military assistance against Charles I. The covenants were revolutionary because their adherents were intent upon nothing less than the complete overturning of the political order, the more extreme among them seeking to establish a republic of Jesus Christ in its place.[7] Why then, we may reasonably ask, was Archibald Campbell, scion of one of the most distinguished aristocratic families in Scotland not only totally implicated in these tumultuous developments but would soon be recognised as leader of the entire covenanting faction?

Part of the answer must be sought in his complex Campbell

heritage. Argyll's father, Gilleasbuig Gruamach, the seventh earl, almost wrecked the fortunes of the entire clan when, in 1617, he went off to Spain and converted to catholicism. This man had hitherto been a loyal Crown servant willingly taming the Gàidhealtachd on behalf of his master, James VI, and fabulously enriching himself at the same time through the engrossment of fines and the acquisition of lands and jurisdictions. Gilleasbuig was entrusted with the extermination of the MacGregors, a process which it was intended to continue until the king was satisfied that only twelve of them remained alive. He received a bounty on each clansman slain and a hefty percentage of the fines levied on those who sheltered MacGregors all the way from Loch Lomond to Sutherland. As a consequence the Campbells earned much of the legendary hatred for which they became so famous throughout the Highlands. The earl was also charged by the king with the suppression of the MacDonalds of Islay. There were thus many clans with vengeance on their minds when Gilleasbuig turned catholic. In the event the great Clan Campbell pulled together to overcome their chief's unforgivable treachery but one of the consequences was that strong measures were taken to ensure that young Archibald Campbell, was raised as a devout presbyterian. In a sense he was trapped by his own history, a calvinist opposed by predominantly catholic clans intent upon the restoration of their ancestral lands. Munro's allusion to the return of Argyll's father from Spain (p.18) is intriguing because historians have totally overlooked the incident, assuming that he never again visited his old haunts. In fact he did return to Edinburgh, Stirling and Rosneath in 1634 but few of his clansmen were interested, reluctant to forgive the shame and danger he had inflicted upon the kindred as a whole.[8]

Archibald Campbell, later Marquis of Argyll, has continued to suffer from an extremely bad press which was first apparent in the course of his own lifetime. Clarendon in his famous *History of the Rebellion*, praising with faint contempt, observed that he 'wanted nothing but honesty and courage to be a very extraordinary man, having all other talents in a great degree'. Patrick Gordon of Ruthven was prepared to credit him with some admirable qualities, 'if the iniquitie of the tyme had not carried him away with the maine current'. He thought him homely and tending towards simplicity rather than consumed with 'a loftie and unsatiable ambition, although he proved the deepest statesman, the most craftie, subtill and over-reaching politician, that this age could produce'.[9] Wishart, who was no admirer, alluded to 'the man's cunning and natural propensity to intrigue and treachery'. Of later historians that Neil Munro might have consulted, Malcolm Laing was inclined to admire Argyll but admitted that 'his prudence was apt to descend into craft, and the apprehensions which his subtle dexterity excited occasioned his destruction',[10] while Mark Napier further trashed the Campbell reputation in several studies devoted to the apotheosis of James Graham, Marquis of Montrose.[11] Of admirers, Hill Burton considered Argyll as 'one whom many adored as a saint and martyr ... his political conduct was not that of a coward and his death was heroic'.[12] After *John Splendid* made its appearance John Willcock produced a chronicle-like and remarkably unimaginative biography in which 'the virtues possessed by Argyll vastly outweighed the faults'.[13] Peter Hume Brown was one of the first historians who truly tried to understand Archibald Campbell:

> To his type of mind and character, the Calvinistic scheme of thought and rule of life presented a natural affinity which permitted him to embrace it with genuine conviction. He was the one Scotsman of his time who can be regarded as a statesman; and to him more than any other was it due that the main body of the Covenanters maintained a united front against their successive adversaries.[14]

John Buchan for his study of Montrose, which remains astonishingly popular though much dated, cribbed most of his information from Mark Napier. Buchan was largely responsible for the idea that Argyll found his *alter ego* in Montrose but he did make an honest attempt to come to grips with the man:

> His troubles came primarily from a divided soul – a clear, practical intellect pulling against an obscurantist creed, the Highland chief at variance with the Presbyterian statesman, a brain, medieval for all its powers, fumbling with the half-understood problems of a new world. With such a one subtlety will appear as irresolution, perplexity as cowardice, and a too quick mind will seem to argue a dishonest heart.[15]

All that need be said is that generalisation obscures the particular; to highlight the specific detracts from the bigger picture. There was remarkable complementarity between Montrose and Argyll, the one with the type of terrifying closed mind sometimes exhibited by military men, the other a vacillating politician, Montrose gallant and heroic, Argyll courteous and circumspect.

The John Splendid of the novel is Iain MacIver of the Barbreck, another mercenary and one who was called 'Splendid', 'not for his looks but for his style' (p.16). And a wonderful creation he is, a cousin albeit a poor one, of Argyll himself, a failed cattleman now manager of the silver mines and surely inspired by Scott's Dugald Dalgetty who was, in turn, modelled on Sir James Turner a cynical seventeenth century Scottish soldier-of-fortune who revealed much of himself in his fascinating *Memoirs*. Historically many Scots served in the Thirty Years War and many returned to fight the battles of the covenant. Part of MacIver's 'style' is to agree with everybody. He is a man who is 'twenty at heart, at the heart man, and do my looks make me more than twice that age? I can sing you, or run you or dance you' (p.93). He knows many tales, composes poetry, speaks English and French, can 'witch the eye of women' by looks alone and good humour but to his regret he cannot play the pipes and he has a poor regard for books (p.23).

Neil Munro's inspiration, if not his script, owed a very great deal to Scott's *A Legend of the Wars of Montrose*. Inveraray is depicted as the very Valley of the Shadow of Death (p.66), but we also see the place, in its magnificent setting beside Loch Fyne, in the company of Dugald Dalgetty who, more intent on sustenance than scenery, encounters the terrible spectacle of feudal power with all its symbols – the gibbet, the block and the head on the pole (pp.90–1). Dugald provides the perfect model for the character of John Splendid. He had sat with princes, was not a man to be browbeaten; 'he was naturally by no means the most modest man in the world, but, on the contrary, had so good an opinion of himself, that into whatever company he chanced to be thrown, he was always proportionally elevated in his own conceit' (p.93). Dugald mocks the use of bows and arrows (p.117, 132) as a sign of primitivism although histori- cally Argyll began to stockpile such supplies before he had even declared for the covenant in 1638. Bows were preferred because they were more easily come by and, in the right hands, were faster and more accurate than musketry; hence they were much favoured by Gaels in the wars. Scott lauded Gaelic military prowess while deploring their tendency to desert (pp.125–6). In *Legend* it is Montrose's idea to attack Inveraray, though modern opinion would give the accolade to Colkitto. Scott acknowledged the latter's accomplishments as a warrior but considered that his 'jealous and presumptuous disposition' often negated his personal gallantry. Nonetheless he admitted that Colkitto made a much greater impact upon Gaelic tradition than did the deeds of Montrose (p.121–2).

Argyll's notorious withdrawal from the battle of Inverlochy is brilliantly handled with a kind of bitter resignation not totally lacking in condemnation:

> when the still small voice within a man's own breast, which tells him that his life is of consequence to himself, is seconded by that of numbers around him, who assure him that it is of equal advantage to the public, history affords many examples of men more habitually daring than Argyle, who have consulted self-preservation when the temptation to it were so powerfully increased. (p.150)

Munro's treatment is rather different but still owes a good deal to Scott. In John Splendid's view MacCailein Mór had been corrupted by books; they had spoiled his stomach. He cannot fathom how Argyll can believe that 'a man might readily show more valour in a conclusion come to in the privacy of his bed-closet than in a victory won on the field' (p.23). John has catholic sympathies which sustain his suspicions of the likes of Master Gordon the minister and of the impact that he and his ilk will have on the Highlands, 'I hate the very look of those Lowland cattle sitting here making kirk laws for their emperors, and their bad-bred Scots speech jars on my ear like an ill-tuned bagpipe' (p.49).

Elrigmore's celebration of Loch Fyneside parallels Dalgetty's view which is as unseeing as Scott's when the witness of the native is compared. Munro understood the beloved landscape which had nurtured him, with nature conferring its 'biggest cup brimmingly', in a way that Scott never could. The comparison is instructive. Sailing across Loch Fyne Dalgetty was oblivious to 'one of the grandest scenes which Nature affords', careless of the rivers pouring into the loch from their dark woods, and heedless of 'the noble old Gothic castle, with its varied outline, embattled walls, towers' etc which, wrote Scott lapsing into Tourist Board mode, 'so far as the picturesque is concerned, presented an aspect much more striking than the present massive and uniform mansion', an anachronistic and unwelcome intrusion. Dugald also missed the picturesque peak of Duniquoich, 'raising its scathed brow into the mists of middle sky, while a solitary watch-tower, perched on its top like an eagle's nest, gave dignity to the scene by awakening a sense of possible danger' (p.89). The present watch-tower was built at the same time as the castle and so would not have been seen by Dugald, nor did the scene require the enhanced dignity of possible danger – whatever that means.

By way of contrast Munro's description teems with life as he details the 'fine fat land' thick with herds, 'rolling in the grassy season like the seas'. The wilds of Ben Bhuidhe and the hills beyond are home to the stags and the chase while among the cot-houses bairns toddle and women sing. The hazel trees were laden with nuts, 'the hip and the haw, the blaeberry and the rowan, swelled grossly in a constant sun...birds swarmed in the heather', deer abounded and the rivers boiled with fish. Truly 'a land laughing and content', its prosperity, in the time-honoured Celtic tradition, a reflection of the benign rule of Gilleasbuig Gruamach (pp.51-2).

Munro also handles the subject of prophecy much more effectively than Scott whose use of Second Sight (p.36, 39, 42, 44, 48) is somewhat forced. Prophecies attributed by Munro to the Macaulays about the demise of the Marquis of Argyll (pp.61-3) can be paralleled in contemporary sources. Cameron of Lochiel knew that a squint-eyed, red-haired earl of Argyll would be the last of his race while pro-Campbell seers predicted that Lord Archibald would one day 'cry king'. Even the 'Prophecies of Merlin' were invoked on his behalf when it was claimed that he was 'eighth man from Robert Bruce' and thus a legitimate future ruler.[16] For some reason humankind is quite forgiving of prophecies which are not fulfilled as in Argyll's case for although he personally had a date with 'The Maiden', as did his son, their posterity flourished.

Just why Munro insisted on designating the Macaulays (p. 62) 'the children of the mist' is unclear since, as every reader of Scott knew only too well, the label was reserved for the MacGregors. Was he making fun of Scott's over-use of this over-romanticised term? Did he believe that the Macaulays had been victimised every bit as much as the MacGregors? Or was he mischievously suggesting that the MacGregors did not deserve the appellation since, as he well knew, Rob Roy's house was at the head of Glen Shira and the outlaw's wife was a Campbell?

In Munro's account the true leader of the Royalist forces was Colkitto rather than Montrose and with this most modern commentators would agree. It was Alasdair historically who told Montrose that he had no option but to descend on the lion's den at Inveraray. The army was guided through the mountains by the MacIans of Glencoe upon whom savage vengeance would be wreaked in 1692. So it was that in late 1644 Inveraray was sacked, houses were burned, livestock haughed, stores spoiled and 900 Campbells killed.

The 37 MacDonalds murdered in the Massacre of Glencoe almost fifty years later afforded poor compensation; several of the attackers on that fateful February morning articulated their inherited bitter memories of the devastating descent on the caput of Argyll. Rape was always a concomitant of seventeenth century warfare. There is no reason to believe that Campbell women escaped in 1644 for neither did MacIan's elderly wife in 1692. At the Battle of Inverlochy, 2 February 1645, the victors slaughtered over 2000, many of them Campbells, MacCailein Mór having fled down Loch Linnhe. Argyll's cowardice, supposed or real, is central to *John Splendid*; the theme runs right through the novel.

Historically Argyll did abandon his people when news reached Inverary of the descent of Montrose and Colkitto. The splendid MacIver encourages the chief in his desire to retreat with his family, and this after he has lauded Argyll's bravery on other occasions.

Do you know, I put a fair face on the black business to save the man his own self-respect. He'll know himself his going looks bad without my telling him, and I would at least leave him the notion that we were blind to his weakness. After all it's not much of a weakness – the wish to save a wife and children from danger. Another bookish disease, I admit: their over-much study has deadened the man to a sense of the becoming, and in an affair demanding courage he acts like a woman, thinking of his household when he should be thinking of his clan. (p.78)

Later Argyll confesses his own doubts. He can detect his own cowardice in the eyes of those about him, among his clansmen, in his gardener, at table. He had failed in his 'most manifest duty', leaving 'the blood of his blood and skin of his skin to perish for want of his guidance and encouragement', waking 'to find it no black nightmare but the horrible fact'. He had been raised to keep the burning hatred of the feuds in the forefront of his mind but he now doubts the wisdom and righteousness of such sentiments; 'Dubiety plays on me like a flute'. Yet MacCailein is not so consumed with self-pity that he cannot still strike out. He tells John Splendid that he can read him like an open book, he and his kind who are 'the weak, strong men of our Highland race. The soft tongue and the dour heart; the good man at most things but at your word!' (pp.136, 138–9, 142).

It is words that have prevented Argyll from performing his duty. He is allowed to present one brief glimpse of what might have been as he and his companions ceilidh by the campfire in Glen Noe, but what is reinforced as the story unfolds is how trapped John Splendid is in a world that is doomed as he stumbles along, 'a carouser of life in a mirk and sodden lane' (p.191). A key chapter is XXV in which MacIver overhears the discussion between Master Gordon and Elrigmore. It is the minister's belief that sometimes God puts two men in the one skin, a man to love and blame, the generous oppressor, the pious libertine who is the result of his history and who has on hand flatterers for all seasons. Argyll is a man of peace and intellect but yet 'a remnant of the old world of Highland sturt and strife' (p.240–2).

Later, back in Inveraray, John erupts in the dialogue which forces him to quit the town, telling Argyll that he is for the cloister and not for the field. It is the chief's love of books that has ruined him to the point that Splendid is so embarrassed that he will deny he was ever at Inverlochy. Argyll's spirit is 'smoored among books. Paper and ink will be the Gael's undoing' (p.284).

There can be no doubt whatsoever that Argyll actually did quit his clan at both Inveraray and at Inverlochy. For the latter we have the devastating testimony of the Gaelic poem 'The Lament of the Widow of Campbell of Glen Faochain'.

O, I am sadly wounded since the day of the Battle of
Inverlochy. The Irishmen's onset was searing, they,
who came to Scotland empty-handed, who owned not even a cloak;
they gave mettle to Clan Donald.

They slew my father and my husband and my
three fine young sons; my four brothers hewn
asunder, and my nine comely foster-brothers.

O, I am spent on account of Campbell of Glen
Faochain. Every man in this land weeps for you;
Here and there about Inveraray women wring their
hands, their hair dishevelled.

O, I am despoiled on account of the rider of
bridled and pillioned horses who fell in battle
with his followers. Great MacCailein took himself
off to sea, and he let this stroke fall on his kin.[17]

The doubts which Munro attributes to Argyll were real, perhaps not quite as he described them, but credible nonetheless. He was conscious of his role as 'the mainstay of a great national movement' (p.243) and he believed in the wisdom of fleeing to fight another day even if he was trapped in a heroic code which despised him for so doing. Neil Munro shows no signs of having read Argyll's *Instructions to a Son* but in that small book, written at Edinburgh Castle as he awaited trial and execution in 1661, he would have found further ample corroboration for the portrait he painted of the 'Great Marquis' in *John Splendid*. His great rival Montrose could pen lines such as:

He either fears his fate too much,
Or his deserts are small
That puts it not unto the touch,
To win or lose it all.[18]

MacCailein Mór could never be quite so certain or single-minded. In his *Instructions* he most movingly wrote:

I did not look upon our intended reformation as any way taxable, since it had the whole stream of universal consent of the whole nation; I never thought of those dire consequences which presently followed, till by that confusion my thoughts became distracted and myself encountered so many difficulties in the way that all remedies that were applied had the quite contrary operation; whatever therefore hath been said by me and others in this matter, you must repute and accept them as from a distracted man, of a distracted subject, in a distracted time wherein I lived: And this shall serve to let you know how far I waded unwarily in that business.[19]

Considering the ethos of the age Argyll's remarks were truly heroic in their honesty.

Both Scott (p.150) and Munro allude to MacCailein's brave death which, so far as both their stories were concerned, was to take place at some distance in the future, 1661 to be precise. His execution was witnessed, according to Munro, by Elrigmore, who saw his 'head up and his chin in the air' before the marquis was decapitated by 'The Maiden', Scotland's guillotine, in 'Edinburgh of the doleful memories' (p.286). There is ample testimony to the composure with which Argyll met his end. The mask allegedly fell briefly as the tears welled but he turned to poke the fire in order, as

Marquis of Argyll in 1652. *Gilleasbuig Gruamach, MacCailein Mór*

he hoped, to avoid detection. A later story related that he consumed partridge for his final meal and that when his body was later opened up it was found to be perfectly digested, a sure sign that the Campbell's nerves were as steady as his pulse which was taken by his physician just before he made his closing speech.[20]

The best historical novels should capture something of the flavour of a period which is alien to our own. All too many novels about the Highlands depict them as an anachronism, glorious or otherwise, whose time has gone. The time had not yet quite come for John Splendid and his ilk though the writing was on the rocks and the bloom was off the tartan. Bibles, books and commerce were in the process of conspiring in the destruction of a culture.

In his article on Stevenson Munro talked of RLS 'in the happy sanctuary of Samoa, a little king in exile, experiencing the joys of a sort of feudal lord'. Munro understood the feeling of exile even if he was only as far away as Glasgow. Only an exile could have written the powerful and brilliant ending of John Splendid when Betty Brown finally realises the truth, and I would think that every native of Inveraray reads it blinded by tears:

> ... the rider passed on his way with the piper's invitation the last sound in his ears. He rode past Kilmalieu of the tombs, with his bonnet off for all the dead that are so numerous there, so patient, waiting for the final trump. He rode past Boshang Gate, portal to my native glen of chanting birds and melodious waters and merry people. He rose past Gearron hamlet, where the folk waved farewells: then over the river before him was the bend that is ever the beginning of home-sickness for all that go abroad for fortune. (p.334)

Through his exploration of the tensions and conflicts in one man's mind and soul Neil Munro encapsulates an essential historical truth that many historians have not yet grasped. The horror of Culloden and its aftermath may seem to mark the destruction of the Gàidhealtachd but its culture had been suffering a process of attrition for well over a hundred years before that fateful battle. When John Splendid rounded that last bend in the view from Inveraray he was heading a procession of his people on the History Highway, bravely, splendidly even, confronting the inexorable forces which were in process of consigning John himself, Gael and mercenary, to the long road of oblivion along with the Gaelic way of life. The Gaels themselves would survive but the certainties of centuries could no longer be taken for granted. The future lay with the confused philosophies and the much-adored books of MacCailein Mór.

Notes

1 Cowan, Edward J., 'Intent upon my own race and place I wrote': Robert Louis Stevenson and Scottish History' in *The Polar Twins: Scottish History and Scottish Literature*, Eds.Edward J.Cowan and DouglasGifford, Edinburgh: John Donald, 2000, pp. 187–214
2 All references to *John Splendid,* are to the B&W Publishing edition (with introduction by Brian D. Osborne), Edinburgh, 1994
3 All references to Scott's *A Legend of the Wars of Montrose,* are to The Edinburgh Edition of the Waverley Novels, Edinburgh University Press, ed. J.H. Alexander, Edinburgh, 1995

Edward J. Cowan

4 Watson, W. J., 'Unpublished Gaelic Poetry', *Scottish Gaelic Studies*, 3 (1931), pp.143–51; Edward J. Cowan, 'The political ideas of a covenanting leader: Archibald Campbell, Marquis of Argyll 1607–1661' in *Scots and Britons. Scottish political thought and the union of 1603*, ed. Roger A.Mason, Cambridge: Cambridge University Press, 1994, pp. 241–61

5 Argyll Transcripts, Inveraray Castle, nos. 469, 708

6 Wishart,George, *Memoirs of James, Marquis of Montrose 1639–50*, Eds. A.D. Murdoch and H.F.M. Simpson, London: Longmans, Green and Co.,1893

7 See in general Cowan, Edward J., 'The Making of the National Covenant' in *The Scottish National Covenant in its British Context 1638–51*, ed. John Morrill, Edinburgh: Edinburgh University Press,1990, pp. 68–89 and 'The Solemn League and Covenant' in *Scotland and England 1286–1815*, ed. Roger A. Mason Edinburgh: John Donald, 1987, pp.182–202

8 See for example Stevenson, David, *Alasdair MacColla and the Highland problem in the Seventeenth Century* Edinburgh: John Donald,1980, pp.49–50, 'he never returned to Scotland'. For a corrective see Edward J. Cowan, 'Fishers in Drumlie Waters' Clanship and Campbell Expansion in the time of Gilleasbuig Gruamach', *Transactions of the Gaelic Society of Inverness* 54, 1984–6 (1987) pp.269–312

9 Gordon of Ruthven, Patrick, *A Short Abridgement of Britane's Distemper*, Aberdeen: Spalding Club, 1844, pp.56–7. This is probably the most readable and entertaining of contemporary accounts of 'The Troubles' though like all of them it is pro-royalist and anti-covenanter and thus overwhelmingly hostile to Argyll

10 Laing, Malcolm, *The History of Scotland from the Union of the Crowns to the Union of the Kingdoms* 2 vols. Edinburgh: Constable, 1800, vol. 2, p.16

11 Napier, Mark, *Montrose and the Covenanters* (Edinburgh 1838), *Life and Times of Montrose* (Edinburgh 1840), *Memorials of Montrose and his Times* 2 vols Edinburgh: Maitland Club, 1848, *Memoirs of the Marquis of Montrose* 2 vols. Edinburgh: T.G.Stevenson, 1856

12 Burton, John Hill, *The History of Scotland* 10 vols. Edinburgh: William Blackwood, 1870, vol. 8, 133 note, p. 190

13 Willcock, John, *The Great Marquess. Life and Times of Archibald, 8th Earl, And 1st (And Only) Marquess of Argyll (1607–1661)* Edinburgh and London: Oliphant, Anderson and Ferrier, 1903 p.335

14 Brown, Peter Hume, *History of Scotland* 3 vols Cambridge: Cambridge University Press, 1905, vol. 2, p.309

15 Buchan, John, *Montrose* London and Edinburgh: Thomas Nelson and Sons, 1928, p. 94

16 Cowan, Edward J., *Montrose For Covenant and King*, 1977; Edinburgh: Canongate, 1995, p.94

17 Cowan, *Montrose*, p.186. Translation by John MacInnes

18 Cowan, Edward J., 'Mistress and Mother as Political Abstraction: The Apostrophic Poetry of James Graham, Marquis of Montrose, and William Lithgow' in *The European Sun,Proceedings of the Seventh International Conference on Medieval and Renaissance Scottish Language and Literature*,Eds.G.Caie, R.J.Lyall, S. Mapstone and K. Simpson , Edinburgh: Tuckwell Press, 2001, pp.534–44

19 Archibald, Marquis of Argyll, *Instructions To a Son Written in 1660 during his confinement*, Glasgow: R. Foulis, 1743, p. 5

20 Willcock, *The Great Marquess*, Chapter 20

Mr Neil Munro's *John Splendid*

(from *The Bookman*, October 1898)

I. By ANDREW LANG[1]

To a crawling Saxon interested in things Celtic, Mr. Munro's *Lost Pibroch* seemed a delightful and valuable work, full of the poetry of 'nature-folk.' The 'Lost Pibroch, however, was esoteric, and appealed to the few. In *John Splendid* Mr. Munro addresses the many, I trust with the success which he deserves. His plan is ambitious. Who can handle Montrose's wars, and Gillesbeg Gruamach, after the creator of Dugald Dalgetty? Mr. Munro may reply that he sees the affair as a Celt of the Campbell faction; our beloved Rittmeister looked with the eyes of a Lowlander. The answer is valid, we now behold these old frays and forays from both sides. Mr. Munro is a Celt, following two Border Scots into the hills. His theme is Sir Walter's, his manner is Mr. Stevenson's. These wanderings in the heather inevitably recall the pilgrimage of David Balfour. The style, too, is (I think) reminiscent of Mr. Stevenson's, though in no servile fashion. It is an excellent style, though, of course, Elrigmore could never have written it. This reflective, elaborate, copiously descriptive, deftly psychological manner is as modern as the telephone. That is of no importance; there is but one 'Esmond,' and even 'Esmond' is modern.

As to the story, Mr. Munro rightly says, 'it is a picture of times and manners,' a charming picture of these, as of landscape. I cannot say that the story, as a story, the plot, as a plot, the love affair, as a love affair, very much absorb me. The heroine is a heroine *de convenance*, not a Catriona, still less a Barbara Grant. Of the plot, there is hardly enough to keep the matter alive. There are *longueurs*, and I do hold that the psychology of the timid Marquis is overdone. Conceive Argyle saying to two soldiers of fortune, 'dubiety plays on me like a flute!' Argyle had not read Mr. Stevenson. But these things are not essential, though of these things there is too much. Essential is Mr. Munro's reading of Celtic character, 'the soft tongue and the dour heart; the good man at most things but at your word.' (p.142) Far be it from me, thinking of Lochiel, Keppoch, Glenaladale, and Young Clanranald, to say that this *mot* of Argyle applies to all Highlanders. But it does apply to Mr. Munro's brave, gay, kind, vain, superstitious hero, John Splendid, an excellent creation. In brief, Mr. Munro makes the past live, with its men of the past, its clan hatreds (the Macdonalds and Stewarts must raise up their own advocate in fiction), its beliefs, freits, poetry, and intense love of the most delightful country in the world. Dame Dubh and the widow of Glencoe are worthy of the best artists in fiction, and the atmosphere of hill and salt loch, the scent of gale and heather, are what you may breathe. I am anxious to make a raid on the historical part of the narrative, but a novelist may have it as he will, and give to a Macdonald the credit due to a Graham: the military credit. But I refrain, merely thanking Mr. Munro for so many hours of enjoyment, so many pictures of such various men and scenes, and especially for the song of 'The Sergeant of Pikes' (p.149).

II. By FIONA MACLEOD[2]

I would like to say what I have to say about this book from the personal and Highland rather than the strictly critical standpoint – if, indeed, there be any vital criticism without the leaven of predilection.

Frankly, then, for me there is too much of the Campbell in Mr. Munro's book. It has ever been the way with Clan Diarmid to consider itself as the Gaelic section of the chosen people. I have never loved the clan, or its glib way either with its tongue or its sheath, nor does it in history, save in individual instances, touch those heroic levels overrun by the clans of northern and western Gaeldom. There is not a chapter in *John Splendid* wherein I have not found a nettle behind every obtrusion of the bog-myrtle, the badge of him and his. It's well to a Campbell to be a Campbell; but I take it that it is not every one from Sutherland Ord to the Rhinns of Islay who would rather doff the cap to MacCailein Mòr than to any other chief. Even in the Gaelic southlands there are Macdougalls and McLeans, Camerons and Lamonts, Maclachlans and Macfarlanes and Macgregors, who would be as slow to kiss the myrtle-spray of the Campbells as would any Macleod or Macdonald.

There will be few in the Highland north, I fancy, who can read this book without some such feeling. Clan Diarmid is summed up in Mr. Munro's tale; the book is over faithful, one would think, to be wholly pleasant reading betwixt Lochfyneside and green Lorn. Vain, resentful, at once brave in desperate straits and commonly mighty careful, boastful, with an eye upon other men's lands and goods, fair to speak but with treachery in the hollow of the left hand; that is how the Campbells of history have ever seemed to me and to many others of the north, and that is how, in a general impression, they are revealed in this book, from Gillesbeg Gruamach, Marquis of Argyll, to the commonalty of his followers, always excepting that brilliant cavalier of fortune, John Splendid (as the nominal hero, McIver of Barbreck, is commonly called, though the Gaelic name, Iain Aluinn, would rather mean Handsome John) and the actual chief personage, the teller of the tale, known by his territorial name, Elrigmore. There are many episodes of bravado and daring, but perhaps these are rather the fiery accidents of driven men than the swift valour of those born under the fighting star.

This, however, is a sentiment that will be restricted to the north or to those of Highland blood. What is a more serious drawback, from the general Highland standpoint, is that in this romance there is not one prominent personage who has the nature to withstand all the things and to win against all odds. Elrigmore himself, though the least winsome and in some ways the most exasperating of heroes of romance, has grit for much, though little real stomach for a fight, and yet it could never have been men such as he who would have carried the Stewart cause through the gates of fate, had that great issue been sealed against failure. There is but one man in the book who has the masterful virility of those who do first, and argue or ignore the point afterwards; and that is Master Alexander Gordon, the Lowland Covenanting minister, as hateful for his doctrines and teaching as admirable for his indomitable courage and unvanquishable zeal.

As for the ordinary reader, surely the common objection will be that Elrigmore, the real 'hero,' is too dull and heavy a person. My own feeling throughout the story he tells was from the first one of vague resentment against him. He begins by an unchivalrous deed, on the night of his advent, when wantonly he breaks an old woman's window; and slight, and excused, as this episode is, it seemed to me, then and afterwards, indicative. His meeting with his stricken father sends a chill to the heart. As a lover he is slow in understanding, and with little of the Campbell honey in his mouth; and if I had been pretty Betty Brown, the Provost's daughter, it is not staid Colin of Elrigmore who would have made my pulse leap, but laughing 'Barbreck,' who in the end rides slowly through the old Arches of

Inveraora and out upon the white road that is the road for all broken
or adventurous men.

But having said this much – though, indeed, there is much more
in *John Splendid* for which I would like to take Mr. Munro to task –
it is time that I wrote on the other side. This I can do with cordial
pleasure. Take it all in all, *John Splendid* stands as the truest and
finest Highland romance written since Scott. I do not compare it
with the simpler, more moving, more convincing, and far more
unforgettable masterpiece of Robert Louis Stevenson; though I may
add frankly I would rather any day read the Highland chapters of
Kidnapped than even the finest pages in *John Splendid*. But as a
Highland romance, written by a Highlander, from the Highland
standpoint, it seems to me hardly less remarkable an achievement
than it is interesting, often fascinating, sometimes wholly delightful
as a moving tale.

Mr. Neil Munro has matured as a writer since he gave us *The Lost
Pibroch*. The obvious fault of that otherwise delightful book was an
altogether exaggerated use of Gaelic idiom – with minor faults of
diction and statement conspicuous enough to a Highlander, or to
Highlanders of the Isles and the West, though, it is only fair to add,
there is no universally accepted authority on Gaelic spelling, idiom,
and even grammar; Argyll differing from Inverness, and Islay from
the Lewis, almost as much as the Iona-Gaelic or the Irish-Gaelic of
Barra and Uist from either. In *John Splendid*, also, Mr. Munro's style
is still much too conscious, and I confess to an occasional weariness
of it; but that he will reach to a freer and suppler handling I am
confident, and that he has all the makings of a writer of genuine
distinction I believe. But henceforth and for ever let him avoid,
under any archaical pretence, such bastardy as this: '[if I set down
here what was said] it must not be in homologation on my part of
such latitudinarianism.' What was best in his first book is best in his
second: his intimate familiarity with all the aspects of sea-loch and
hill-side, and his faculty for vivid, novel, and convincing description.
Here, as before, there is a tendency to 'enamelling,' and sometimes
in the too free yielding to a native instinct he demonstrates the peril
of an acquired habit. But I know nothing finer or truer than innumerable depictive passages from his pen – a delight to read, a delight
to realise, a delight to recall. Let the reader turn to the masterly
description of the sudden oncome of winter, at the opening of
Chapter VIII; the breaking of the ice at pp.79–81; the coming of
dawn at p.120; of a grey day on the Moor of Rannoch in Chapter
XXVIII – but no, let him rather come upon these and a hundred

others as one comes suddenly, out of a barren pass, upon leagues of windy sunlit heather, or upon moonlit tracts foam-flecked with canna and fragrant with loneroid and bracken.

I put down *John Splendid* with some regrets and many reserves, but with the conviction that we have a new romancist of power and promise.

III. By WILLIAM WALLACE[3]

Mr. Munro, and not Mr. Crockett, is the Elisha on whom the mantle of Elijah Stevenson has fallen. In saying so I mean no disrespect whatever to Mr. Crockett, and not too extravagant respect for Stevenson. Not being an ultra-Stevensonian, and holding that a frayed sleeve belonging to the busy and slovenly man of affairs who wrote *The Antiquary* is worth the whole velvet coat of the invalid-student that wrote *Kidnapped* for boys, who knew buccaneers but was ignorant of men, who did not know women at all, and who, according to Mr. Charles Whibley, 'wrote English as a foreign tongue which he had acquired after painful effort,' I am glad to see that Mr. Crockett is emancipating himself from the fetters of hero-worship, and in his latest work, which seems his ripest, is simply himself. The author of *Clegg Kelly* and *A Woman of Fortune* is more of a romanticist, and if he were to get rid of certain exuberances of style, and to linger a little less than he is in the habit of doing in the 'hinterlands' of vernacular conversation, he would make a vigorous yet admirable realist. Even in romance his mission is that not of a second-rate Stevenson, but of a superior – a very superior – James Grant. Mr. Munro, on the other hand, is the heir of Stevenson, and in point of blood, not to speak of breeding, has a better claim to the heritage of Highland romance. Stevenson's love of nature, of open-air life, of the purple heather and bleak rocks of highland scenery, tragedy, and brigandage, is genuine and as intense as it is genuine. But at the best Stevenson is a Sassenach – for the Edinburgh middle-class man is the most unmitigated Sassenach in the United Kingdom – and his Highlands are the Highlands of a very accomplished and enthusiastic student of history. One is told on all hands that Alan Breck Stuart is the best Celt that was ever created. Possibly so; but would he be as popular as he is but for the 'tarry pirate' element in him which is not Highland at all, but pure Stevenson? Mr. Munro, on the contrary, is born to the manner – and still more to the manor – of the West Highlands. In *John Splendid* he walks the streets of

Inveraray as if he were his own Elrigmore, and when Montrose has raided it, jogs on surefootedly over moor and through heather listening to the 'Gude Gospel' sermons of Gordon and the sagacious braggadocio of McIver. In no romance that was ever written before is there so much of the colour and the air of the Highlands, and still more of the water, as there is in *John Splendid*; indeed, there is such an amount of a certain 'smirr of rain' in the book, that the best method of enjoying it is to put on a waterproof and read it during a heatwave in an umbrella tent. As a story, indeed, *John Splendid* is exasperatingly lacking in 'go'; every tenth page you wish for a Napoleon or a Kitchener to put a little energy into the marching and the counter-marching. The love 'business' is not strong. It is not easy to get enamoured of the Provost of Inveraray's daughter. She is born to haunt not the heather, but the saloon of the *Columba*; the 'randiest' of Mr. Crockett's byre-lasses is more attractive. Mr. Munro is a careful and not too pretentious stylist. Although some of his purple patches savour too much of loose-jointed special correspondence, and although he sometimes dallies on the moor in the spirit not of the romancist, but of the lyrist, the writing in *John Splendid* is a great advance upon that of *The Lost Pibroch* in point at once of grip and of ease. Some of the by-play, such as that in which Montrose's kindliness saves his life, is exquisite. Then the leading characters in the book – happily there are not too many of them – are one and all admirably drawn. Young Elrigmore, in spite of his smattering of what Mr. Munro too persistently calls 'the humanities,' is a good specimen not of the walking gentleman – except when he is engaged in limp love-making – but of the stalking clansman. The Argyll of Mr. Munro is not the Argyll of history – not, at least, the Argyll who held out in Inveraray Castle against Cromwell after Worcester. But as Gillesbeg Gruamach, as the Highland feudal superior, in closest touch with clansmen, servants, and Inveraray citizens, he is a unique and perfect study. Finally, although John Splendid, the soldier of fortune and of Argyll, a compound of Dugald Dalgetty and Alan Breck, is disappointing as a man; although one cannot help wishing he had taken a page out of Dalgetty's book, and when he had a chance, shaken the bookworm cowardice out of his master, he is a genuine Campbell. I am too much of a Lowlander to guess whether or not *John Splendid* will have a great vogue, and it is too soon to make any confident prediction as to the future of its author. Yet there is no doubt whatever that he has the makings of a great literary artist, and that he has already created genuine and genuinely romantic figures that have no superiors in fiction.

IV. By WILLIAM SHARP[4]

Of all the ways of romance, that is best which deals in the simplest and most direct manner with stirring events and momentous issues. It is the way of Defoe, of Scott, of Dumas, and, in our day, of the author of *Kidnapped, The Master of Ballantrae,* and *Weir of Hermiston.* But colloquialism, archaic or modern, is not necessarily the simple and direct way, which is a matter of the shaping mind far more than of literary discretion. If we turn to *Captain Singleton* or *Kidnapped,* or to any of their kind, we find a simple colloquial speech, but at the same time perceive how this is the very triumph of art, which is to transmute the matter of fiction into the substance of reality. It is in this direction that, in my judgment, Mr. Neil Munro falls short. His style is laboured throughout, for all that it bristles with obsolete epithets and discarded phrasings that in the period of his romance (about 1644) were a natural and living part of the common speech. His continual effort after surprise, after the unwonted turn, the novel note, acts as a drag upon his brilliant and picturesque tale. This is as noticeable, is indeed more noticeable, in those descriptive passages (fine and often of rare excellence, as these are) where it is really Mr. Neil Munro and not the Laird of Elrigmore who writes, as in those pages which set forth the sayings and doings of John Splendid and his friends.

Whether intentionally or unintentionally, Mr. Munro does not present the Highland people in a favourable light. If we accept, as trustworthy accounts, books such as *John Splendid,* Mr. McLennan's *Spanish John,* and others of the kind, we must arrive at the conclusion not only that the collapse of 'the Highlands' in any sustained undertaking was inevitable, but that it is just as well the Hanoverian musket came to replace the dirk and claymore.

It is, of course, as a romance pure and simple that we must look at *John Splendid.* Its predecessor, *The Lost Pibroch,* was a book of altogether exceptional promise, and many of its readers must have anticipated a masterly historical romance from the man who could deal so ably with dramatic episodes, who was so intimate with the life and circumstances and natural environment of the people with whom he concerned himself, and who wrote in a style at once virile, picturesque, and original. I have read *John Splendid* with constant pleasure and interest, and though because of its constant straining after effect I cannot account it a masterly work, I do look upon it as a valuable addition to Scottish fiction. But as an historical romance, it disappoints me. Mr. Munro had splendid material to hand. Out

William Sharp, 1896. Etching by William Strang

of the famous Marquis of Argyle, Gillesbeg Gruamach or Archibald Grim-face, as he was nicknamed, might have been wrought one of the great figures of art. All Argyle's indecision, evasiveness, mental cowardice, and occasional personal poltroonery are depicted, but we are left with little or no indication of that subtle, scheming mind, that calculating wide-seeing genius which made him the foremost man in Scotland in his turbulent day. No historical romance can be a success where the central historical figure is a failure, and a failure Mr. Munro has made of 'the great Marquis,' who neither in words, actions, nor leadership shows himself 'king of the Highlands,' but only as an incompetent chief, at times as a man unworthy, and more than once as a poltroon. His cowardice, indeed, has contagion in it, at least in Mr. Munro's story, for all the endless succession of brave shows of brawl and battle. In single episodes Mr. Munro is often masterly; it is in his weaving of episodes into an epical whole that he fails. The actuality which characterised most of his personages in the short stories of *The Lost Pibroch* is not so conspicuous in *John Splendid*. And one of the two 'heroes' – for the narrator, Colin (his surname is never mentioned, but presumably he is a Munro!) of Elrigmore, more than shares with John Splendid the leading part – has the fatal disadvantage of constantly recalling an elder brother in art, the ruder, more heroical, perhaps less winsome, but more absolute Alan Breck Stewart.

It is difficult to believe that a book written in this archaic Highland-Scots style can have a wide appeal. If so, so much the better. It is genuine and fine work, done with spirit, verve, and determination. No one, surely, will read it without admiration of many pages, delight in many chapters, and interest in all. It is one of the ablest Highland romances I have read; that it is not a great historical romance is another thing. This, I feel sure, Mr. Munro will yet achieve.

Notes

1 Andrew Lang, born Selkirk 1844, died Banchory 1912, was a leading literary critic, scholar and folklorist. His edition of Walter Scott's novels became a standard work and his collections of fairy stories remain significant contributions

2 'Fiona Macleod' – author of *The Sin Eater, Pharais* and numerous other works of Highland fiction. The female pen-name and *alter ego* of William Sharp (q.v.) Munro would later criticise 'Fiona Macleod' for knowing no more of the Highlands and Gaelic than could be got from a trip on a MacBrayne's steamer and a Gaelic dictionary

3 William Wallace, born Culross 1843, died Glasgow 1921, assistant editor of the *Glasgow Herald* 1888 – 1906, and editor, 1906 – 1909. A prominent Burns scholar and critic, he received an honorary doctorate from St Andrews University. Wallace spoke at a presentation dinner to Munro in November 1897 on the occasion of Munro's leaving the staff of the *Glasgow Evening News*. Munro was one of the pall-bearers at Wallace's funeral

4 William Sharp, born Paisley 1855, died Sicily 1905. Poet and biographer who adopted the personality of 'Fiona Macleod' in the 1890s. Strenuously denied that he and 'Fiona Macleod' were connected in any way – as can be seen in both authors contributing essays to this Symposium

'*From so trivial a thing*': Tradition and the Individual Talent in Neil Munro's *Gilian the Dreamer*

BETH DICKSON

Neil Munro's second novel, *Gilian the Dreamer,*[1] was published in 1899. He had already published *The Lost Pibroch and other Sheiling Stories* in 1896 and the novel *John Splendid* in 1898. The action of *John Splendid* took place during the harrying of Argyll by the Marquis of Montrose in 1644. In *Gilian* Munro moves the historical focus forward by about a hundred and seventy years to Inveraray in the period of peace after the end of the Napoleonic Wars. Despite this change of historical setting, Munro continues to examine the dreamer character who in *John Splendid* was Elrigmore and in *Gilian the Dreamer* is the eponymous anti-hero. Gilian's passivity, however, is not complemented by the activity of a John Splendid, an adventurer in the tradition of Alan Breck Stewart. Rather, Gilian is pitted against his active contemporary, Ensign Islay. It is through this split between vision and action that Munro analyses the relationship between the artist and Highland society which is the burden of *Gilian the Dreamer.*

The plot focuses on Gilian, a young orphaned boy, brought up by distant relatives; Miss Mary Campbell is delighted to have a child to care for as she never married. Her brothers are more forbidding. Major General Dugald Campbell and Cornal Colin Campbell are veterans of the Napoleonic Wars. The Paymaster, Captain John Campbell, was an army quartermaster and is looked down on by his brothers and others in the town for not having seen active service. Ironically, he is the most active and business-like of the three and it is 'the Paymaster', as he is known locally, who decides to take Gilian in. Gilian, a dreamy boy, grows up unsure of what he wants to do with his life. The paymaster wants him to join the army but Gilian's dangerous inability to respond quickly in emergencies puts paid to this. Gilian and Islay are both fond of Nan Turner, the daughter of

General Turner who is still likely to be called to further active service. Gilian's rival, Islay, rescues Nan from drowning, and in due course marries her, Gilian not being able to summon up enough resolution of purpose to secure Nan's love.

It is on the fretwork of this seemingly insignificant, even trivial, plot that Munro works out his analysis of the relationship between the artist, more particularly the writer, and Highland society. This essay will explore that relationship and then seek to answer the question, why, given this question is so important, is it so hidden in the text?

One of Inveraray's unusual features is that it is the home of a number of retired soldiers, whose Highland regiments played their part in the Peninsular and Napoleonic Wars. These men, have come home to grow old and die in the rosy glow of memories of old campaigns. The Paymaster says that without war the country will rot. He sees fighting as a means of ensuring the survival of the fittest, which thereby ensures the fitness of the country. This is surely ironic as the soldiers who laze about the town are fat, drunken and choleric. There is not much to do except stand around the street and talk, attend funerals, or go in for a drink now and then. The most ferocious aspect of the old society – its absorption with fighting – is seen as dangerous by the schoolmaster, who, when asked why he does not drink with the old soldiers, says:

'I find more of the natural human in the back room of Kate's there where the merchants discourse upon their bales and accompts than I would among your half-pay gentry who would have the country knee-deep in blood every day in the calendar if they had their way of it.' (pp.82–3)

The half-pay officers may be joined by the sheriff, the innkeeper or the schoolmaster. The rest of the inhabitants are made up of 'merchants and mechanics and fishermen' and are despised by the old soldiers as civilians (p.82). Spencer, a shopkeeper of a General Store is a Londoner who has come to make a living among a people now at peace with London government. The coming of trade is a sign of peace.

People make their own entertainment and supper-parties are popular. Highland songs are sung but although these songs are enjoyed, people are not keen to encourage others to maintain this culture. In the past poets who wrote songs which reflected Highland society were respected but no honour now attaches to a writer. Evan

MacColl, 'bard of the parish' so called, has only one couplet recorded, and a trivial, ironic comment at that:

Captain Mars, Captain Mars
Who never saw wars. (p.12)

Somehow the quality of society has deteriorated. Munro does not go into great detail as to why this should have happened. He mentions economic and social changes which have taken people from the country to the town and have resulted in a debasement of the culture: supper-parties were to make up for the 'lost peat-side parliaments or supper nights that for their fore-folk made tolerable the quiet glens' (p.71).

Parts of this older culture can be seen in the home of Jean and Aliset Clerk, to whom Gilian takes the news of his grandmother's death. Jean realises what has happened before Gilian tells her because she had a premonition of it the previous night:

'I dreamed last night I saw a white horse galloping over Tombreck to Ladyfield and the rider of him had his face in his plaid.' (p.9)

This sort of dream was a distinguishing feature of the Highland outlook. However, the old world of the second sight has gone and the reality is that the sisters live, not on a croft, but in a room, in a web of closes, in a town by the sea. Physically and spiritually, they are displaced people.

Jean cannot afford to bring Gilian up, but she ensures he will have a good home by persuading the Paymaster to adopt him. His new family shows a less appealing trait of Highland culture – touchiness which leads to feuding. At his grandmother's funeral, Gilian's prospective guardian, Campbell, and General Turner insult each other and inflame an old quarrel. Campbell ends the altercation swearing he will train Gilian to hate Turner's very name. They cannot fight or raid each other's cattle, but Turner 'revenges' himself on the Campbells by not inviting them to his next supper party; the trivialisation of life could not be more obvious.

In addition to feuding, the inhabitants of this society have a tendency to dream. The Paymaster's brothers, General Dugald and Cornal Colin are old and only happy when recounting their fighting days. Their day is regulated by routine and simple actions which pass the time but do not fill it. The overwhelming atmosphere of

Gilian the Dreamer is of complete enervation, mainly because so many of the characters are old and in indifferent health. When the news reaches Dugald that the country corps is to be billeted in the town overnight, he seems to lose years and returns to that lively youth, whose memory haunts him. But his romantic reverie is betrayed by his advancing decrepitude and inflexible reality – the army marches in during the hours of darkness, thus eliminating the possibility of a civic welcome.

Miss Mary, sister to these men, seems to be healthily rooted in reality. But her dream has arisen because of disappointment in love. When she finds she is to look after Gilian, the reality of having a child to care for is too great for her. Huge stores of love are poured on a small boy to an extent which impedes his development. Miss Mary can live with dreams more easily than reality. When Gilian arrives she wants him to remain a child for ever. As Gilian grows up, Miss Mary will not hear a word against him. The schoolmaster cannot tell her about Gilian's truancy because he knows he would 'shatter her illusion' (p.166). After years of keeping house for her undemonstrative brothers, Gilian wakes in Miss Mary the need to be loved and, closely associated with this affection, her buried but undestroyed attachment to the old world:

> 'I once had my own fancies, but I think they must have been sweat out of me in my constancy to my brothers' oven-grate and roasting-jack. It must be the old, darling, foolish Highlands in us, my dear, the old people and the old stupid, stories they are telling for generations round the fire, and it must be the hills about us, and the constant complaint of the sea –' (pp.46–7)

The schoolmaster is also involved in playing games with the real world. He does not wear his spectacles in class, preferring to see his pupils in a 'vague mist', rather than having to admit to needing glasses (p.82). The persistence of dream and illusion among these people points to a dissatisfaction with society as it is. Munro describes this aspect of the town as 'A stopped and stagnant world, full of old men and old plaints...' (p.22).

General Turner also harbours illusions about his society. He wears an 'antiquated queue that made him always look the chevalier' (p.192). The queue was a pendant braid of hair at the back of the head and wearing his hair in this fashion, General Turner associates himself with a romantic version of the past, with a particular version of the Jacobite Rebellion and Bonnie Prince Charlie. If the General's perception of the past is romanticised, so too is his perception of the present. General Turner tries to placate his daughter's desire to return to the bustle of Edinburgh in these words:

> 'Bide at home, my dear,' said he softly, 'bide at home and rest. I thought you would have been glad to be back from towns among our own kindly people in the land your very heart-blood sprang from.' (p.193)

Into the society described above comes Gilian, a boy who is acutely sensitive to nature and stories, but who is weak and not able to make a good and healthy relationship between his vivid imagination and the real world. Gilian's powers of imagination are quickly established in the novel. His ability to identify with an external situation of which he can have little knowledge is seen in his first meeting with the Paymaster's brothers. He surprises them with his ability to read from a painting the emotions of a wounded soldier. The child's insight disturbs the Cornal who thinks Gilian is 'not canny' and is unsuited for soldiering, having 'only the makings of a Dominie' (p.58). This failure to interpret Gilian's gift correctly becomes more acute as the novel progresses.

Miss Mary's understanding of Gilian's gift is at the same time a blessing and a curse. Gilian understands her feelings completely when she shows him the rusty sword of her brother James who died in battle. He knows the mixture of horror, sorrow and guilt that she would feel on drawing the sword. Miss Mary's response is set to mirror the Cornal's but she changes it in a way that helps Gilian:

> 'You are uncanny – no, no, you are not uncanny, you are only ready-witted...'
> Gilian was amazed that at last someone understood him. No one ever did at Ladyfield; his dreams, his fancies, his spectacles of the inner eye were things that he had grown ashamed of. (p.45)

Munro itemises quite clearly the influences on Gilian's imagination. First of all there is Nature itself:

> When hail or rain rattled on the branches, when snow in great flakes settled down or droves of cattle for distant markets went bellowing through the street, it was with difficulty the boy kept himself to his seat and did not rise and run out where his fancy so peremptorily called. (p.84)

Secondly, Gilian is aware of the stories of the Celtic tradition. He
tells Miss Mary that:

> from so trivial a thing as a cast-off horseshoe on the highway he
> was compelled to picture the rider, and set him upon the saddle
> and go riding with him to the King of Erin's court that is in the
> story of the third son of Easadh Ruadh[2] in the winter tale. (p.45)

Although the values attached to men of action in the old culture still
remain in the axiomatic respect for soldiers, those attached to the
bard and shenachie have vanished. Gillesbeg Aotram, from whom
Gilian learns folk-tales, is shunned as a tramp and Gilian is taught
to feel ashamed of even knowing Gillesbeg. Gilian's society supplies
him with no adequate role model for his gifts.

In addition, the 'Highland' side of his nature leads to an affinity
with two other characters. Gilian meets Black Duncan, the sailor,
who is presented to Gilian in almost magical terms. Black Duncan
tells Gilian of his adventures in what are imaginary worlds. Besides
Black Duncan, Gilian meets Nan Turner – the daughter of the man
with whom his guardians are conducting a respectable feud – who
sings to him the old songs, thus bringing to him 'new and potent joy'
(p.69). Gilian recognises that just as he becomes whatever role he
adopts, so Nan 'is The Rover' when she sings (p.70). Clearly there
is an identity between Gilian and Nan; it remains to be seen how
close it is. Gilian's friendship with Nan and Black Duncan represents another world which stimulates his creativity and presents him
with the hope of his calling which is almost universally denied in his
ordinary world.

Thirdly, Gilian is a member of a small lending library and reads
anything the lady who runs the library will allow him: *Mysteries of
Udolpho, Thaddeus of Warsaw, Moll Flanders, Roderick Random,
Belinda* and *Robinson Crusoe.* The parts he likes best are the parts he
makes up himself after the written adventure has come to an end.
He wants to read the poetry of Walter Scott after having been
impressed with it at school, but the librarian thinks he is too young
for poetry. It is interesting that Scott is introduced here only to be
dismissed. What might Gilian have made of *Waverley* or *Rob Roy*?
Both Scots and Gaelic models are denied Gilian and even if he had
known Scott, is it not more than possible that he would have
responded like Tommy Sandys in *Sentimental Tommy* (1896),
reducing Jacobite history to children's games?

However, Gilian's unschooled imagination is problematic. It is finely-tuned and the real world can easily become different for him if it triggers his transforming imagination. What his imagination creates is more intensely present to Gilian than the world where he feels out of things. Other people recognise that there is something different about Gilian. His schoolfriends are amazed at the reality he can inject into their games. For the most part though, other people do not know how Gilian should use his gift, if indeed they consider it a gift at all. When Islay finds Gilian reading two days in a row, he provokes him with the insult, 'you should have been a girl!' (p.88).

Gilian covers up for his weaknesses by acting. He is concerned about how his actions will look to other people and so he tries to manipulate them into seeing him as he wants them to see him. Taking the news of his grandmother's death to the town, Gilian spends most of the journey planning his entrance for maximum effect. However, because of Jean's premonition, his grand entrance is spoilt by his inability to cope with life as he finds it.

Although Gilian is good at imagining all sorts of varied events, he cannot bring them to pass. He finds it difficult to respond spontaneously to reality and instead assumes various roles. This happens most conspicuously when the country corps is billeted in the town overnight and Gilian becomes enchanted with the role of soldiers. After listening to the campaign tales of the Paymaster's brothers, Gilian dreams vividly about being a soldier. When the troops arrive, Gilian is fascinated by them and marches behind them as they move out:

> Gilian was walking in step to the corps, his shoulders back, his head erect, a hazel switch shouldered like a musket. But it was the face of him that most compelled attention for it revealed a multitude of emotions. His fancy ran far ahead of the tramping force thudding the dust on the highway. He was now the army's child indeed ... (p.101)

The Cornal mistakes Gilian's dream of the army for a sincere expression of boyish ambition but as Munro points out, when something new comes to take up Gilian's attention, his 'dream of the army fled' (p.104). It is Nan Turner who dispels this dream and she is very aware of Gilian's inadequacies:

> 'I think when you can pretend so much to yourself you cannot so well do the things you pretend. You can be soldiering in your mind so like the real thing that you may never go soldiering at all.' (p.107)

Some boys who 'dream of being a soldier' use the dream to motivate them to take actions which will make the dream a reality. However, for Gilian, making dreams come true is not simply impossible but also irrelevant. He is not interested in dreaming because it brings reality closer, he is only interested in dreaming for its own sake. His inconsistent actions reflect his multitudinous dreams. As a dream is dreamt then abandoned for something else, the actions which the dreams inspired are also abandoned, making the boy seem capricious.

The negative consequences of Gilian's dreaming soon become apparent. Gilian's imagination, which allows him to 'playact' so brilliantly, grows in inverse proportion to his will to act – to implement those decisions which are the stuff of ordinary life. This tension is so deep that the pun on 'act' which sums it up grows into the structure of the last part of Book One.

Gilian's undisciplined imagination is obvious when he takes Nan on a walk through the Duke's gardens. During their conversation Nan sets up this tension between the man who acts and the man who thinks. Nan prefers men who act but Gilian knows that, though she says she does not like 'the kind of boy' he is, she did recognise in him a kindred spirit when she sang for him on board the 'Jean' (p.106–7). However, Nan is annoyed with Gilian when the heron's nest that he promised to show her turns out to exist only in his imagination. There is a nest, but Gilian never climbed up to verify whether or not it belonged to a heron. He did not check the nest because he did not want to be disappointed should it have been the nest of a less splendid bird. Gilian is using his imagination to insulate himself from reality. Instead of enhancing reality, it is falsifying it. Indeed he is sentimentalising reality because it takes its co-ordinates from the world as he would like it to be, not the world as it is. And Nan is not impressed by this for she asked him if he climbed the tree 'looking him through with eyes that then and always wrenched the prosaic truth from him' (p.109).

The climax of Gilian's indecisiveness occurs one afternoon when he is on board the *Jean* with Black Duncan and Nan. Gilian begins the afternoon by feeling ashamed of his dreaming in the presence of Nan's active nature:

A fury at the futility of existence seized him. He would give anything to be away from this life of ease and dream, away where things were ever happening, where big deeds were possible, where the admiration and desire were justified. (pp.132–3)

But Black Duncan, seeing his perturbation, says he will tell another story. He asks if Gilian is frightened by things that are not there. Gilian says he is and Black Duncan assures him that this is a sign of his affinity with the old world. Duncan related his tale of an encounter with the supernatural and at the end Duncan makes it clear that he was destined for that encounter. He thereby implies that the power of the old world may still be felt. This possibility so arouses Gilian that he jumps off the ship onto the shore.

As he comes to, he realises that a gathering storm will sink the *Jean* in a short time. A bridge has been dislodged and is careering downstream, set to collide with the *Jean* at the river's mouth. Gilian sees all this in an unreasonably detached way. He runs down to the boat to warn Black Duncan who responds by loosing the boat from her mooring and allows her to be driven by the wind. Unfortunately, the ship is headed straight for a rock and will founder if she hits it. The seamen cry to Gilian and point but he cannot understand their meaning that there is a boat nearby which he could sail out to the *Jean* to rescue Black Duncan and Nan.

As he follows the boat's progress and realises its danger, he anticipates in his imagination what will happen when the ship founders. Indulgently, he wishes he could be a hero and save the ship. Just then he sees Islay push out in the small boat and make for the distressed ship. Gilian was so wrapped up in dreams, it never occurred to him that the possibility of action was real:

> Then the whole folly of his conduct, the meaning of the seamen's cries, the obvious and simple thing he should have done came to Gilian – he discovered himself the dreamer again. A deep contempt for himself came over him … (p.144)

Gilian's self-contempt only lasts as long as it takes him to get home. He acts out the adventure to the General and the Cornal. They think his use of 'the boy' as he narrates the story is a modest way of referring to himself, and this is confirmed to them when, halfway through the story, Gilian switches to first person singular narration. Gilian can act Islay's part but he cannot perform Islay's actions. The old General finds the disappointing knowledge that Gilian has been proved the dreamer again too much to bear. He takes to his bed and dies shortly afterwards.

Book One ends on this pessimistic note. Gilian has talent but because he places more importance on dreams than reality, he actually endangers life. In the second book, these aspects of his character are developed to their conclusion but Munro steers the book away from the tragedy, which this last episode perhaps suggests, and the book ends on a note of unfulfilled promise. The plot now centres around Gilian's romantic relationship with Nan and his rivalry with Islay for her affections.

Islay has joined the army and is on leave. He visits Nan at Maam House and declares his love for her. Gilian who has been eaves-dropping, hears this and thinks how fine it would be to be Islay in love with Nan! Gilian is only slightly depressed by Islay's success and soon thinks himself an eligible lover for Nan. The plot falls out (again rather oddly) that General Turner arranges a marriage for his daughter without informing Nan.

Not knowing her father has picked Islay for her, Nan decides to go with Gilian to find Old Elasaid, Nan's former nurse. Gilian finds himself hoping Nan will take cold feet. Nan finds that Gilian is not sufficiently alive to the romantic possibilities of the situation for her liking:

'I was – I was – kissing you a score of times in fancy and all the time you were willing in the actual fact.' (p.244)

On their journey they find an old, broken-down summer sheiling and Gilian is perfectly happy. Immediately he conjures up the people who dwelt there and the atmosphere of domesticity that surrounded them. Gilian thinks the land melancholy because it has lost its people but in his imagination he is able to people the glens and to bring the old customs and culture to life again (p.246). In Gilian's final debacle, we catch glimpses of how his imagination could have grown strong but as it had no guidance, dreams are punctured by reality, which finally breaks in on Gilian when Islay finds Nan and is accepted by her, after suitable protestations.

Although Nan marries Islay, Gilian's irresponsible imagination confirms him in the belief that Nan loves him, not Islay. Even Miss Mary cannot make Gilian see what has happened. Out of the expe-rience has come one positive result. Gilian has written a poem. It is one of the few things that Gilian has done on his own initiative and his guardians wish to put a stop to it immediately. Gilian has written about 'love and idleness among the moor and heather' (p.294). Although the love was wholly illusory, just as was his heroism on the day the boat sank, the utterly paradoxical thing is that to the readers of the poem, the emotions and actions are real in every aspect. Munro steps into the story at this point:

It was the first of those heart-wrung fancies that went to the making of the volume that lies before me as I write – the familiar lament for the lost 'Maid of the Moor' that shepherds are still singing on his native hills. (p.294)

There is no development or explanation of this startling conclusion to Gilian's story. Like so many other aspects of the novel, no interpretation is made by the author. Yet it does explain implicitly the prominence given to Gilian's dreaming. His dreaming is the result of his imagination which seems to have no relation to the ordinary world. Yet finally, Munro seems to imply that everyone in the book has been making wrong evaluations about Gilian's imagination. Instead of seeing it as something to be ignored or something that should be disciplined to the common uses of imagination, it should have been seen as a gift which marked Gilian out as a creative artist. Such was the cultural decline of Gilian's tradition, however, that there was no one left who could recognise his individual talent.

Given that Munro is discussing the problems of tradition and the individual talent in the Highlands, why does the novel read ostensibly as if it is a book about a worthless boy? The main difficulty in interpreting the novel lies in explaining the discrepancy between the apparent lightness of the plot and the seriousness of the theme. Of Munro, Hugh MacDiarmid said:

Neil Munro is the lost leader of Scottish Nationalism... He is a promise that has not been kept and while it is not permissible, and perhaps not possible, to describe here just how and why it came to be broken, I may speak of such a thing as a disabling fear of life, a soul destroying tyranny of respectability, ... So I think unworthy hesitations – whatever their nature, economic, moral, psychological – have made Neil Munro 'unequal to himself'.[3]

This comment that Munro's inadequacies come from what he does not say rather than what he does are very similar to the interpretative crux of *Gilian the Dreamer*. Munro makes observations but he rarely expatiates. There are a number of possible reasons for this. Firstly, Munro did not know how his society had come to such a pass or, secondly, he was not willing to say what he knew to be true, perhaps because, as MacDiarmid suggests, it would have led to a radical political view with which he, as a member of the Scottish literary establishment, did not want to be associated. However, there is a third possibility which is present in the language of the novel and that is the Highland characteristic of not discussing those things about which one feels most deeply. This is usually a virtue but it can be a terrible vice. It cannot operate unless the person who is spoken to shares the same outlook on life as the speaker and can interpret the silences or the allusions correctly. However, if that unity of vision is not shared then communication breaks down and silence and allusion can be interpreted as lack of interest or deliberate mystification. Both of these characteristics, especially the latter, are sometimes associated with stereotypes of Highlanders.

It is now time to look at the silences and allusions in *Gilian the Dreamer*. While it will be helpful to compare these with the interpretations of Highland life offered by later writers, it should be remembered that Munro was not a Modernist and because his interpretation is not the same as theirs, he should not be thought to have 'failed'; he should be interpreted on his own terms.

In 1746 the Duke of Cumberland, son of King George II, routed the forces of the Young Pretender, Charles Edward Stuart, at Culloden, thereby ending the Stewart claims to the British throne and the threat to British political stability which emanated from the Highlands. After the battle, survivors were killed and homes were systematically burnt. Weapons and bagpipes were confiscated. Wearing tartan was prohibited. The estates of Jacobite chieftains were confiscated until 1784 and Highland chiefs were deprived of their traditional rights to dispense justice. The King's courts alone were to do that. Another drastic blow was dealt when the chiefs themselves left the Highlands for London and began to exploit their own people in order to support their new aristocratic life-style, close to the centre of political power, preoccupied primarily with English affairs. Chieftains began to think of how to make money out of their estates and from the beginning of the nineteenth century onwards the infamous process of the Clearances began as landowners 'cleared' resident populations to make way for sheep because sheep farming was more profitable. Many Highlanders moved on to coastal strips and many others emigrated. Further disruption took place during the Napoleonic wars when many young Highlanders were recruited to Highland regiments which fought in the Napoleonic campaigns.

These convulsive events are not described by Munro. However, he points to two features which imply them: depopulation and employment. He writes of the depopulation of the glens – when Nan and Gilian 'elope', they shelter in a derelict summer sheiling, one of many ruins which would have been inhabited in previous summers but are no longer needed because the farming techniques which made them necessary are not practised as the people are not there. In addition, Jean and Aliset Clerk who used to live in the glens now live in the town. Secondly the jobs available to Gilian are either shepherding or soldiering – Inveraray is stiff with ex-soldiers. Without stating it in so many words, Munro is dealing with the body-blow dealt to Highland life by the Clearances and yet the word is not mentioned in the whole of the novel. However tacitly, Munro is criticising the Clearances for reasons which were overtly expressed by twentieth century novelists such as Neil Gunn in *Butcher's Broom* (1934), Fionn MacColla in *And the Cock Crew* (1945) and by Iain Crichton Smith in *Consider the Lilies* (1968). Whatever reasons Munro may have had for not making this theme more explicit, so fundamental were the changes brought about in the Highlands by the Clearances, that he cannot build a picture of Highland society without reference to them.

In parallel with the Clearances, Munro perceives the army as a key factor in Highland life. Parliament finally subdued the Highlands when it made Highlanders fight for Britain instead of against it. The Paymaster is proud of the Highland record in the Napoleonic wars but both Neil Gunn and Iain Crichton Smith clearly show how the lack of a generation of young men, who had left home to fight in foreign wars, were, because of their absence, made unwitting contributors to the subjugation of their own. Munro makes this observation:

> Gilian looked and saw Young Islay, a smart ensign home on leave from the country corps that even yet was taking so many fine young fellows from that community. (p.171)

and the following quotation, which is taken from the description of the troops entering Inveraray, on their way elsewhere is enigmatic and suggestive:

> And now they were the foreign invader, dumb because they did not know the native language, pitying this doomed community but moving to strike it at the vitals. (p.99)

Is Gilian here imagining what it would be like if the army were marching in to destroy a foreign community? Is he seeing them as if it were his community which was to be invaded? Is Munro suggesting that although there are valuable things in the society, for some reason it has become doomed and therefore the army is doing an unpleasant but necessary job in destroying the place altogether? If this is true then it implies that Munro's feelings about Highland culture are split. On the one hand he sees a social tradition to be treasured, while on the other, he knows that the life has gone out of society and because it has become so stultified, it is not worth saving. This split attitude is close to that shown in the early novels of Neil Gunn, who in *Grey Coast* (1926) and *The Lost Glen* (1932), shows the same blend of regret and pessimism which characterises Munro here. Perhaps more tellingly in *Land of Our Fathers* (1933), however, Ian MacPherson points to reasons within Highland communities which resulted in their doing little to resist destruction. The view that fatalism was a factor in Highland decline was vehemently dismissed by writers such as Gunn, MacColla and Crichton Smith but the fact that some Highland writers felt like that about their own communities should not be overlooked.

Munro shows too that the vitality and range of possible action which characterised the old community now serves to emphasise the deterioration which is apparent in contemporary society. This deterioration can be seen in the lives of Islay – the man of action – and Gilian – the dreamer – the boy who is linked with such a 'feminine' quality as imagination. There is still a place for Islay but there is no place for Gilian that he can easily see. Interest in the arts has become feminised and therefore seemingly closed to male writers. In addition to that the energy of Highland soldiering is dispersed all over the world with the Highlands acting merely as a recruiting depot.

The reason people dream themselves into other worlds, or delude themselves about the one they are in, is that their society provides them with no frame of reference in which to exist. The only man who links this area of the Highlands to Parliament, and the centre of power, is the Duke and, though he appears in church sometimes, he does not seem to know or be involved with the local community. He speaks to no one; when at home, he merely 'threw a glance among his clan and tenantry' (p.186).

General Turner's admonition to his daughter to content herself in the Highlands sounds conspicuously hollow coming from a man who is himself only passing time in the Highlands until a new posting comes up and who carries on mindless quarrels with his neighbours. The realistic hopes and ambitions of General Turner and his daughter shed light on why this dissatisfaction is endemic:

[Nan, his daughter, was] uplifted marvellously with his ambitious dreams of State preferment. For General Turner was but passing the time in Maam [his estate] till by favour promised a foreign office was found for him elsewhere. (p.193)

Socially significant activity takes place outside of the Highlands. Nan knows this and her problem is that she may not be allowed to accompany her father. When the news comes through of a posting to Sierra Leone, in West Africa – known then as the White Man's Grave because of the number of colonisers who died of disease there – Nan realises she is in an even more invidious position than her father. Because she is a girl she might not even get the chance to exchange social stagnation for an uncertain future. For her the possibility of action is preferable to the certainty of boredom:

'But this is Glen Shira ... it's the white girl's grave for me ... Should not I be glad to be getting out of it?' (p.228)
'... I must have something that is not here; I must have youth and life – and – life.' (p.193)

The fact that Nan's liberation is a version of her father's liberation is yet another indication that Munro's implicit criticism of Highland society is an incipient expression of what we would now call a post-colonial view. Feminism would argue that Nan's position is doubly difficult because of her gender. However, it is obvious that although her father has more power than she does, his power is significantly modified by the British State. The Highlands, though not 'colonised' in the same way as, say, India, were subjugated and some of the effects of subjugation were similar in nature if not, perhaps, in degree.

Perhaps the most intense irony of *Gilian the Dreamer* is that the positions of Gilian and Turner are much closer than they themselves realise and than the reader easily sees. Turner needs 'permission' to act, literal permission from the government. Gilian cannot act because the educating and enabling bardic traditions of the old society have been destroyed in the subjugation and are now no longer respected by the descendants of the old society. Both Gilian and Turner are vitally affected. Gilian's true identity is hidden from him but Turner's identity is literally taken away. Before the reader knows anything about Turner, Munro writes:

the man himself was little more than in his prime, straight set up like the soldier he was till he died of the Yellow in Sierra Leone, where the name of Turner, Governor, is still upon his peninsula. (pp.34–5)

General Turner's fate is introduced so proleptically and without comment that it is quite conceivable that readers could miss it. Again Munro makes it as hard as possible to piece the interpretative jigsaw together. Turner may think Gilian a 'failure' but both men are disposed of in different ways by an alien power.

Munro knows that the Clearances and the role of the Highland Regiments were significant features in the change. They are the obvious and continuing expressions of the Highland subjugation. He implies that the peace which exists is not a good peace because it has been achieved by defeat, desolation and displacement. The life and colour of the old world has gone. Trivialisations and falsifications have been set up. The people who are walking about are shadows with their minds full of dreams. Munro points out that the remnants of the old world which exist in this doomed community create a vast, searing regret for the world that has gone; a regret he links with the separation of the lambs and ewes in August; a regret which he expresses in one Gaelic word which simultaneously evokes and mourns for the old world:

that far-extending lamentation of the flocks was part of some universal *coronach* for things eternally doomed. (p.169)

Gilian's particular difficulties in relating to this decaying society are similarly shrouded in silence and implication. Gilian is linked with the old story-telling traditions of the Gaelic people. However, Munro never says about Gilian what Gunn says about Kenn in *Highland River*, that much of his society cut him off from seeking them out. It is interesting though, that at key passages, Gilian's imagination is fired directly by Gaelic songs or stories. At various stages in the novel it is suggested that Gilian could be a clerk, a dominie, a playactor or a soldier. He becomes a shepherd and poet. The difficulty in defining his gift brings about most of the misery he feels as he grows up as a misfit in his own society.

Gilian's problem here bears a close resemblance to that of Tommy Sandys in J.M. Barrie's *Sentimental Tommy* who finds himself constantly wishing he were a child again. The same pattern appears fitfully in MacDougall Hay's *Gillespie* (1914) where Eoghan wakes up after a nightmare to hear children singing, 'Again the unappeasable yearning to mingle with them, to be a boy again!'[4] Does Munro mean that though Gilian would never be able to stand in relation to the ordinary world as most people do, this different standpoint allows him to produce art? Is he suggesting that Gilian is able to find a role in society by writing songs from the experience of the people which the people recognise and sing? Munro's final attitude to Gilian is difficult to gauge. When Gilian's poetry is published the Campbell brothers are scornful and Gilian is protected by Miss Mary just as he was when he first came to the house as a child:

> She looked at her dreamer and stifled a sigh. Then she saw her brothers in the doorway, silent, and her hand went down and met his and fondled it for his assurance as on the day he first stood, the frightened stranger, on that floor, and she had sheltered his shyness in the folds of her bombazine gown. (p.295)

This direct verbal echo of chapter five (p.50) implies that at 17 the boy has not grown up and is still in need of adult protection. And yet there is the book of poetry. Is it perhaps that the only model that Gilian can find for his imagination is that of the wonderstruck, instinctive child, before society began to impose patterns on his behaviour? Certainly the return to childhood is a prominent theme in many Scottish novels. Munro gives one reason why this preoccupation should be so intense, perhaps. The unclouded vision of the child must become the touchstone of artistic integrity to all those potential artists who grew up without meeting a literary tradition which might have helped them develop. Instead they were told that literature was a worthless pursuit. When they found nothing in external reality to correspond to the inner experience, they have to return to the sure intimation of their gift – the untrammelled imagination of the child.

Munro is writing about the relationship between the writer and society and the tension between action and passivity in the Highland worldview. Although in *John Splendid* and *Gilian the Dreamer* it appears he is writing historical fiction or adventure stories this is only half true. If Munro, the artist, could but dimly see what was going on, it was little wonder that friends did not understand either and encouraged his talents in the wrong direction. As Anne Smith has pointed out in a reappraisal of Munro, Norman Bruce confirmed this view in an earlier *Scotsman* article by quoting from Munro's diary and commenting:

[The entry was] an anathema against those (unspecified) who had encouraged him to pursue the vein he had adopted in his fiction. One can only suppose that he had in mind those friends, critics and possibly publishers who had seized on his writing 'in the Highland manner' and by their acclamation led him into an artistic cul-de-sac.[5]

By now I hope to have shown that Munro in a rather obscure way did recognise the social consequences for Highland culture after the Clearances. Munro shows the debilitating effects of false realities on society and on Gilian. He is quite well aware that romantic self-indulgence has dangers which are to be recognised and condemned. *Gilian the Dreamer* displays an instinctive knowledge of the decline of Scottish society and its baleful effects on the potential artist as did *The House with the Green Shutters* (1901) and *Gillespie*. While Brown and Hay ended their novels tragically, Munro did not choose to close in that manner. Gilian becomes a poet but of what ability we do not know. Munro is confronted on all sides with problems which he refuses to simplify. For Munro there are no questions, only instinctive, and perhaps subconscious, interrogative shadows.

Notes

1 The edition referred to in this essay is Munro, Neil, *Gilian the Dreamer*, Edinburgh: B&W Publishing, 2000
2 See Campbell, J.F., *Popular Tales of the West Highlands*, Edinburgh: Birlinn, 1994, pp.91-109
3 MacDiarmid, Hugh, 'Neil Munro' in *Contemporary Scottish Studies*, Edinburgh: 1976, pp.5-6
4 Hay, John MacDougall, *Gillespie*, Edinburgh: Canongate, 1979, p.410
5 Smith, Anne, 'In search of the essential Celt' *The Weekend Scotsman*, 11 December 1982, p.1

The Post '45 Novels

Doom Castle, The Shoes of Fortune, Children of Tempest

RONALD W. RENTON

Following in the tradition of *John Splendid* Neil Munro published three further historical romantic novels between 1901 and 1903. These were *Doom Castle, Shoes of Fortune*, and *Children of Tempest*. Common to all three is their setting in the aftermath of the Jacobite Rising of 1745. *Doom Castle* is, in the last analysis, an elegy for the Jacobite movement. *The Shoes of Fortune*, set mainly in France, deals with the last throes of Jacobitism – the dissipated Charles Edward Stuart's attempt to join the French in an abortive invasion of Britain in 1759. *Children of Tempest*, is a moral fable set in the Outer Hebrides which has as its mainspring the search for a hoard of French gold which had been intended to help finance the '45.

Doom Castle (1901)[1]

Doom Castle owes its principal inspiration to Dunderave Castle, a fortified tower house on the shores of Loch Fyne, about five miles north of Inveraray in Argyllshire. This building was restored by Sir Robert Lorimer in 1911 – a restoration to which Munro was later to object vigorously.[2] The book, however, was written when the building was still in a ruinous state and it is its decaying condition which Munro was to make an important symbol throughout the novel.

In terms of its literary roots this novel catches the time and atmosphere of Stevenson's *Catriona*. It is set in 1752 with the trial of James of the Glen taking place during the action.[3] During the trial the town is full of lawyers, dominated by the powerful figures of Argyll himself, the Justice General, and Lords Kilkerran and Elchies. The French Count Victor, hero of the story, finds it unwise as a foreigner to go into Inveraray immediately after the trial because 'there was associated with the name of the condemned man as art and part in the murder that of a Highland officer in the service of the French' (p.94) – a reference surely to Stevenson's Alan Breck whom we are told in *Kidnapped* wore the French army uniform.

Another strong influence on *Doom Castle* is Scott's *The Bride of Lammermoor*. The character of the proud domestic, Mungo Boyd, who devises all kinds of strategies to give the impression that his impoverished master is, in fact, quite wealthy has close affinities with Caleb Balderstone[4] (although Mungo has a very definite personality of his own), and the crumbling castle of Wolf's Crag with its decaying splendour and the general atmosphere of *The Bride of Lammermoor* clearly provide a Gothic prototype for Munro's novel. Add to this Munro's boyhood familiarity with Radcliffe's *The Mysteries of Udolpho* and *The Italian* and Walpole's *The Castle of Otranto* and it is easy to see that he was well equipped to exploit the Gothic genre.

Doom Castle is a Highland Gothic novel and at the same time it satirises that genre. The castle itself is a place of eerie staircases and echoing rooms set on a shadowy off-shore island where winds moan through the mainland trees. There are mysterious midnight visits and violent skirmishes and the haunting sound of a flageolet is heard often at night.[5] One of the old domestics is a seer and has the Evil Eye of which all the inhabitants are afraid. And in this castle an

Dunderave Castle

apparently wicked father keeps his beautiful daughter locked away – for the simple reason that he knows (quite rightly) that the man who is courting her is an out and out rogue! The story is shot through with satire and irony at the expense of the genre – at one point, for example, Count Victor says to himself of his miraculous escape down a secret tunnel:

> But figure a so-convenient tunnel in connection with a prison cell! It was too good to be true. (p.222)

– as well as the more obvious humour provided by the shrewd, well-meaning but officious Mungo Boyd.

The plot deals with the arrival at the castle of a very romantic and honourable French Count and Jacobite sympathiser, Victor de Montaiglon. He has come on a mission to seek vengeance on a Highland double agent called Drimdarroch who had drawn his pay from the British Government whilst also taking sides with the Jacobites and, as a result of these intrigues, was responsible for the death of Cecile Favart, Victor's sweetheart. The Count takes up residence in Doom and is intrigued by the playing of a flageolet by the urbane and handsome Sim MacTaggart, the Duke of Argyll's Chamberlain, for the benefit of his sweetheart, the Baron of Doom's daughter Olivia (in spite of the fact that the same MacTaggart had trifled with the affections of her mother twenty years before!) (p.178). It turns out that this romantic suitor is also the unscrupulous rogue who has defrauded the Baron of his property of Drimdarroch. He makes several attempts on Victor's life to protect himself from eventual detection – for he, in fact, is the double agent who had been using the name Drimdarroch when abroad in France – and because he is jealous of the favour which Victor has found with Olivia. In the end he is slain by the Baron when, demented, he comes to seek his final revenge on Victor. At bottom the gallant suitor was merely a sordid self-seeker.

Like *John Splendid* the plot has action in plenty – although on a less grand scale – with the opening attack on Victor by a band of hired thugs masquerading as MacFarlanes, the two night raids on Doom, the beautifully described duel at dawn between Victor and MacTaggart, and the latter's death at the hands of the Baron. If there is a weakness in the story it is that the plot becomes somewhat convoluted towards the end and is difficult to follow. Indeed, Munro appears to confuse the name of Doom's late wife, calling her Christina at one part of the novel (p.185) and Mary at the end (p.287). Furthermore, the reader identifies the villain just beyond the half-way mark and waiting for confirmation of his identity by the main characters becomes a little wearing.

The surface theme of *Doom Castle* is the triumph of good over evil and this is characterised, on the one hand, by the scrupulously honourable French count who surrenders himself after severely wounding the Chamberlain and in the end will marry the thinly written maiden of Doom, Olivia ('Miss Milk and Water' as she is called by her rival Mrs Petullo (p.263)), and, on the other, by the smooth-talking unscrupulous MacTaggart who has all the *panache* of Stevenson's James Durie in *The Master of Ballantrae*. Although the undoubted villain, he creates much interest by being a Jekyll and Hyde figure. His good side shows him to be, like Gilian in Munro's *Gilian the Dreamer* (1899), a man of great sensibility, a 19th Century 'Man of Feeling' who insists that his drinking companions savour the beauty of a moonlit scene (p.148), who enjoys playing the flageolet and who is moved to tears by a piper's tune (p.190). He is a man who wants to be good but the Hyde in him is too strong. When trying to distance himself from Mrs Petullo he says:

'There's my punishment: by something sham ... I must go through life beguiled from right and content. Here's what was to be the close of my folly, and Sim MacTaggart eager to be a good man if he got anything like a chance, but never the chance for poor Sim MacTaggart!' (p.78)

But as with *John Splendid* there is a deeper underlying theme which questions the direction of Highland society. The novel has two locations, Doom Castle and Inveraray Castle, and these locations are powerful symbols. Doom Castle, as its name suggests, signals gloom and despair. Crippled by poverty it is falling into steady decay. It is the seat of Lamond, Baron of Doom, a supporter of the ill-fated House of Stuart which is destined never to return. Inveraray Castle with its new town, on the other hand, signals prosperity and order. It is the new castle of the Enlightenment, the seat of Archibald Campbell, 3rd Duke of Argyll,[6] supporter of the Hanoverian Government and the Lord Justice General, who commissioned Roger Morris, architect, and William Adam, clerk of works, to undertake its construction. It is the home of many books, the venue for learned disquisition by fine minds like Lords Elchies and Kilkerran and the scene of sophisticated musical gatherings.

The personalities of the owners of these castles reinforce their symbolism.

The melancholy figure of the Jacobite Lamond, the Baron of Doom, broods over the whole book. He supports the Jacobite James of the Glen whose execution is intimated in the novel and of which he says:

'Murder was done this day in the guise of justice.' (p.88)

The only way in which he can demonstrate loyalty to his cause and defiance of the new regime is by the charade of dressing up in Highland regalia in the old chapel of his keep:

He drew them out hurriedly upon the floor but yet with an affectionate tenderness, as if they were the relics of a sacristy, and with eagerness substituted the gay tartan for his dull mulberry Saxon habiliments. (p.131)

Although he strikes the final blow for justice in the novel, he must still go into exile in France where the majority of the Jacobites are men of less than honourable character and

'James [Stuart, the 'Old Pretender'] and Jacquette were often...indifferent enough...about the cause our friends were exiled there for.' (p.127)

and

'[Prince] Charles... was not... an inspiring object of veneration.' (p.127)

The Duke of Argyll, on the other hand, is a scholar and a lawyer. He is usually good natured and cheerful but firm on matters of grave importance of law and order, even with his wife who can normally manipulate him. Of Victor after the duel he says:

'No more of that, Jean; the man must thole his trial, for I have gone too far to draw back even if I had the will to humour you.'
There was one tone of her husband's his wife knew too decisive for her contending with, and now she heard it. (p.217)

Despite the rights and wrongs of the James of the Glen trial and Argyll's part in it (and here there is an implied resemblance between

Argyll and Stevenson's Lord Prestongrange in *Catriona*) there is no
doubt that he represents the new Scotland of the Enlightenment and
a more civilised Highlands. Referring to imprisoning Victor so that
he can stand trial for his part in the duel against his Chamberlain he
says:

> 'My father would have been somewhat more summary in circum-
> stances like these.' (p.207)

– civilisation has moved on in Argyll. And Victor himself has reasonable expectations of fair play:

> Count's Victor's breakfast [in his cell]...was generous enough to
> confirm his belief that in Argyll's hands he was at least assured of
> the forms of justice. (p.209)

In addition to his skilful use of symbolism in *Doom Castle* Neil
Munro's technique shows considerable development in another
important area – his portrayal of female characters. Maurice Lindsay
accuses him of depicting women who are mere 'verbal wraiths'.[7]
Whilst this is arguably fair comment on the character of Betty Brown
in *John Splendid* and Olivia in this novel it would be less than fair to
the portrayals of Kate Petullo and the Duchess of Argyll.

Kate Petullo, a 'small town Argyllshire Emma Bovary' as Francis
Russell Hart calls her,[8] is no cardboard cut-out. She is powerfully
drawn and closely observed. She has a sharp, cruel beauty:

> Opposite the unhappy lawyer sat a lady of extraordinary beauty –
> a haughty, cold supercilious sort of beauty, remarkable mainly
> from the consciousness of its display. Her profile might have been
> cut from marble by a Greek; her neck and bust were perfect, but
> her shoulders, more angular than was common in that time of
> bottle-shape, were carried too grandly for a gentle nature. (p.72)

She delights in her gauche husband's discomfiture when he spills a
compote over himself at dinner in Inveraray Castle while she flirts
strongly with Sim MacTaggart. He had been her lover until lately
but now he wishes to relinquish her for Olivia. In an endeavour to
retain his love she uses all the seductive powers at her disposal:

> (she) lifted up her mouth and dropped a swooning lash over her
> passionate orbs. (p.102)

Indeed, such is her passion for him and her contempt for her husband that she openly courts MacTaggart in front of her husband in her own home. To please him she admits to having got her lawyer husband to ruin Doom by defrauding him of the Drimdarroch estate and she threatens further vengeance on that family:

'You made me pauperise her father, Sim; I'm sorry it was not worse. I'll see that Petullo has them rouped at the door.' (p.163)

Then realising that she is making no progress she embarrasses him by announcing his forthcoming marriage to Olivia when such a happening was far from certain.

Later, ironically, she causes a distraction for Sim in the duel with Victor which results in his serious injury and, while tending his wounds, she is driven to distraction when in a fever he reaffirms his love for Olivia. She has her revenge when a letter she wrote to Sim indicating his identity as the double agent who had used the name Drimdarroch was intercepted by Doom, Olivia and Victor.

The Duchess of Argyll,[9] likewise, is no two dimensional character although her part in the action is much smaller than Mrs Petullo's. She is a warm person who in her sixties is still very much in love with her husband. She is not a Gael and has brought some of the sophistication of the outside world to the Ducal court. She has an unerring female intuition when dealing with men and is quick to identify Victor as the victim and MacTaggart the villain long before the evidence has been discovered. Indeed, whilst cunningly appearing to maintain a politically correct stance, she gives sound advice to Victor for his safety:

'If I were to meet this person we speak of [i.e. Victor himself], I should – but for the terror I know I should feel in his society – tell him that so long as he did not venture within a couple of miles of this castle he was perfectly safe from interference.' (p.229)

Furthermore, although she knows that she has very real influence over her husband, she is shrewd enough to know when it is no longer judicious to interfere (p.217).

As regards language, when one compares *Doom Castle* with Munro's previous work in the Highland historical tradition, *The Lost Pibroch and Other Sheiling Stories* and *John Splendid*, one notices immediately a considerable lessening of Gaelic-inflected English;

indeed the only heavily marked use of it is in Olivia's speech in Chapter XVI:

> 'Isn't that a father, Count Victor!' cried Olivia...' But he is the strange father too, that will be pretending that he has forgotten the old times and the old customs of our dear people...' (p.125)

although individual Gaelic words are deployed throughout the novel and there is evidence of the use of Nicolson's *Gaelic Proverbs*:

> '*Ni droch dhuine dàn da féin.*' 'A bad man makes his own destiny.' (p.282)[10]

The major linguistic innovations in the volume, however, are the wide deployment of French and the protracted use of Scots.

Much of the book is seen through the eyes of the chivalric Count Victor and the copious use of simple French phrases and French-inflected English in his speech helps to reinforce *his* perception of all that is going on. Indeed, a lasting impression that we have is of the sophistication of France compared with the decay of Doom. This language also strengthens our awareness of the life of the Jacobite community in France who are referred to throughout and whom Doom and Olivia are soon to join.

The *tour de force* of the novel, however, is the racy Scots of Mungo Boyd, the small, shrewd and cunning East Coaster from Dysart who is an alien in the Gaelic speaking lands of Argyll. His language and character are inseparable. Mungo is dedicated to his master and, in order to save the reputation of the house, he resorts to all sorts of ploys the execution of which provide some hilarious incidents e.g. he promises jugged hare for Victor's dinner on the night of his arrival – only to be able to provide rabbit! When confronted with this fact he replies:

> 'A rabbit!...Weel if it was a rabbit it was a gey big ane, that's a' I can say.' (p.28)

In a desperate bid to save the menage from penury he actively encourages the relationship between Olivia and MacTaggart:

> 'I aye keepit my he'rt up wi' the notion that him doon-by the coat belangs to wad hae made a match o't and saved us frae beggary.' (p.253)

His summing up of the situation when hope is past and exile inevitable is a moving epitaph for the house of Doom and the now decadent cause to which it gave support:

'And noo' it's a' by wi't; it's the end o' the auld ballant...I've kent auld Doom in times o' rowth and splendour, and noo I'm spared to see't rouped, the laird a dyvour and a hameless wanderer ower the face o' the earth. He's gaun abroad, he tells me, and ettles to sit doon aboot Dunkerque in France. It's but fair, maybe, that whaur his forbears squandered he should gang wi' the little that's to the fore. I mind o' his faither gaun awa' at the last hoved up, a fair Jeshurun, his een like to loup oot o' his heid wi fat, and comin' back a pooked craw frae the dicing and the drink nae doot among the scattered-brained white cockades.' (p.252)

Doom Castle, then, is an experiment in the Gothic tradition which not merely satirises the genre but also goes much further in that, continuing the tradition begun in *John Splendid*, it makes a statement about Highland society. Like Scott's *Redgauntlet* but in a less serious tone it rings the death knell on the Stuart cause and implies that the new way of the enlightened House of Argyll is the way forward. In addition Munro enhances his novel by the deployment of French nuances and widespread use of protracted passages of fluent demotic Scots in the mouth of Mungo Boyd. Both of these strands he develops further in his next novel *The Shoes of Fortune*.

The Shoes of Fortune (1901)[11]

The Shoes of Fortune differs, quite refreshingly, from Munro's previous historical romances in that it is not set in the Argyllshire Highlands and, indeed, most of it is set outside Scotland itself. The Scottish parts of the book are set mainly in the area around the old village of Newton Mearns, near Munro's home at Waterfoot where he lived before moving to Gourock. The other parts are mainly set in Dunkirk and Helvoetsluys (perhaps influenced by Stevenson's *Catriona* which also uses these places) and a large section is located in Paris and Versailles.

The story is divided into seven movements and, like Stevenson's *Kidnapped*, the opening and close of the novel deal with the most romantic episodes where the hero leaves home in unfortunate circumstances and in the end returns to take up his rightful place.

David Balfour claims the House of Shaws as his inheritance. Paul Greig, the hero of *The Shoes of Fortune,* returns the innocent and honourable son of Quentin Greig of Hazel Den and future husband of Isobel Fortune of neighbouring Kirkillstane. The intervening sections, however, grow more interesting because the heroes of both books become involved in major political events connected with the Jacobite cause and the significance of the respective plots is transformed from local to national and beyond. (As the plot of *The Shoes of Fortune* is complex and the book is currently out of print the following summary has been included in italics.)

'The Shoes of Fortune' opens with a lively scene in Glasgow where Paul Greig to the shame of his family is rusticated from the university for throwing snowballs at a Baillie. He returns to Hazel Den near Newton Mearns where he helps his father work the family croft. He meets and falls in love with his neighbour Isobel Fortune but is too naive to see that his love is being reciprocated and thinks her affections are meant for David Borland of whom he quickly becomes inordinately jealous. In the meantime his Uncle Andrew, a wild and depraved Jacobite, comes home in a poor state of health and soon dies. He leaves his few belongings which include a pair of red shoes of Eastern origin – 'The Shoes of Sorrow' or 'The Shoes of Fortune' – to Paul. These give Paul the desire to travel and explore and are a symbol of reckless restlessness and wanderlust which Quentin Greig regards as his family's curse. Wearing them one evening Paul goes to Isobel's home merely to see the light in her room but encounters Borland coming away from the house. Insults are exchanged and a duel arranged for the next morning at which Paul thinks he has killed his opponent.

After a hurried leave-taking of his parents he rides frantically for the port of Borrowstouness where he encounters a Captain Dan Risk, a figure not unlike Stevenson's Hoseason in 'Kidnapped', who seems to know the nature of his crime and offers him terms for a passage to Nova Scotia. Once the ship is underway Paul discovers from a friendly and honourable seaman called Horn that Risk and the crew are rogues who intend to scuttle the ship and claim insurance for the cargo which they have secretly landed at Blackness. The ship founders and Risk and his crew take to the boat, leaving Horn and Greig to their fate. They are saved, however, by the timely appearance of the 'Roi Rouge', captained by Antoine Thurot, a gentleman corsair (and genuine historical character); and, as at the similar point in 'Kidnapped' where Alan Breck is taken aboard the doomed 'Covenant', the novel enters the political arena.

Ronald W. Renton

*The ship reaches Dunkirk where Paul enjoys the hospitality of
Thurot and his friend and lukewarm Jacobite supporter, the Irish Lord
Clancarty. He meets a fat Jesuit priest, a Fleming who goes by the
name of Father Hamilton, and a young Scottish woman, Clementina
Walkinshaw. Paul is immediately attracted to Clementina and in a
short time she arranges to get Paul employment as Fr. Hamilton's
secretary on a European tour which he has to undertake although she
clearly dislikes Hamilton intensely. Knowing their mutual antagonism
Thurot finds it incredible that Clementina should have arranged a
position for Paul with the priest and at the same time hints are dropped
of a connection between her and Prince Charles Edward. Meanwhile
Paul goes to thank Clementina who regrets that he may be being
corrupted by the 'sophisticated' society of Dunkirk. Paul at once
assumes that her reason for sending him away with Fr. Hamilton is to
protect him from this and she herself leaps at such an explanation:*

*'Am I no the careful mother of you to put you in the hands o' the
clergy?' (p.116)*

*By now it is obvious that Paul has fallen in love with Clementina
and, observing her loneliness, he offers to cancel the position with
Hamilton to stay near her. At this she grows angry and accuses him of
making fun of her. Then she tells him to write to her each day so that
she will know exactly where he is, but the priest is not to be told of this
correspondence or its means of delivery (as yet unknown). Finally,
banking on his obvious infatuation, she tells him to wear his red shoes
for her. Obviously Paul is being exploited as a means of spying on the
priest's whereabouts and activities.*

*The setting of the novel now moves to Paris. The priest wakes Paul
at 5 a.m. three days earlier than arranged to set off on their tour,
obviously a ploy to give the slip to unwanted observers of his whereabouts. Walkinshaw's servant, Bernard, however, has secured
employment with the priest after being 'sacked' by his mistress and tells
Paul that he will see to the delivery of correspondence between Paul and
the lady. On arrival in Versailles they visit the Place d'Armes where
Paul recognises Prince Charles Edward whom he had seen once in
Glasgow as a boy. A few days later Hamilton gives Paul a letter in Miss
Walkinshaw's handwriting to deliver to the prince. This is in fact a
trick to get the Prince to meet Hamilton who had intended to shoot him.
The plan, however, is forestalled and Buhot, a police inspector, substi-
tutes for the prince and the bullets are removed from the gun. Paul and
the priest are arrested. Buhot tells Paul that there have been a number
of attempts on the Prince's life by the Jesuits and the real object of their
attention is one of the Order's superiors, Fr.Fleuriau. He asks Paul to*

132

try to get further information from Hamilton while in prison. Paul refuses to stoop to this method and accepts the possibility of long term imprisonment in Bicêtre and Galbanon. Whilst in Bicêtre a sous-officer gives him a letter from Bernard informing him that the correspondence with Miss Walkinshaw can be continued – and it does. When he meets Hamilton he finds him to be extremely happy that his attempt on the Prince had failed because it meant that he could live with his conscience. Then Paul is threatened with the Galbanon, the most severe of French prisons. At this news Hamilton decides that they should attempt to escape and they set out across the prison roofs at night, finding windows and trapdoors etc. conveniently open to assist their escape. They then go into hiding in Paris. Hamilton finds out that Paul is sending letters to Clementina through Bernard and that Bernard took the bullets out of his pistol. Hamilton then admits that the letter to the Prince in Clementina's handwriting was a forgery. So we have plot and counterplot: the Jesuits seeking to kill Prince Charles Edward and Clementina, the Prince, Buhot and Bernard spying on the Jesuits through Paul's letters to Clementina. At this point, an Alan Breck character, MacKellar of Kilbride, the brother of Paul's room mate at Glasgow University, happens to meet Paul in a tavern and warns him off Hamilton.

Hamilton disappears and Paul decides to go back to Dunkirk where Thurot tells him he and the priest were pawns in a game, that neither are now in danger and that Hamilton had been permitted to escape by Buhot in the hope that he would lead them to the Jesuit superior Fleuriau who had by now been captured. Then Paul goes to see Clementina but is too naive and still too infatuated with her to see her part in all of this and believes that she sent Bernard to spy on them to protect him! She tells him she has arranged a commission for him in the Auvergne Regiment, but he does not want to avail himself of this opportunity since he will be separated from her. He then declares his love for her. She tells him she is merely a proxy for Isobel Fortune and besides she has a preference elsewhere. Meanwhile Paul has seen a debauched Charles Edward on the streets of Dunkirk calling himself M. Albany and soon after he is challenged to a duel by an apparent drunk called Bonnat who later admits to having been instructed to get Paul out of the way by the Prince. Paul then visits Clementina to seek an explanation of the Prince's behaviour and to his surprise finds the Prince staying at her house. The Prince admits to having spoken to Bonnat after dinner when he was drunk but had no recollection of the order he gave. At this point Paul declares his complete opposition to the Jacobite cause.

Paul then goes to fight with his regiment in Prussia and is wounded in battle. By chance he is tended by MacKellar of Kilbride who assists him to desert. They make for Helvoetsluys where MacKellar knows Hamilton to be. Kilbride explains to Paul exactly how he has been used and that his letters were the means of informing the French Cabinet of Hamilton's movements. Bernard had passed on all his letters to Buhot. Clementina had organised all this on behalf of her lover, the Prince, to get to the source of the Jesuit plot and now the Order had been suppressed in France. The Prince had set Bonnat on Paul because he was envious of his friendship with Clementina. In the meantime Hamilton is being threatened by his own Order because they blame him for betraying Fleuriau. They return to Dunkirk. On a visit to Thurot's house Paul overhears a plan being discussed by the Prince and Thurot for the French invasion of Britain on behalf of Charles Edward. He is captured because he is recognised by his red shoes but eventually escapes with MacKellar and Hamilton across the Channel in a small boat.

When they reach London Paul seeks an interview with Pitt who is more inclined to believe Paul's information of the invasion than that of another Scot because Paul is not seeking to bargain with it. Then Paul makes a clean breast of his crime against David Borland and tells Pitt he is going to hand himself over to the Lord Advocate in Edinburgh. When he reaches Edinburgh by chance he hears that Captain Risk is in a sorry plight in prison and goes to visit him. Struck by the appalling prospect of what he saw there he decides not to give himself up but to go to America. This necessitates him travelling west and so he takes this opportunity to have a last look at his old home at Hazel Den without informing his parents. His horse goes lame, however, and he has no choice but to stay the night at the inn at Newton, is recognised by his red shoes and is reconciled to his parents. Furthermore, as it happens, David Borland is not dead (Paul's shot had merely grazed his temple) and he had married, not Isobel, but Jean Fortune, so the way is clear for Paul to marry Isobel who had been waiting faithfully for his return.

The Shoes of Fortune, then, has two distinct aspects to it. On the one hand, it is a romance which depends for much of its action on the device of the red shoes by which the hero will be recognised as a Greig all over Britain and France and as a result his fortunes will be affected for good or ill. Closely connected with this are other frequent and unlikely coincidences which occur throughout the story and keep the action moving. On the other hand, at a deeper level, Munro tackles matters of historical interest: he speculates albeit somewhat sensationally, but nonetheless pioneeringly in Scottish fiction, on the position of the Jesuits in France in the 18th

Century before the suppression of the Order in 1762 and, like Scott in *Redgauntlet*, seriously questions the wisdom of further support for Jacobitism after the failure of the '45.

As regards the former, there is no doubt that Munro knew exactly what he was doing for in the opening words of the story the narrator warns us of the way our lives are influenced by chance and coincidence:

> It is an odd thing, chance – the one element to baffle the logician and make the scheming of the wisest look as foolish in the long run as the sandy citadel a child builds upon the shore without any thought of the incoming tide. A strange thing, chance; and but for chance I might this day be the sheriff of a shire...if it had not been for so trifling a circumstance as the burning of an elderly woman's batch of scones. (p.1)

and again

> I began these chronicles with a homily upon the pregnancy of chance that gives the simplest of our acts ofttimes far-reaching and appalling consequences. It is clear that I had never become the Spoiled Horn [failed student] and vexed my parents' lives had not a widow woman burned her batch of scones, and though perhaps the pair of shoes in the chest bequeathed to me by my Uncle Andrew were without the magic influence he and I gave credit for, it is probable that I had made a different flight from Scotland had they not led me the way of Daniel Risk. (p.272)

Munro, then, is quite deliberately exploring the use of coincidence and chance in his story and the red Shoes of Fortune become the device which unifies the plot. He was clearly enjoying the entire idea and not only does he end with the amusing pun on Paul's wife's maiden name:

> My Shoes of Fortune, she will sometimes say, laughing, brought me first and last Miss Fortune. [i.e. herself, Isobel Fortune] (p.324)

but it was also a family a joke for Munro's wife's mother's maiden name was, in fact, Fortune and his second daughter's name was Euphemia Fortune Munro (born 1890). Other 'in' jokes which Munro clearly enjoyed are the naming of the tenement in Glasgow where he stayed as a student as Crombie's Land (in reality the house where he was born in Inveraray) and calling his room mate in that house MacKellar after Archie MacKellar, his boyhood friend, whom he roomed with when he first came to Glasgow. Indeed, it is worthwhile remembering what Munro said of his novels when looking back on them in 1921; it is particularly true of the fantastic elements of *The Shoes of Fortune*:

> I fancy I shall never write the story of my own childhood, though there were tragic and pathetic elements in it which would make a dozen novels of the grimy sort now in vogue. I sought escape from them in the imagination for so long, and so ardently, that I couldn't help becoming a romancer in the end.[12]

When the setting moves to France we are introduced to the first part of the 'political' plot of the novel which deals with the Jesuit conspiracy against the life of Prince Charles Edward. The idea of Jesuits being a subject for major, if rather superficial and conventional, treatment in Scottish literature is certainly new although Munro does refer to both Catholicism and Jesuits frequently throughout his work. It is interesting to note, however, that Munro's friend R.B.Cunninghame Graham published his study of the Jesuits in Paraguay *A Vanished Arcadia* (on which the film *The Mission* was based) also in 1901. The source for this episode appears to be *Pickle the Spy* (1896), a study of the government spy in the Jacobite ranks, Alasdair Ruadh, 13th Chief of Glengarry, written again by a person whom Munro admired, Andrew Lang. The key passage would seem to be:

> He admits that he acted as a *mouton*, or prison spy, and gives a dreadful account of the horrors of Galbanon, where men lay in the dark and dirt for half a lifetime. MacAllester next proses endlessly on the alleged Jesuit connection with Damien's attack on Louis XV, and insists that the Jesuits, nobody knows why, meant to assassinate Prince Charles. He was in very little danger from Jesuits.[13]

Munro takes up this challenge and constructs a completely fictitious conspiracy in which the Jesuits use Hamilton, an apparently disreputable member of their Order, to attempt the assassination of Prince Charles. Galbanon is pointed out to Paul as his fate if he fails to co-operate in traducing the priest, and the escape from Bicêtre, the smaller prison (clearly based on Inveraray jail, even to the parrot in the cage)[14] near Galbanon, is for sheer tension one of the best recounted episodes of the book – the more so because the coincidences of open windows and trapdoors which have been deliberately arranged to permit Hamilton and Paul's escape provide a satirical humour and counterpoint beautifully the 'conventional' coincidences in the rest of the novel. The counter-conspiracy masterminded by Walkinshaw is masterly, using Paul and his red shoes and letters as a way of providing the Jacobites with news of the Jesuit plotting against the Prince and it is these letters in the end which lead to the capture of the Jesuit superior Fleuriau and the suppression of the Order in France. In Ch.35 Kilbride tells Paul:

> '...the Marshal Duke de Bellisle, and Monsieur Florentin, and Monsieur Berrier, and all the others of the Cabinet, had Fleuriau's name and direction from yourself, and found the plot had some connection with the affair of Damiens.' (p.260)

and

> 'She [Walkinshaw] made you and this Bernard the means of putting an end to the Jesuit plot upon his Royal Highness by discovering the source of it, and now the Jesuits, as I'm told, are to be driven furth the country and putten to the horn.' (p.261)

The Jesuit episode is followed by news of the planned invasion of Britain by pro-Jacobite France. This, of course, has a basis in historical fact and refers to the abortive invasion of 1759. Paul overhears the plan for this being discussed by Prince Charles Edward Stuart and Thurot and it is clear to him that he must prevent it at all costs. His family had been Jacobite in sympathy but the more he saw of Prince Charles the more he had become disillusioned with his dissoluteness until the last time he was in his company he spoke of him in these terms in his hearing:

> 'Neither prince nor king of mine, Miss Walkinshaw...No, if a hundred thousand swords were at his back. I had once a notion of a prince that rode along the Gallowgate, but then I was a boy, and now I am a man.' (p.247)

Now he is in no doubt that he must take decisive action and, as soon as they reach England, he seeks an interview with Pitt to inform him of the invasion plans. Significantly, as in Scott's *The Heart of Midlothian*,[15] such an important audience is gained through the intervention of a Duke of Argyll (in this case, Archibald, the third Duke):

It was more by good luck than good guidance, and had there been no Scots House of Argyll perhaps I had never got rid of my weighty secret after all. (p.295)

For all Paul's naiveté and irritating slowness to see the *realpolitik* of what has been going on around him and how in his boyish infatuation he has been used by Walkinshaw and that she is Charles Edward's mistress, this major decision which saves Britain makes him a more successful man of action than the David Balfour of *Catriona*, who for all his strong intentions to prove the innocence of James of the Glens[16] finds his hands tied at every turn even although as a character he is much more strongly drawn:

For upon a retrospect, it appeared I had not done so grandly, after all; but with the greatest possible amount of big speech and preparations, had accomplished nothing.[17]

During the interview with Pitt Munro's tongue in cheek humour surfaces again when the statesman tells Paul that another Scotsman had also come to him with news of the invasion but he was prepared to give Paul's information more credibility because Paul was not seeking to bargain with his knowledge. This is almost certainly meant to be a reference to the historical Pickle's proposal.

The character of MacKellar of Kilbride is also interesting in this context. Like Alan Breck he is a Highlander and had been out in the '45 but now he is disillusioned and is only too anxious to throw in his lot with the Hanoverian government:

'The breed of them [the Stuarts] has never been loyal to me, and if I could wipe out of my life six months of the cursedest folly in Forty-five I would go back to Scotland with the first chance and throw my bonnet for Geordie ever after like the greasiest burgess ever sold a wab of cloth or a cargo of Virginia in Glasgow.' (p.290)

Although MacKellar only comes in towards the end of the book he has the charisma and attractiveness of an embryonic Alan Breck figure. By making such a character pro-Hanoverian, and a potential follower of the life-style of Scott's Bailie Nicol Jarvie, Munro is shifting the emotional conviction of the book profoundly away from the Jacobite cause, a device which will become even more marked in the similar placing of the much more fully developed character of Ninian Campbell in *The New Road* (1914).

Although the portrayal of the dissipated Charles Edward is slight in the novel it nonetheless justifies both Paul and MacKellar's scepticism about the House of Stuart. Clancarty calls him, not unfairly, 'a madman, a sotted madman tied to the petticoat tails of a trollope' (p.281) and, when Paul goes to confront the Prince about the duel in which he had him involved with Bonnat and which was nothing less than an assassination attempt, it appears he has no recollection of giving the command since he gave it after dinner when he was habitually drunk:

'I do not wonder that M. Albany has lost so many of his friends if he settles their destinies after dinner.' (p.246)

Our last picture of the Prince is of him discussing the invasion of Britain with Thurot and insisting, against Thurot's obviously superior advice, that the attack should begin, like the ill-fated '45, in the West Highlands.

Clementina Walkinshaw, the daughter of a Glasgow merchant, is a complex and interesting creation. She is clearly dedicated to Charles Edward yet out of a sense of patriotism is ambivalent about the invasion of Britain and Scotland in particular and does not believe it will help the Jacobite cause:

'The cause will suffer from this madness more than ever it did, but in any case it is the most miserable of lost causes...Where is your heart, Mr Greig, that it does not feel alarm at the prospect of these *crapauds* making a single night's sleep uneasy for the folk you know?' (p.118)

To protect Charles she masterminds the whole plot against Hamilton and the Jesuits but at the same time she cruelly exploits young Paul Greig's infatuation for her in making him the unwitting spy in the Jesuit camp. She obviously does, however, feel an attraction towards him, sufficient to rouse Charles Edward's jealousy, and at the same time he reminds her of her lost innocence. She says of him at their parting:

'The honest and unsuspecting come rarely my way nowadays and now that I'm to lose them I feel like to greet.' (p.242)

He also, of course, reminds her of Scotland. Significantly she uses Scots for intimacy and affection as when imagining herself back home:

'Look! look! ye Mearns man, look! look! at the bairn playin pal-al [hopscotch] in the close. 'Tis my little sister Jeannie that's married on the great Doctor Doig – him wi' the mant i' the Tron kirk – and bairns o' her ain, I'm tell't, and they'll never hear their Aunt Clemmie named but in a whisper.' (p.94)

Perhaps, however, Munro's most interesting and adventurous creation in *The Shoes of Fortune* is Fr. Hamilton, the Jesuit priest. Hamilton is enormously fat, self-indulgent and good-natured:

He was corpulent beyond belief, with a dewlap like an ox; great limbs, a Gargantuan appetite, and a laugh like thunder that at its loudest created such convulsions of his being as compelled him to unbutton the neck of his soutane, else he had died of a seizure. (p.86)

As a somewhat disreputable priest he is considered expendable by his Order and is used as an instrument to kill Charles Edward. He undertakes the mission because he feels that there is little chance of him ever finding him and he is terrified when he is eventually informed that Charles is at Versailles. When the attempt is fore-stalled and fails he is delighted because he can now live with his conscience:

'Now my part is done, 'twas by God's grace a failure, and I could sing for content like one of the little birds we heard the other day in Somme.' (p.162)

He is happy to go to prison and only decides to attempt an escape to prevent Paul being sent to Galbanon. The description of his attempt to drag his girth across the precipitous prison roof is all the more heroic in that it is entirely altruistic. In hiding in Paris he is a St Francis figure who attracts the affection of birds and children and in the end, having escaped to London, having been pursued across Europe by his fellow Jesuits for, as they believe, betraying their

superior, he dies protecting the life of a child who is being mercilessly beaten by her father. He dies a picture of essential goodness,
saying to Paul:

'Be good, be simple, be kind! 'Tis all I know.' (p.305)

Such generosity to Catholicism and to a Catholic priest is relatively
unusual in post-Reformation Scottish literature and for the time in
which Munro was writing. Interestingly, his next book *Children of
Tempest* has another priest as a main character, although of a very
different type.

The Shoes of Fortune is, then, a romance heavily dependent on
coincidences and the device of the red shoes but at the same time it
has important things to say about Jacobitism and the nature of
goodness as personified by the priest. It is also a good spy novel of
the Jacobite period, an idea which was touched on in the behaviour
of Sim MacTaggart as double agent in *Doom Castle* and which was
to be taken up again by Violet Jacob in *Flemington* (1911) and later
by Munro himself in the *New Road* (1914). Munro was fully aware
of the fact that he was exploiting the devices of coincidence and the
red shoes and, had he been writing only at the level of fantasy or fairy
tale, the result might well have been more successful. This approach,
however, sits uneasily with the more important historical judge-
ments at the end of the book and make them less credible. That said,
there is no doubt that the book is heavily influenced by Stevenson's
Kidnapped and *Catriona* and, although inferior to them artistically,
it, nonetheless, makes a sharp political statement where *Kidnapped*
does not, and, although Paul is much less sharply drawn than the
David Balfour of *Catriona*, his decisiveness in going to Pitt and
averting invasion is a major advance on David's inaction.
Furthermore, the alliance of the Alan Breck character, Mackellar,
with the Hanoverian side is a significant change on the Stevenson
model. Finally, although there is a similarity with the ending of
Scott's *Redgauntlet* in that both books end with the failure of Charles
Edward's cause, in Scott the tone that is elegiac for the end of the
auld sang; in Munro there is no doubt left in the reader's mind that
right has been done.

Children of Tempest (1903)[18]

Children of Tempest can claim to be the first novel to deal with the Outer Hebrides in an authentic manner. It is set for the most part on the island of South Uist, but also on Benbecula, Mingulay and, briefly, North Uist. The inspiration for the novel would appear to be Munro's own visits to Barra, to the Uists and Benbecula in 1901 where he was fascinated by the fords which connect the islands at low tide[19] and especially to the island of Eriskay where he met Father Allan McDonald, Maighstir Ailein (1859–1905) as he is still known in Gaelic throughout the Southern Outer Hebrides. Fr. Allan was parish priest first of Dalibrog (1884–93) and later of Eriskay (1893–1905). Munro visited him in Eriskay and corresponded with him intermittently thereafter.[20] He was a heroic pastor who in putting his people before all else seriously overworked and damaged his health. He was clearly very charismatic and much loved by his people for whose welfare he campaigned relentlessly. In addition he was a fine Gaelic scholar: he edited *Comh-Chruinneachadh de Laoidhean Spioradail (A Collection of Spiritual Hymns)* (1893),[21] for use in Catholic Churches and, indeed, wrote many of them himself, and he collected many note books of folk tales, traditions and vocabulary of the Outer Hebrides which are invaluable to scholars today. He also corresponded with and assisted the folk collector Alasdair Carmichael in his researches for the *Carmina Gadelica*, his great collection of Hebridean hymns, prayers and invocations, some dating back to pre-Reformation times.[22] Not surprisingly, then, Munro found in Maighstir Ailein a model for Father Ludovick, his priest hero in *Children of Tempest*, and much of the novel is set in Boisdale in the South of South Uist, the area roughly corresponding to Mghr Ailein's first parish of Dalibrog. The church, however, which plays a central part in the novel takes its name, *Stella Maris*, from the church in Barra which Munro admired[23] and the building itself on its rocky eminence is modelled on *St Michael's* in Eriskay, which Mghr Ailein built himself and was particularly dear to him.

Children of Tempest is set in the Scotland of 1795–6 and deals with the supposed fate of the famous Loch Arkaig treasure or *ulaidh* of 40,000 louis d'ors (£20,000) which was actually sent from France to support the Jacobite cause but arrived too late and was buried at Loch Arkaig and then disappeared. Unlike *Doom Castle* and *The Shoes of Fortune* this novel deals only very loosely with the aftermath of the Rising of 1745 and makes no overt political statement.

(As *Children of Tempest* is currently out of print the following summary in Italics is included.)

'Children of Tempest' is a romantic love story in which the heroine Anna, the sister of Father Ludovick, priest of Boisdale, is sought after by two brothers from Corodale. One of them, Duncan, a 'stuck' priest, is an honourable young man who goes to Anna's aid when she is cut off from the rest of the party as they cross the North Ford on their return from her Uncle Dermosary's funeral in North Uist. He finds her and stays with her on the islet of Trialabreck until the tide subsides (p55).[24] The other suitor is named Col. He is a mean, selfish and acquisitive individual – something of a ruthless entrepreneur – who, aided by the old man, Dark John whom he had rescued from drowning at the opening of the book, seeks Anna's hand because she is the heir to the Loch Arkaig ulaidh *which has been left her by her Uncle Dermosary and which she will be eligible to receive in about a year's time. In order to achieve his aim Col persuades Dan MacNeil (nicknamed Flying Jib-boom), the Captain of his sloop the 'Happy Return', to sing a song with an interpolated defamatory verse about Duncan (a device which Munro was to modify and use again in 'The New Road') to a crowd of Boisdale fishermen whom he has got drunk. The verse is :*

> *'Duncan, Duncan, what is you wishing?*
> *A crock of gold and an easy life.*
> *Come over from Corodale, then, and welcome,*
> *To make the crock of gold your wife.' (p.159)*

This spreads like wildfire among the people and, when Duncan himself hears it and its suggestion that he is only after Anna for the ulaidh *and realises that he has nothing to offer her in the way of prospects, he feels honour-bound to leave Uist at once without taking leave of Anna. This, of course, leaves the way open for Col to try his suit but Dark John finds out that the people have discovered his deception and plan to have Duncan home by the Autumn.*

In the meantime another unscrupulous and acquisitive rogue, the Sergeant, who keeps the inn at Creggans in Benbecula becomes involved. He extracts from Dark John the information that Col's romance with Anna is doomed to failure and suggests that he and Dark John (unknown to Col) kidnap Anna in order to extract from her the location of the ulaidh. *She is captured aboard the 'Happy Return' and taken to the inn at Creggans where after subjection to rough treatment by the Sergeant she is rescued by Jib-boom who takes them all back to Boisdale on the sloop. He suggests she do a deal with the Sergeant telling*

him, *in exchange for the letters of Duncan which he has been with-*
holding from her, the location of the ulaidh. *She agrees and tells him*
that:
'*It's in the Long Gallery in Mingulay, then, on the ledge below the*
blood of the Merry Dancers.' (p.250)
When they reach Boisdale Dark John is forced to disembark with
Anna and she is restored to Ludovick. In the meantime Jib-boom
punishes the Sergeant by sailing, not for Mingulay, but for the Clyde
where he discharges him. Dark John, however, meets Col and
persuades him to sail for Mingulay only to find that the treasure is no
longer there below the fuil nan sluagh *or the blood of the Merry Dancers*
(a piece of red lichen high up on the side of a cliff lit by the reflection of
Aurora Borealis in a creek in Mingulay). Upset when Dark John
climbs up the cliff and touches him unexpectedly from behind, Col
wards him off and sends him hurtling to his death. A few days later he
himself drowns as he tries to reach his boat when it floats back into the
creek.
The ulaidh *had, ironically, been discovered and squandered twelve*
years before by Col's father. Only two people knew this – Jib-boom who
had been Old Corodale's co-plunderer and Father Ludovick who was
bound by the seal of the confessional.
Duncan returns to Uist and he and Anna marry and go to live in
Corodale.

Although the bald narration of the plot of this novel suggests
melodrama with stage villains opposed to saintly characters, a closer
examination shows that Munro's treatment of good and evil
produces a novel with the qualities of a parable. Indeed, he himself
described it as a fable.[25]

Like the stories 'Boboon's Children' and 'Black Murdo' in *The*
Lost Pibroch and Other Sheiling Stories, *Children of Tempest* has as its
mainspring a proverb (probably of Munro's invention, and not taken
on this occasion from Nicolson's *A Collection of Gaelic Proverbs* and
Familiar Phrases (1881)). In Chapter 2 Bell Vore says,

'It is not lucky to save a man from drowning: take its spoil from
the sea and the spoil itself will punish you.' (p.15)

This refers to the heroic act of rescue which Col performs at the
opening of the novel when he sees Dark John's little boat in trouble
on the open sea and rushes out to save him from drowning. It immediately becomes the key idea in the novel. Throughout the story

frequent references are made to this proverb as a piece of folk wisdom and we realise that Col, although intending a kind act, has in fact been guilty of *hubris* in interfering where he had no right. The situation is similar and may, in fact, owe something to that in Stevenson's *The Merry Men* where Gordon Darnaway and others are punished for looting sunken ships, the sea's spoil.[26] Indeed, Col himself becomes aware of its reality early on when he considers that bad luck in his commercial/smuggling activities may be punishment for his *hubris*:

> he... looked from the little window into the garden and over the fields and out as far as he might upon the sea, that he had robbed of its spoil, and now – it might be in the first of its revenge – had robbed him of his sloop. (p.35)

The old man, Dark John is, of course, the spoil and in the *ceilidh* house immediately after his rescue he declares to Col:

> 'I drink...to the gentleman of Corodale. I am his man from this on. Is it the fire? – there is the hand! The knife for him? – here is the bosom!' (p.18)

He dedicates himself entirely to Col and is his complete servant. The grotesque imagery which is used to describe the old man, however, makes us realise that there is something very unpleasant about him and he is to be treated with grave suspicion:

> He might have been a monster of the deep, some uncanny soulless thing, in the form of man briefly borrowed for villainous devices, slobbering the stuff that feeds itself on ooze and slime. (p.205)

and

> She looked down and saw Dark John like a toad, his eyes shut up to slits, his jaws industrious, gave him a look more of repugnance than of blame, and stood upon the deck. (p.224)

It gradually becomes clear that Dark John, like Gilmartin in James Hogg's *The Private Memoirs and Confessions of a Justified Sinner* (1824), appears to be there spurring Col on whenever his greed for the *ulaidh* appears to wane:

A thought came to him with a sense of revelation that this old wretch haunted him, a ghost in moments critical, led him first astray, and always spurred his interest in the fifty years' fortune at any time the same might seem to flag. (p.260)

Even after he lashes the old man's face with a switch the old man still will not forsake his allegiance to him. There is, therefore, a strong suggestion that Dark John is a demonic being, who drives Col on to his inevitable doom in a magnificent climax in Mingulay. In the yawl which they had commandeered John directs Col to the foot of the cliff below the blood of the Merry Dancers and, spurred on by his greed, he climbs up. He finds no treasure and then finally stops to take stock:

No ease of his mind had been for him since he dragged its prey from the sea, to be the spur to schemes that somehow seemed to end in foolishness and mockery. It was *trom-lighe* [nightmare] – it was Incubus he had lifted from the Barra Sound; there was something after all in the ancient proverb. (p.273)

Finally, after he has lashed out at Old John who has climbed up behind him and sent him to certain death Col descends to the water's edge to find that the boat has disappeared. After a day or two it drifts back in an atmosphere that has all the eeriness of Part III of Coleridge's 'The Ancient Mariner' with the body of the old man before the mast:

'Twas Death come back for him. (p.281)

Col leaps into the water to reach the yawl but his weight capsizes her:

The yawl heeled over with his weight; the body fell on his shoulders; the tide was sucking his feet, and he sank with his burden, with *trom-lighe* – incubus – spoil of the sea he had robbed at Michaelmas – to the dark, expectant, patient depths. (p.281)

'Incubus' is, of course, the term Stevenson used to describe James Durie, the Master of Ballantrae[27] whom he had earlier described as 'all I know of the devil'.[28] There is also a verbal echo of The Merry Men (the name given to the breakers which seduce Gordon Darnaway to his inevitable destruction in Stevenson's story of that name) in the Blood of the Merry Dancers, the red lichen on the Mingulay cliff which fascinates Col and leads him on to his ultimate doom.

Although Col does have a few redeeming features (at one point he does seem to have genuine love for Anna for herself (p.105) and not for her money and he does show regret for having duped Duncan with the song (p.172)), he is almost completely selfish and unscrupulous. One of the interesting things about him, however, is the fact that he is a cunning and unscrupulous entrepreneur in a *Hebridean* setting :

> '... but nowadays too many of the curing-barrels belong to Corodale Col, and the bounty and price he pays for the cran are hardly worth a God-fearing man wetting his boots or putting his breath in a net-bow for.' (p.109)

Along with the Sergeant, his equally grasping but much less subtle business partner, they make a formidable pair. The Sergeant is brutal in his treatment of Anna when he kidnaps her and considerably more so in his treatment of his pathetic and slatternly wife:

> ...when he turned to shut the door behind him, and saw her, he put his foot out and thrust her down the stair. She fell to the bottom with a cry of pain that he paid no heed to. (p.231)

His ultimate punishment of exile for all his greed, however, is much less severe than Col's, presumably because he did not steal the sea's spoil.

It is certainly possible to see in these two men approximations to the small town entrepreneurs Gibson and Gourlay in George Douglas Brown's *The House with the Green Shutters* (1901). Indeed, the similarity between the Sergeant and his wife and Gourlay and his wife is particularly marked and when the Sergeant taunts the terrified Anna with the phrase

> 'I wonder what I'll do next' (p.230)

one is reminded of John Gourlay's taunt to his terrified son,

> 'What am I to do wi' ye now?' [29]

and when Jib-boom fells the Sergeant with a blow so that

He fell with a crash among the ashes of the hearth (p.245)

we are reminded of the death of Gourlay after he had been struck with a poker by his son:

Gourlay thudded on the fender, his brow crashing on the rim.[30]

Although Munro's business characters are pale reflections of the starkness of Douglas Brown's they will almost certainly have been influenced by *The House with the Green Shutters* since Munro was familiar with that book and a friend of its author,[31] and they, in turn, may have contributed to the character of Gillespie Strang since John MacDougall Hay's *Gillespie* (1914) was dedicated to Neil Munro.

The character of Dan MacNeil, nicknamed Flying Jib-boom, captain of the sloop 'Happy Return' is a 'bridge' character between the good and evil groups in the book. Although he has been the unwitting promulgator of the scandalous verse in the song and has been manipulated to kidnap Anna and was one of the two original plunderers of the *ulaidh*, he is, when left to be his own man, a decent person who is in the end responsible for Anna's safe return and for the punishment of the Sergeant. He has a sense of fun and lives to enjoy life and is clearly a literary predecessor of Para Handy. When he brings Duncan back to Boisdale he says:

'Two or three splendid dances have I lost this week in Arisaig, that I might be the one to take him back. I'm not complaining a bit, though I'm the boy for the dancing.' (p.284)[32]

In opposition to the dark characters Col, Dark John and the Sergeant we have the characters who represent unalloyed goodness: Father Ludovick, Duncan and Anna – all kind, honest and devoutly religious characters.

Ludovick, clearly based on Maighstir Ailein, is a much loved and popular but rather lonely priest whose presence seems to permeate the narrative although his actual participation in the action is comparatively small:

To its south they saw Ludovick rising on the brae, his tall figure bent against the furrows of a little field beyond his dwelling. When he reached the summit he stood dark against the sky. He stopped a moment there, and turned and looked across the islands and over the sea, the genius of the place, a lonely figure. (p.120)

He is a mystic who is at one with nature and who very quickly sees into the heart of things. He sees through Col:

> A shallowness in his spoken sentiments made the priest distrust him, and come at last to the sad conclusion that here was a vulgar mercenary, so they went their own ways searching. (p.254)

At the same time his reputation for justice terrifies Dark John and the Sergeant when they realise their folly in kidnapping Anna:

> Father Ludovick's wrath, they felt, would follow them to the remotest of the Outer Isles. (p.250)

Above all, however, it is the strength of his priestly calling and his attention to his priestly duties which impress us. All along he was in possession of the agonising knowledge that the *ulaidh* had been stolen by Old Corodale but he could not stop the mad speculation and problems connected with it because he could not break the seal of the confessional. But most impressive of all is his belief in the power of prayer: when Anna is discovered missing, perhaps drowned, he goes into *Stella Maris* and prays all night. He emerges from the church at the same hour as her release is secure. When he meets her he says:

> 'I knew you were coming... Since the break of day I never had a doubt of it.' (p.258)

Duncan, too, is a religious figure. He is a described as a 'stuck priest' i.e. a student for the priesthood who leaves seminary before ordination. He is a highly honourable young man who, unlike his brother Col, is completely unselfish. Although the older son, he cedes his rights to Corodale to his brother since he feels that enough of the family money has been spent on his priestly training which he never completed. Above all his sense of duty and fairness to Anna forces him to leave her to seek his fortune on the mainland when he realises that people are saying that he is after her merely for the *ulaidh* and that he has no means or prospects to offer her for support in married life. His return to Uist and to Anna in the end is, of course, right and fitting.

Anna herself, Ludovick's sister and housekeeper, is again a person with strong religious connections. Although she is not portrayed with great depth, she has a sparkling personality and is extremely popular on the island, particularly with the women and the children. Where Ludovick is aloof and remote, she complements this. She is not naive in that she suspects Col's integrity; she 'was always dubious of her visitor' (p192) but she never fully sees through him. She is courageous and plucky during most of the time of her kidnapping. Above all, however, she is a strong loving personality (as can be seen in the way she goes back to kiss the Sergeant's feckless and much abused wife when they are leaving Creggans). She is generous to all and a strong force for good.

In addition, of course, to Munro's use of Highland English which is, appropriately, sustained throughout this novel, one of the most interesting aspects of *Children of Tempest* is the tremendous mass of traditional material of a religious nature which the author has researched and introduced to give the story Hebridean authenticity. This adds to the artistic strength of the book in reinforcing the role of the 'good' characters.

The most obvious religious material referred to is Carmichael's collection of *Carmina Gadelica* – hymns, invocations and prayers which cover every aspect of the Hebridean life – to which Munro is clearly referring in the following passage:

> The fisher of the Uists begins no enterprise but in the spirit of prayer, nor rises at morn nor sleeps at night, nor kindles cruisie light nor smothers an evening fire without some invocation of the saints. (p.108)

Munro refers to four specific examples from the *Carmina* on pp.25, 91, 140, 176. The example on p.91 he puts into the mouth of Anna as her morning prayer. This is his own accurate translation except that he omits the fourth line of the original, presumably for rhyming purposes:

> *Iosda Criosda*, thanks to Thee
> That brought me from the deeps of night
> Into the solace of the light,
> Through blood atoning shed for me. (p.91)

> *Taing dhut Iosda Criosda,*
> *Thug mis a nios o'n oidche 'n raoir*
> *Chon solas soillse an la'n diugh,*
> *Chon sonas siorruidh a chosnadh dha m'anam,*
> *An cion na fal a dhoirt thu dhomh.*[33]

In addition to the traditional Uist hymns he also includes extensive reference to the Latin Mass and, very interestingly, to the Gaelic translation of the *Veni Creator Spiritus* (*O Thig a nuas, a Spioraid Naoimh*) the ancient hymn to the Holy Spirit. Ludovick and the others sing this for comfort as they are crossing the dangerous North Ford:

> *Ur naimhdean fuadaich fad bhuainn,*
> *'Us builich oirnn do shith gu buan.* (p.51)

> (Far from us drive your foes
> And award us everlasting peace.)

Munro would have got these lines from the *Comh-Chruinneachadh de Laoidhean Spioradail* which had been edited by Maighstir Ailein and the hymn itself translated by the priest's relative D.C MacPherson.[34]

The baking of Michaelmas cakes was also traditional in Uist for the feast of St Michael on the 29th September and these were distributed to the island's poor, suggesting a caring and supportive community:

> Some... were running with bee-skep baskets round the poorer huts of the nearer town land, giving, as custom compelled, and their good hearts in any case had prompted, something of their bounty in St Michael's morning food to the less fortunate of their fellows. (p.9)

Lastly, there are many references to St Bride who is particularly revered in Uist. She has taken on the attributes of a previous pagan goddess of Spring and her feast coincides with Candlemas in the Catholic Church. In the novel Anna is rocking Brideag (little Bride) in a cradle when Duncan first comes to see her. Brideag, in reality, was 'a sheaf of corn, ornamented with flowers and ribbons' (p.112). This practice was the vestige of a fertility rite performed to ensure good crops in the coming year and is referred to in Frazer's *The Golden Bough*.[35] Indeed, for her virtues and the regenerative spirit she brings to the community Anna virtually becomes identified with the saint. When in the end she is united with Duncan the islanders hear her singing and

> Her voice came over the water from Orosay's lee, a sound enchanting –

Bride's voice that hushes the children and wrings the hearts of men. (p.286)

When we review the novel as a whole, then, it would seem that the inclusion of so much reference to Christian tradition suggests the strength of faith in the island way of life which is there to support Ludovick and the other good characters and will ensure their ultimate triumph against the brutality of the Sergeant, the scheming of Col and the demonic incubus, Dark John.

Finally, although there is no major political statement in this novel as there is in *Doom Castle* and *The Shoes of Fortune*, Ludovick does enjoy visiting the township of Kilbride where there are still the 'ashes of revolt' after the '45. But the reason he likes this place is not for its active part in the campaign but because it has retained the old way of life that was disturbed by the '45 and all that came after it. He loved this place because there he feels himself 'separate by some freak of the imagination from that new world of fretting influences that came with books and letters to the Bay of Boisdale' (p.252). In Kilbride 'people were content and never had a doubt of God' (p.252).

In this section (as in the passage 'I know corries in Argyll' in *John Splendid*[36] and a number of other passages throughout his work) Munro seems to be harking back to a Golden Age in the way that is to become one of the basic tenets of the mythopoeic novels of the Scottish Renaissance of the 1920's and 30's. It is interesting that here he is doing it through the eyes of a Catholic priest. Indeed, it is remarkable that he, an orthodox Presbyterian, should have invested so much effort into research on the Catholic Church in this novel and in *The Shoes of Fortune*. It may be that like Fionn MacColla, Compton MacKenzie and George Mackay Brown he was using the older faith of the Catholic Church as a means of getting back to a Golden Age of a wholer, more harmonious Scotland without, of course, going so far as they did in becoming converts to Catholicism.

Notes

1 The edition referred to is Munro, Neil *Doom Castle*, ed. Brian D. Osborne, Edinburgh: B&W Publishing, 1996
2 Munro,Neil *The Looker On*, Edinburgh: The Porpoise Press, 1933, pp.44–9
3 The action of the book is clearly intended to be set in 1752 although Munro has Argyll tell MacTaggart to 'wake up! this is '55.' (p.97). Munro's chronology is not infrequently imprecise
4 '... No, Mungo Boyd (*Doom Castle*) was not your waiter. He was, partly, a tailor

in this neighbourhood, who had for obvious reasons to be considerably altered in the outlines. I had rather a curious experience with Mungo; the beggar was pretty well written up (I mean mostly completed) and I thought him no' that bad ava, when it occurred to me that he seemed completely familiar. I have a wretched memory and I had to read over half a dozen of Scott's novels to discover – alas! – that I was unconsciously plagiarising Caleb Balderstone! I had to re-write the character; in spite of that I fear sometimes a little of Caleb lingers, and at least I know my Mungo is not so good as he was in the first draft.'

Letter from Neil Munro to Pittendreigh MacGillivray, 17 June 1901 in Hermann Völkel, *Das literarische Werk Neil Munros*, Germersheim, 1994, p.211

5 The playing of the flageolet by the suitor to attract his lover's attention may owe something to Scott's *Guy Mannering* Ch.18 where Bertram indicates his presence to Julia Mannering by serenading her with a melody on the flageolet. Sir Walter Scott, *Guy Mannering*, ed. P.D. Garside, Edinburgh: Edinburgh University Press, 1999, pp.94–5

6 Although work on the new castle would have been started in 1752 the building was not habitable until 1758. See Osborne, *op. cit.*, p.x

7 Lindsay, Maurice *History of Scottish Literature*, London: Hale, 1977, p.346

8 Hart, Francis Russell *The Scottish Novel*, London: John Murray, 1978, p.166

9 Duchess Jean is fictitious. Archibald, third Duke of Argyll, married Anne Whitfield who died in 1723. See Osborne, *op. cit.*, p.xi

10 Nicolson, Alexander, *A Collection of Gaelic Proverbs and Familiar Phrases*, Edinburgh: MacLachlan and Stewart, 1881, p.333. Munro frequently incorporates proverbs from Nicolson throughout his stories and novels

11 The text edition referred to is Munro, Neil *The Shoes of Fortune*, Edinburgh and London: William Blackwood and Sons, 1935 (Inveraray Edition)

12 Letter from Neil Munro to Lynn Doyle, 10 March 1921. (Property of Lesley Lendrum)

13 Lang, Andrew, *Pickle the Spy*, London, 1897, p.299

14 Munro, Neil, *The Brave Days*, Edinburgh : The Porpoise Press, 1933, pp.30–4

15 The Duke of Argyll (the second Duke, 'Red John of the Battles') makes it possible for Jeannie Deans to meet Queen Caroline in order to plead her sister's case. Sir Walter Scott, *The Heart of Midlothian*, ed. Claire Lamont, Oxford: Oxford University Press, 1982, Chs 35–38 pp.344–77

16 James Stewart, the victim of the Appin Murder, is referred to as James of the Glens by Stevenson and James of the Glen by Munro. Local tradition in Appin refers to him in Gaelic as Seumas a'Ghlinne, James of the Glen

17 Stevenson, Robert Louis, *Kidnapped and Catriona*, ed. Emma Letley, Oxford: Oxford University Press, 1986,Ch 20, p.38

18 The edition referred to is Munro, Neil *Children of Tempest*, Edinburgh and London: William Blackwood and Sons, 1935 (Inveraray Edition)

19 Munro, Neil *The Looker-On*, ed. George Blake, Edinburgh: The Porpoise Press, 1933, pp.79–91

20 Munro, Neil *The Brave Days*, ed. George Blake, Edinburgh: The Porpoise Press, 1933, pp.302–8

21 McDonald, Fr Allan, *Comh-Chruinneachadh de Laoidhean Spioradail*, Oban, 1893

22 Carmichael, Alexander, *Carmina Gadelica*, Vols I and II, Edinburgh, 1928

23 Munro, Neil, *The Looker-On*, ed. George Blake, Edinburgh, 1933, p.80

24 This incident may owe something to Sir Walter Scott's *The Antiquary* Chs 7and

8 where Lovel rescues Isabella in similar circumstances. Reference to the 'blue gown' of the beggar on p.66, the garb of Edie Ochiltree the gaberlunzie of Scott's novel, would seem to confirm this

25 Letter from Neil Munro to unnamed male correspondent in Völkel, *op. cit.*, p.220. (The letter is erroneously dated 4 July 1903 in this text. The date should read 9 July 1903.)

26 *Robert Louis Stevenson: The Scottish Short Stories and Essays*, ed. Kenneth Gelder, Edinburgh: Edinburgh University Press, 1989, pp.99–141

27 Letter from Robert Louis Stevenson to Henry James, March,1888, *The Letters of Robert Louis Stevenson*, ed. Sidney Colvin, London: Methuen and Co.,1901, p.87

28 Letter from Robert Louis Stevenson to Sidney Colvin, 24 December 1887, *The Letters of Robert Louis Stevenson*, ed. Sidney Colvin, London: Methuen and Co., 1901, pp.88–9

29 Brown, George Douglas, *The House with the Green Shutters*, ed. Dorothy Porter, Harmondsworth: Penguin Books,1985, Ch25 p.219

30 *Ibid.*, Ch 25, p.226

31 Munro, Neil, *The Looker-On*, Edinburgh, ed. George Blake, Edinburgh: The Porpoise Press, 1933, p.277–82

32 Compare the boast of Para Handy in 'The Leap Year Ball': ' I can stot through the middle o' a dance like a tuppeny kahoochy ball.' Para Handy, Eds. Brian Osborne and Ronald Armstrong, Edinburgh: Birlinn, 1992, p.273

33 Carmichael, Alexander *Carmina Gadelica*, Vol. I, No. 41, Edinburgh, 1928, p.96

34 McDonald, *op. cit.*: No. 20 p.44. Also Campbell, J.L., 'The Sources of the Gaelic Hymnal, 1893', Innes Review, Vol. VII, Number II, 1956, pp.101–11

35 Frazer, Sir James, *The Golden Bough*, London: MacMillan and Co. Ltd., 1963, p.177

36 Munro, Neil, *John Splendid*, ed. Brian D. Osborne, Edinburgh: B&W Publishing, 1994, p.223

Some Reflections on Neil Munro's
The Daft Days

RONALD ARMSTRONG

The burgh town turned on its pillows, drew up its feet from the bed-bottles, last night hot, now turned to chilly stone, rubbed its eyes, and knew by that bell it was the daftest of the daft days come.[1] (p.1)

New Year (the Daft Days of the title) dawns on the (unspecified) Scots 'burgh town,' and with the dawn comes an orphan child to a family called Dyce, bringing with her mirth and joy as well as a constant struggle by relatives, who are no longer young, to provide her with a sound and proper upbringing. The seven or eight-year-old child at the centre of Munro's 1906 novel is Lennox (also known as 'Bud') Dyce, who, after losing her Scots father and American mother, both professional actors in Chicago, comes to stay in Scotland with her two paternal aunts and uncle. We follow her through the trials and excitements of her growing up, her education and developing enthusiasms and finally leave her on the threshold of an astonishing success as an actress.

This charming if rather odd little book is very unlike Munro's other novels. Neither is it a swashbuckling tale like *John Splendid*, nor is it a meditation on Highland and Lowland society like *The New Road*. If anything, to one reader at least, it most closely resembles the short stories Munro was writing in these early years of the twentieth century about Jimmy Swan the Joy Traveller who is a 'commercial' travelling in haberdashery and ladies garments.[2] These charming and amusing tales first appeared in the *Glasgow Evening News*, as did the Para Handy and Erchie stories.

Given the West Highland setting of *The Daft Days*, it might be expected that many of the characters would have a touch of Para Handy the puffer skipper about them. Certainly, Munro does give us a seaman, Charles MacLean, who has a somewhat Handyish turn of phrase and one of the key figures in the story, Kate MacNeill, the

Dyces' maid, is a most endearing emigrant from the island of Colonsay. Overwhelmingly, however, the tone and manners and language of the main characters – Bell and Ailie and Uncle Dan Dyce – are those of Lowland Scots, very like the bien and decent citizens encountered by Mr. Swan on his journeys around Scotland. Miss Minto, proprietor of the Millinery and Manteau Emporium in the 'burgh town' of the novel, could easily be one of Jimmy Swan's customers and the comings and goings of the townsfolk are reminiscent of those in places he visits like the fictitious Burrelton. Similarly, Jimmy Swan's knowledge and love of poetry and music echoes that of Bud herself, or key characters such as Aunt Ailie, an embryonic 'new woman', or her brother Dan Dyce the lawyer.

Mention of the West Highland setting of the book leads us to touch on Munro's skill in evoking a sense of place in his writing. *The Daft Days* will come high in the estimation of any reader who loves Inveraray and Loch Fyne, because such a reader will instantly recognise that the town and its environs are described with the true sympathy of a native son.

Clearly, the setting of the novel – 'the burgh town' of the opening paragraph – is Inveraray. Equally clearly, Munro, for whatever motive, chooses not to name it, not even to give it a fictional name. When he describes the arrival of young Lennox Dyce, she gets off the train at the nearest station, which Munro calls Maryfield. This is clearly Dalmally, which in the Gaelic has been thought by some to mean 'the field of Mary.' The railway to Dalmally opened in 1877, giving us a useful time reference and suggesting that the story is inspired by the period of Munro's adolescent years, when he was still working in a lawyer's office in Inveraray (and perhaps acquiring useful background for the character of Daniel Dyce.) So the location of the town is Munro's birthplace, and further reinforcement of the point comes when we read of a nearby loch and castle (although there is an earl instead of a duke in residence).

The internal topography of the town also offers many clues. Here, for example, is Daniel Dyce the lawyer's office – 'at the windy corner facing the Cross' (p.65). His house, too is recognisable as the one 'with the brass knocker,' (p.31) and the native son shows his colours in wonderfully evocative passages like the following:

> The strangers had gone south with the swallows; the steamer no longer called each day to make the pavement noisy in the afternoon with the skliff of city feet, so different from the customary tread of tackety boots; the coachman's horn, departing, no longer

sounded down the valley like a brassy challenge from the wide, wide world. Peace came to the burgh like a swoon, and all its days were pensive. Folk went about their tasks reluctant, the very smoke of the chimneys loitered lazily around the ridges where the starlings chattered, and a haze was almost ever over the hills. When it rose, sometimes, Bud, from her attic window, could see the road that wound through the distant glen. The road! – the road! – ah, that began to have a meaning and a kind of cry, and wishfully she looked at it and thought upon its other end, where the life she had left and read about was loudly humming and marvellous things were being done. (p.140)

This novel is full of descriptions of bird-life like the swallows and starlings – elsewhere we read of seagulls and rooks; most memorable of all are the wild geese. The descriptions of these avian travellers are the book's most obvious – and most familiar – use of symbolism (one might point out that Henrik Ibsen's archetypal and influential symbolic work, *The Wild Duck*, had appeared in 1884). The *motif* of the wild geese is one that Munro uses throughout the book as a kind of evocation, sometimes of freedom and escape, but also sometimes of the supernatural – of the ghosts of Scotland:

Over the tenements of the town the song of the bell went rollicking, and with its hiccuping pauses went wonderfully another sound far, far removed in spirit and suggestion – the clang of wild geese calling: the 'honk, honk' of the ganders and the challenge of their ladies come down adrift in the snow from the bitter north. (p.3)

Another, more personal, Munro image is that of the road – we saw it in the previous extract and here it is again:

'My road,' said the child. 'The one I see from my window: oh how it rises and rises and winds and winds, and it just *shrieks* on you to come right along and try.' (p.147)

Munro's greatest novel, *The New Road*, of course, was to take this idea to its ultimate conclusion.

* * * * *

'I do perceive here a divided duty:
To you I am bound for life and education;
My life and education both do learn me
How to respect you.'
(p.279 [*Othello* by William Shakespeare, Act I, Sc. 3, lines 181–4])

At the end of the novel Lennox achieves tremendous success as an actress in the role of Desdemona in *Othello*. All of the family go to London for the opening and in a somewhat strange chapter the unnamed narrator seems to add an oddly nightmarish tinge to the description of the glamour of the metropolis – this contrasts markedly with the provincial manners and attitudes of Aunt Bell and her relatives and at the same time appears to assert a kind of moral superiority:

They sat in silence in the darkness of the cab, and in silence drifted into the entrance-hall of the theatre to mingle with the pompous world incongruously – with loud vainglorious men, who bore to the eye of Bell some spirit of abandonment and mockery, with women lovely by the gift of God, or with dead-white faces, wax-red lips, and stealthy sidelong eyes. (p.276)

This is quite at variance with the generally benevolent tone of the book; a page or so further on, however, and Munro is once again on reassuringly familiar ground, as he describes the reception of Lennox's first great speech as Desdemona:

To the box where she knew her friends were sitting she let her eyes for a second wander as she spoke the opening lines that had so much of double meaning – not Desdemona, but the loving and wilful child asking forgiveness, yet tenacious of her purpose. (p.279)

Lennox, like Desdemona, has been 'bound' to her family – in this case *in loco parentis* – for her 'life and education,' and is now ready to break free and make her own life. Bud is one of her chosen names, a word which suggests a flowering or growing. *The Daft Days* could be described as what the German critics called a *Bildungsroman* – a novel dealing with a young person's growth and development. More specifically, the account given in this book is one of an educational awakening.

Munro's ideas about education were no doubt influenced by his own schooling – apart from spells at the rural school in nearby Glen Aray he went to the Church Square Public School in Inveraray – but apart from that, his views, I think, are most directly expressed in a sentence he gives to the unnamed narrator of *The Daft Days*. A description of Daniel Dyce's attitude to Lennox's schooling runs:

> (Daniel had) a sort of philosophy that the gate of gifts is closed on us the day we're born, and that the important parts of the curriculum, good or bad, are picked up like a Scots or Heilan' accent, someway in the home. (p.74)

We believe that some of the characters in the book are based on real models. If there were truly any originals of the sisters who ran the dame school, they would undoubtedly have blanched at their portrayal here.[3] A single disastrous day at the Duffs' (or 'Pigeon Sisters') little school in the town ends with the outspoken Bud leaving early and vowing never to return. In fact, that is precisely how it turns out; perhaps because a girl's education was not yet seen as sufficiently important. Also because Aunt Bell's reason for wishing Lennox to attend school was that:

> She deemed it still the only avenue to the character and skill that keep these queer folk, men, when they're married, by their own fire-ends. (p.74)

There is also a realisation by her aunts and uncle of the shortcomings of an establishment where children's learning was stale and unimaginative – this despite the opportunities for imaginative learning presented by the fact that:

> The school lay in the way of the main traffic of the little town: they could hear each passing wheel and footstep, the sweet 'chink, chink' from the smithy whence came the smell of a sheep's head singeing. Sea-gulls and rooks bickered and swore in the gutters of the street; from field behind came in a ploughman's whistle as he drove his team, slicing green seas of fallow as a vessel cuts the green, green wave. (p.78)

Or as we might say, the environment of the school offered limitless potential for learning, potential that was totally unrealised by the Misses Duff, just as was the individual potential of each of their charges:

God only knew the other variations. 'Twas the duty of the twins
to bring them all in mind alike to the one plain level. (p.78)

These poor ineffectual souls meet their match in young Lennox
Dyce and in a comic little scene they have to take cover behind the
blackboard because:

> Bud, used for all her thinking years to asking explanations of what
> she did not understand, never hesitated to interrogate her
> teachers, who seemed to her to be merely women, like her mother,
> and Mrs. Molyneux, and Auntie Ailie, only a little wilted and
> severe, grotesque in some degree because of their funny affected
> manner... she went further, she contradicted them twice, not
> rudely, but as one might contradict her equals. (p.80)

So the plan to send Lennox for conventional schooling is shelved
until much later when, in the fullness of time, she is ready for it
herself. Only then is it decided that she will attend a recognised
leading school in Edinburgh so as to have – as the American Jim
Molyneux puts it:

> The last coat of shellac put on her education. (p.215)

In the meantime, therefore, the steps taken to provide for
Lennox's education – most formally by her Aunt Ailie – had
elements of an age-old way within the home (or the 'Dyce
Academy'), but combined with a more unconventional approach
using ideas resembling those of several well-known educational
reformers later in the twentieth century. Here is how the Dyces set
about it:

> She was learning Ailie's calm and curiosity and ambition; she was
> learning Bell's ideas of duty and ancient glory of her adopted land;
> from her uncle she was learning many things, of which the least
> that seemed useful at the time was the Lord's prayer in Latin...
> (p.89).

and there were the hours that Ailie gave with delight to Bud's
more orthodox tuition. The back room that was called Dan's
study, because he sometimes took a nap there after dinner,
became a school-room. There was a Mercator's map of the world
and another of Europe, that of themselves gave the place the right

academy aspect. With imagination, a map, and the Golden Treasury, you might have as good as a college education, according to Ailie .... Yes, the world is all for the folk of imagination. 'Love maps and you will never be too old or too poor to travel,' was Ailie's motto. She found a hero or heroine for every spot upon Mercator, and nourished so the child in noble admirations. (p.90)

This is a book in which the central figure is a child, but it gradually dawns upon the reader that it is not a book for children. Munro's influences seem to come more from the mainstream of nineteenth century fiction rather than the newer genre of writing for young people, a genre developed by Ballantyne, Stevenson and Barrie to name just fellow Scots. The character of Bud probably owes more to Dickens than any of these – the chapter when she falls ill does have a suspicion of Little Nell-type sentiment – and big themes like the development of character and love of homeland are more dominant than incident or adventure.

A further question about the style of the novel. Mention has been made of the *bildungsroman*, but given the publication date the influence of the kailyard school – if it be a school, or indeed a movement – must be considered. Can *The Daft Days* be classified as a kailyard novel?

Certainly, there is a superficial resemblance to the late nineteenth and early twentieth century movement in Scottish fiction which the *Encyclopaedia Britannica* characterises as 'a sentimental idealisation of humble village life.' *The Daft Days* could be said to be about a single small community and arguably is written in a 'natural and unsophisticated style,' with perhaps slight tinges of sentimentality as already mentioned. Munro's creative vision however, is much wider than the 'parochial viewpoint' of many of the kailyard authors, and certainly this appealing and increasingly fascinating book can never be said to have 'degenerated into mawkish sentimentality.'

The kailyard, of course, provoked a hostile reaction among contemporary Scottish realists and later writers of the twentieth century. Munro positioned himself apart from this. He chose the way of historical fiction for the bulk of his greatest work, so *The Daft Days* can be seen as a rare example of a contemporary, or near contemporary novel of his own lifetime. More than this, however, it is a book which deserves to reach the wider readership that it once had (including a sizeable North American readership) and to enjoy again a much higher critical reputation.

To illustrate the quality of the writing once more and finally, consider this passage from near the end of the novel:

The winds sighed from the mountains, and the mists came mustering to the glens; the sea crept out on long, bird-haunted, wailing and piping sands, nought to be seen of it, its presence obvious only in the scent of wrack and the wash on the pebbled beaches. Behind the town the woods lay black and haunted, and through them, and far upward in the valley, dripping in the rain and clamorous with hidden burns and secret wells, went the highway to the world... (p.234)

Notes

1 Munro, Neil, *The Daft Days*, Colonsay, Argyll: House of Lochar, 2002
2 Munro, Neil, *Erchie and Jimmy Swan*, ed. Brian D. Osborne and Ronald Armstrong, Edinburgh: Birlinn, 1993
3 Munro's own two eldest surviving children, Hugh and Effie, attended a Dame School in Clarkston run by the Misses Gardener for a year in 1898/99, although there is no record of any traumatic incident having taken place there

ARTHUR T. QUILLER-COUCH[1]

A Shining Book:
Mr. Neil Munro's *The Daft Days*

(from *Glasgow Evening News*, 16 May 1907)

Let me allow all possible discount of the delight and admiration that
stay by me as I close this volume, as I shut the covers upon this
shining story. It is true that for months I have eschewed novels, and
so come to *The Daft Days* no doubt with a freshened appetite. It is
equally true, by the same mysterious law which has made so many
friends for me out of Scotsmen, a genuine descendant of the line of
Galt and Moir, Dr. John Brown and J. M. Barrie has only to whistle
and I come to him. These storm-bitten burghs of which they write
are as absolutely strange to me in fact as they are dear to me in imagination: there they belong with Athens and Rome, the Sicily of
Theocritus, the Bagdat (sic) of the Arabian Nights. They are
classical ground. The humours of them lie closer to my understanding than do those of any known or invented town in the middle
or north of England. With the gossip of the wynd these ears are
actually as unfamiliar as with the honk of the wild geese crying over
the roofs in Mr. Neil Munro's story: yet they know it as surely as
these eyes know the Copenhagen of Hans Christian Andersen.

Nay, though the knowledge be all derived from books, imaginings, dreams, so intimately I seem to have it that I dare to detect with
confidence a sham *Mansie Waugh*, a sham *Window in Thrums*, and
be angry as with profanation. Justly or unjustly – but I think justly –
the later kailyarders are abominable to me: they vulgarise sacred
ground: their death beds are odious, and their Sabbaths I cannot
away with.

But this book is of totally different quality, of the right breed and
tradition; native as peat, but also touched with that genius which
makes all countries one; and again differentiated as pure Scots by
that strain of sentiment of which we Southerners fight shy. We are
wise, perhaps. Your literature has purchased its sentiment at a fearful
price – an expense of spirit in a waste of slop; but when one comes

upon a book like this of Mr. Munro's, with its confident delicate handling, he has to admit that the cost has been justified.

Is the story a true one? In a sense it is not true; for it deals only with the sunny side of life, with gentle characters, and with a slight story which it leads, through no difficulties, to a triumphantly happy ending. Save for Captain Consequence (a lightly sketched character, soon laid aside, as the tale and the author's mood have no use for him, or no heart to treat him as he deserves) all the personages are loveable, down to the dog – that admirable dog – Footles. Real life is not all compact of such loveable folk; nor, unless I mistake, is Mr. Munro himself under any such illusion. He writes of the sunny side deliberately, with selection, because he wants to present that side and has a conviction that it will be good for us. So indeed it is; but he does not carry conviction as would a man who wrote of the sunny side simply because he could see no other. The fiction is not of that supreme kind which, probing into the dark shadows of our nature, and daring all depths, lifts out humanity and shows it divine. It passes over all disappointments, all discouragements, in Bud Dyce's progress to artistic excellence and fame; and we know that excellence and fame are not to be attained without these and many of them. Mr. Munro knows it too, of course, though he steadily presents the fairy side of the story.

And the fairy side, after all, is true as it is undeniably beautiful. Such men and women as Daniel Dyce and his sisters do exist in this world and sweeten life; children of genius like our heroine are born and, under such loving influences, must attain. It is good to be reminded of what the best might be; far better than to be reminded of the lets, the hindrances, the pitfalls, that will come without invocation. If this were an impossible story, I should not be found praising it: but it is possible; and, if it happened, this earth would be the glad place it might be and ought to be.

I have laughed over this book, for it is packed with delicate wit and absurdity. I have felt my eyes moisten, here and there, for its joyousness plays over the depths of simple emotion, common to all honest folk who love children and see the child inevitably, cruelly (themselves aiding in proportion to their love), slipping away into a future they cannot share. Tender voices vainly calling upon childhood to linger – hands eagerly, fearfully, promoting the fate their selfishness would delay – household love calling back to protection while the young heart, half regretful, half impatient, leans and listens towards the future – this, the commonest tragedy of good lives, underlies the smiling comedy of Mr. Munro's happy book. We have it summed up for us in the picture of the two good aunts working furiously to prepare their darling's outfit for school – 'the task of love which, in all it does for the youth it cherishes, must ever be digging a grave for its own delight.' And I have called it a shining book because, shutting its covers, I have felt like one pulling down the curtains on a play which – besides introducing me to real friends – has quickened life with a hundred half-forgotten meanings. I think of Turner's retort upon the critic who objected that he had never seen such sunsets, 'Ah! but don't you jolly well wish you could?' Ourselves have seen even such skies as Mr. Munro paints, or guessed them, and should be happy of the reminder.

I do not divulge the plot, for there is no particular plot: and I say little of the characters, because to report of them at second hand would be vain and would moreover defeat the desire with which I write: that your readers hasten to possess themselves of this book, which I have called a shining book, and to make friends with Lawyer Dyce and his two sisters, with the maid from Colonsay and her lover, with Footles, and above all with Bud the incomparable.

Yes: it is a shining book; ending with success, but teaching the Beatitudes by the way, full of the laughter of simple hearts: a book like a morning-room filled with sunshine and Uncle Dan's philosophy, which says,

'The first half-hour in the morning is worth three hours at any other time of the day; for when you've said your prayers, and had a good bath, and a clean shave, and your boots new on – no slippers nor slithery dressing- gowns, the peace of God, and – and – and the assurance of strength and righteousness descends upon you so that you – you – you can tackle wild-cats.'

It deserves to be a little classic, this story so full of good writing, and smiles, and right feeling.

Note

1 Arthur Thomas Quiller-Couch (1863–1944). Novelist, critic and academic. Wrote under pen-name of 'Q'. King Edward VII Professor of English Literature, Cambridge, 1912–44. Knighted 1910

Re-reading *The New Road*[1]

GERARD CARRUTHERS

Neil Munro's *The New Road* (1914) stands in the tradition of Scottish historical fiction, so deeply inscribed by Walter Scott and Robert Louis Stevenson, that deals with the clash of Scotland's history and modernity. This tradition of fiction, though, has lacked critical respect since the early part of the twentieth century. Despite the best efforts of commentators such as David Daiches and F.R. Hart to rehabilitate Scott and Stevenson, the view prevails in many quarters that Scotland's two most famous novelists wrote escapist romance where Scottish history was used merely as a colourful backdrop to whimsical adventure stories. If Scott and Stevenson are viewed in this way, their descendants in the early twentieth century fare even worse so that J.M.Barrie, John Buchan and Neil Munro are supposed to inhabit outworn novelistic romance conventions and noisy, colourful Scottish history, shown in the loudness of the noise and in the tartanry of the colour to be increasingly irrelevant.

The 'line of Scott' has been read as a more or less wilful evasion of the harsh facts of nineteenth and twentieth century Scottish reality, a childish avoidance of the horrible adult, 'modern' nation Scotland had become in the charge towards the British superstate precipitated by the Union of Scottish and English parliaments in 1707. Seen by its detractors as a close ally of the kailyard, the 'line of Scott' is said to dispense historical fantasy rather than historical reality and to be stubbornly anti-modern. These lines of argument are often parroted, but seldom elucidated in any detail. At one end of the scale the Scottish historical writer is accused of focussing upon minor, parochial, antiquarian details to the exclusion of the bigger picture; at the other end, the Scottish historical fiction-writer is charged with a somewhat kinky, at best morbid, interest in the panoramic picture, such as Jacobitism or Covenanting when the time for panoramic history is over and the real historical focus should be falling upon the history of the common folk and the big movements of social and economic history. That is, the focus should be on the history of the Clearances, or industrialisation, or cholera epidemics: the history that Scottish fiction is not really concerned with until Neil Gunn, Fionn MacColla and Lewis Grassic Gibbon appear on the scene.

There, have, however, in recent years been the beginnings of partial reappraisal in the cases of J.M.Barrie and John Buchan. To take the case of Barrie, the *chef d'école* of kailyard fiction, he is forgiven to some extent at least, for his novella *Farewell Miss Julie Logan* (1932).[2] This late Barrie, arguably, is an attempt by the writer to answer the critics who had so long and harshly savaged his output as parochial and unresponsive to the tide of mechanical change which had been transforming Scotland since the 1840s. To take one small but telling detail from the novella, Barrie features the great innovation of the postman's 'velocipede' coming to a small village in the Highlands in the late nineteenth century. When the contraption is broken down the villagers rally round in an attempt to repair it. Implicitly, this might be said to be Barrie showing that sometimes significant, transforming historical change manifests itself in quite small and gradual ways, in this instance with the coming of a bicycle. What Barrie also shows in this example is a community pulling together, or a community still a community in the face of the onslaught of nineteenth century progress. This in contrast to the views of Edwin Muir during the 1930s, who held that the Reformation had smashed any reality of Scottish community and that all Scottish 'individuals' were now sleepwalkers, cogs in the industrialist and capitalist processes of Britain with no minds of their own.[3] Barrie's novella, in details such as the bicycle-repairing incident, perhaps satirises this notion of the automatons that the Scots have now supposedly become. They are not really slavering automatons at the bidding of the slightest sign of progress (the bicycle); rather they exhibit human resourcefulness and curiosity. They are not simply at the whim of historical change; they can accept and control this change to some extent.

Farewell Miss Julie Logan also satirises the desire for concrete, unchanging Scottish identity so despaired over by Edwin Muir and others. It is a work both deeply dark and deeply farcical. Underneath the rural life of the Highlands he presents, Barrie shows the Scottish identity to be deeply trammelled. The community of Barrie's novel is beset by Scotland's troublesome history. The eponymous Julie Logan, it seems, is a Catholic Jacobite ghost though this does not stop the sexually-inexperienced local 'auld licht' minister stepping out with her for a time. Beneath such black comedy, however, as the hinge of that black comedy indeed, is the recognition that Scottish history and identity are hopelessly diverse and entangled. In the face of Victorian English incursion and ridicule, in the face of competing Lowland and Highland, Jacobite and Hanoverian, Catholic and Protestant identities, Scottish life carries on regardless, unable to be summed up in any one neat bundle. It is the suppression of elements of this multifarious identity, such as the minister Adam Yestreen attempts in his sectarian denial of the validity of 'superstitious' folk-culture, or that the Jacobites had any legitimacy in their actions whatsoever, that causes this character to be haunted by these things in the person of Julie Logan. It is significant, I think that Barrie is writing at the high tide of the so-called 'Scottish Renaissance' movement of the early twentieth century. The common hallmark of the thinking of Hugh MacDiarmid, Edwin Muir and many others was that Scotland's precise problem was that it harboured a fractured, contradictory history and identity. Such commentators idealised what they took to be an alternative possibility of an unbroken, coherent, smoothly continuous identity. In Muir's case this meant a starry-eyed worshipping of English culture. In MacDiarmid's, the rejection (at least initially) of anything that smacked of British progress – be this the English language or any kind of accommodation to British history. For both MacDiarmid and Muir at their most extreme, any failure unequivocally to condemn the modern state of Scotland and the course of Scottish history represented either an inability to think, or an engagement in cowardly lies. Barrie recognises from one side, in the figure of Adam Yestreen, the stupidity of trying to mould the reality of Scotland into a single entity. Barrie's uncomplaining recognition of the tragedy and comedy of Scottish history and his failure also easily to apportion blame – to the English or Calvinism or any single cause whatsoever – for Scotland's lack of coherence in *Farewell Miss Julie Logan* was the kind of unpolemical writing that would not go down well with MacDiarmid and Muir, but which today, in our pluralistic, multicultural society we are more likely to be amenable toward.

John Buchan's *Witch Wood* (1927), like Barrie's novel, is increasingly appreciated today for its portrait of a divided sensibility.[4] In this novel, seventeenth-century borderers live the life of pious Presbyterians during the daylight hours and indulge in paganistic orgies in the woods at night. The point of this scenario, which again we can see more clearly than did the generation fired up by the Scottish Renaissance, is not simply that the puritanical side of Scottish Protestantism did not provide for full expression of a complete identity, but that no systems anywhere in any country –

state or church (and perhaps not even folk-systems either) – provide for a full and complete identity which satisfies all of the people all of the time.

Neil Munro's reputation has yet to win much in the way even of the limited reappraisal that those of J.M.Barrie and John Buchan have begun to receive. I am tempted to think that it is the curse of the Jacobites which prevents Munro's *The New Road* from more widespread re-estimation, but then I remember that in recent years we've seen the growing, belated respect for Violet Jacob's novel *Flemington* (1911), very closely contemporaneous to *The New Road*, and on similar subject-matter.[5] The eponymous Archie Flemington is a David Balfour character, attempting impossibly to square the torn circle of Scottish identity. It is a novel, like both *The New Road* and *Farewell Miss Julie Logan*, which graphically deals with the darkest corners of human nature and which punctures any romantic acceptance of the myths of either the pre-Jacobite Highlands or the post-Jacobite Hanoverian settlement in Scotland. Human nature before and after in both locations is both good and evil, according to the personal predilections of characters operating in a state of free-willed morality. Taken together, writers such as Barrie, Buchan and Jacob all belong to the still unfashionable grouping of the pre-1920s and 1930s, pre-Scottish Renaissance cultural scene. Like Barrie, Buchan and Jacob, Munro is a superbly stylish writer, but he is not so largely notorious as Barrie and Buchan have been. On the one hand, a modern defence of Barrie is quite a daring manoeuvre since it has been so long commonly supposed that he is irredeemable as the originating architect-in-chief of Brigadoon. With the potential revisioning of Buchan also, we have the juicy figure of the Tory grandee skilfully helping to guide the cultural and political subservience of the colonies, including Scotland, as well as Canada. Munro's quiet day-job status as 'a hack' makes him not such a tempting, name-making target for the revisionist. The fact that he is not a woman, like Jacob, is the only reason I can see for the deserved reawakening of interest in *Flemington*, alongside the undeserved neglect of *The New Road*. What I want to attempt in what follows is something of a re-reading of Munro's novel in relation to its over-looked modernity, which will suggest both that the seriousness and fruitfulness of the 'line of Scott' in Munro is wrongly overlooked and that Munro belongs to the formation period of Scottish and western 'pre-Modernism' which has remained somewhat invisible in the standard Scottish literary history of the twentieth century.

Let us glance first of all at Munro's disputed literary status in the first part of the twentieth century. Like so many battles in early twentieth-century Scottish letters, one side of this dispute comprised, almost singlehandedly, Hugh MacDiarmid. In 1925 MacDiarmid wrote of Munro:

> Neil Munro is not a great writer, he is not even a good writer – at best he is no more than a (somewhat painfully) respectable craftsman… He has preferred the little wars of Lorn to the conflict of real life in which he ought to have engaged. His literature is a literature of escape – and, in so far as it has succeeded in escaping, in being a sort of antithesis of self-expression, a substitute for it, it is without life… [6]

MacDiarmid here was responding specifically to George Blake's admiration of Munro. Blake had written of Munro in 1919:

> Sensitive to the most minute degree, this artist shrinks from the merest suggestion of professed artistry. He has no mannerisms and no arrogances; he conceals the author beneath the mask of the journalist – he is a bundle of inhibitions successfully decked out as a man of business… His style was exotically beautiful. His romance was pure Celtic, fundamentally different from that of Scott and Stevenson. His plots had all the swiftness and fatality and economy of short story perfection.[7]

What both MacDiarmid and Blake are in agreement over is Munro's artistic self-effacement. With MacDiarmid, this is seen as a fault since lurking behind Munro's lack of 'self-expression' is a typically Scottish (neo-Presbyterian) failure to fully flex the imagination and, instead, a cowardly choosing to stay close to home in his subject-matter. Paradoxically, this staying close to home – writing about 'the little wars of Lorn' – represents somehow also, according to MacDiarmid, 'a literature of escape,' presumably because Munro's historical reflex in his fiction is seen as an evasion of the contemporary world (lurking close by is the classic anti-kailyard taunt of Scottish parochialism). Blake detects in Munro, as does MacDiarmid (albeit grudgingly) craftsmanship; for Blake, this is (rather anxiously) hidden, because of Munro's simultaneous existence as a hard-headed journalist and because of his inhabiting of the medium of 'pure Celtic romance' entailing, notionally, a tradition of storytelling rather than conscious, wilful artistry. Neither the journalist nor the Celt in Munro, so Blake implies, can admit to anything so embarrassingly egotistical or bohemian as working at creativity.

What we see in the utterances of MacDiarmid and Blake are two different views of the modernity of Munro. MacDiarmid, quite clearly, sees Munro as a retrograde, anti-modern 'kailyard' fiction-maker, as an altogether 'too native' writer. Blake, somewhat wryly, sees Munro as a hybrid-man, both no-nonsense journalist and no frills Celt, attributes which happily come together in the 'swiftness and fatality and economy' of his fiction. Blake is actually not sure whether Munro is modern or not and hedges his bets. Blake is not sure himself whether he is joking about Munro's 'Celtic' economical story-telling ability, though I suspect that he suspects that this emanates much more from Munro the hard-bitten journalist. For MacDiarmid, Munro's Celticism is something taken much more seriously and comprises a hidden, trammelled identity. With characteristically ridiculous audacity, MacDiarmid declaims against Munro:

'Had Neil Munro never learned English – and lived quietly in an entirely Gaelic-speaking community – he might have come to his true stature as an artist.'[8]

As indicated, I am going to attempt to take up a position in relation to Munro against the anti-modern judgement of MacDiarmid and beyond the fence-sitting of Blake. I do this first of all because Munro was, in fact, a hugely more sophisticated and modern literary thinker than people have tended to realise.

Munro's literary sophistication is seen in his address, entitled 'The Modern Novel' to the annual meeting of subscribers to Stirling's and Glasgow Public Library of 1906.[9] In this address Munro praises 'the Titan elemental genius of Scott' who is 'the father of them all' and talks of his love of Stevenson, but singles out for particular praise Thomas Hardy, Joseph Conrad, Rudyard Kipling and J.M.Barrie. Amongst all these writers Munro is concerned to chart the development of the modern novel. Here, however, is a passage that most people any time from around fifteen years after Munro was speaking would find wrong-headed in breath-taking measure:

Perhaps some of you may be surprised that I have not sooner introduced the name of Robert Louis Stevenson. There is no modern novelist I like better, but I think Stevenson's work, beautiful though it is, was not a fresh start, and so he does not quite come within the scope of my argument. He simply carried on the romantic traditions of Scott and Dumas, and brought them to that pitch of refinement where it is almost impossible to go further, and refinement is the last stage that precedes decay. And yet Stevenson, working in a convention nearly outworn, contributed his own share to the progressive elements of fiction; he took his characters off stilts in their talk, a posture they had somewhat too often even in Scott. The fresh start is more apparent in the work of Mr. Barrie. *The Window in Thrums*, and its successors are constructed with more art than the stories of John Galt: their humour is more refined than Galt's, though he has nothing like the sheer physique of Galt, who worked at his trade like a blacksmith. The charm of his work lies in his having tried to forget all stock situations and stereotyped characters and gone back to the native kailyard with *naivete* and fresh vision. His contributions [to the modern novel] rise in their treatment from the particular to the general and everlasting truths of human consciousness and human conduct.[10]

Contemporary revisionists of Barrie might do well to enlist and engage these comments of Munro. What I want to draw on from the passage above in relation to *The New Road*, however, is Munro's admiration of avoiding 'stock situations and stereotyped characters' and what he takes to be Barrie's appreciation of the 'everlasting truths of human consciousness'.

Let us also consider Munro's judgement of Thomas Hardy in the same pamphlet:

> He has made the earth speak as no other writer of prose in the last century did. Plains, valleys, cliffs and towers, dawn darkness, weather, and the stars are not, in his books, mere flatly-painted back-cloths, as the stage calls it, but have vitality, soul and impulse. His beautiful prose invests nature with moods as surely as the poetry of Wordsworth does, though it may not leave behind the same comfort and elation that are in the Odes (*sic*) on Intimations of Immortality. He has realised for us that the play of human passion does not take place in a vacuum tube, that in every form of being there is an active principle, that life animates all things.[11]

The misidentification of Munro as fundamentally a Celt plays its part in stereotyping the writer, as MacDiarmid stereotypes him, as a backward-looking anti-modern. However, Munro's skilful attention to nature, from at least as early as *The Lost Pibroch* (1896), results not from Munro's Celtic identity (though it is, of course, informed by his intimate knowledge of the 'Celtic' or semi-Celtic landscape of Argyllshire). It stems rather from a pre-Modernist sensibility promulgated by fiction writers like Thomas Hardy, Rudyard Kipling and E.M. Forster and by anthropologists like J.G. Fraser and later, in an influence I believe we see in *The New Road*, by the psychologist, C.G. Jung. In short, what is the pre-Modernist sensibility in western culture from around the 1890s to the 1910s? It is the increasing suspicion that the optimistic idealisation and pursuit of 'progress' stemming from the eighteenth-century Enlightenment is inadequate as the primary motive and impulse of culture and society. It is perhaps not until the cataclysm of the First World War, and the madness of its ruthlessly efficient killing machinery, that the belief in technocratic progress is truly shaken, but the full-blown Modernist reflex which this conflagration precipitates is prefigured by pre-Modernism. Pre-Modernism sees a move away from the Enlightenment-built, bourgeois, empirical, metropolitan-centred culture of the west and towards the peripheries, often the *non-rational* peripheries of culture, so that, for instance, we see Kipling's interest in Indian culture and, indeed mysticism. And we find an analogous move by Hardy in his fiction in the late nineteenth century with his peasant-centred fiction that precedes such a focus in later, full-blown Modernist writers like D.H. Lawrence and Lewis Grassic Gibbon.

If we are aware of the pre-Modernist context we begin to understand why Munro admired Barrie. Munro felt that Barrie shied clear of simplistic ideas of progress in human nature and society, and dealt instead with the so-called 'primitive' mores, the 'everlasting truths of human consciousness and human conduct' which were to be found among real peasant-people, the 'auld licht' communities of the north-east dealt with by this writer. Barrie's was a focus, we might suggest, on the unchanging bases of human nature rather than the pretence, engendered by both Whig Protestant and Marxist versions of history that the lot of mankind was rapidly changing out of all recognition. J.G. Fraser's great work of anthropology, *The Golden Bough*, published during the 1890s is pivotally influential in seeing the so-called 'primitive' human cultures as containing deep and universally acceptable patterns of custom. A little later Jung's work on psychological archetypes and on folk-memory plays its part in confirming the idea of the deep recurrence of certain myths in human culture, rather than seeing the intellectual, social and cultural trajectories of western civilisation as simply, rapidly progressive.

The pre-Modernist context is pertinent to *The New Road*. The great symbolic trick of the novel is to oppose the old and the new roads, where these do not represent any simple opposition between backwardness and progress. In the novel the young lovers, Æneas and Janet, discuss the new road. To Janet's avowed hatred of the innovation, Æneas replies,

> 'There is something in me too, that little likes it. It means the end of many things, I doubt, not all to be despised, – the last stand of Scotland, and she destroyed. And yet – and yet, this New Road will some day be the Old Road, too, with ghosts on it and memories. In a thousand years will you and I be sitting by Loch Insh -' (p.269)[12]

The old and new roads are variations on a theme like a Jungian recurrent archetype. The new road too will have its history and its ghosts given time. It will be appropriated by human consciousness in ways that go beyond its initial, merely functional motivation. The new road, then, does not represent the path of the new united Britain racing into the bright future, leaving behind the (barbarous) Celtic/Highland past. Time and again, Munro signals dissent from any such simple-minded belief in progress. Toward the end of the novel Æneas and Ninian are on their way home to Inveraray:

> Next day they got to Taymouth, where great woods were blown like corn and fields were flooded; the Road was soft as butter and their wheels ran deep, while, on the drove-track close beside, the folk who came to see them trotted dry of foot. At that was Ninian merry. 'There's our roads for ye!' said he; 'I doubt George hasna got the bottom though he has the breadth! The old folk werena fools!' (p.272)

'The old folk werena fools!' They had adapted their ways with more respect for the powers of Mother Nature than the builders of the new road. There is here an almost Wellsian note of man over-reaching himself with his technology, a note of foreboding about the confidence of the early techno-military establishment, represented by George Wade, which is chillingly appropriate for a novel written at the advent of the Great War.

Æneas stealthily observes the villain of the novel:

> He left the road and walked the grass, invisible to Duncanson, who padded on till he reached the bridge and crossed to the side his house was on. (p.312)

Duncanson, a man who profits from the proscription of Jacobitism so that he is able to appropriate for himself Paul Macmaster's estate, walks the road while Æneas takes to the grass-path at the side of the road (and this, of course, echoes the parallel running of Wade's road and the drove track). Duncanson, a symbol of the new post-Jacobite order to some extent, is evil. While Æneas, walking on the grass or the old way is good. Æneas becomes almost a ghostly presence, a representative of something old. That something old is goodness that is as old and enduring as evil, the novel tells us. The two elements co-exist in human nature in an endless struggle that is never to be resolved or never to be modernised. Good and evil are deeply present in the old history and they are deeply present also in the new ways. The new way or the new road is a new route only through the same unchanging moral terrain. It is not in itself, finally, any kind of new terrain.

We see scepticism toward man's technological sculpting of the landscape, in this case urbanisation, as Ninian Macgregor Campbell says of Inverness:

> 'It's a bonny town enough if one were looking at it from a steeple, but get to the guts of it and it's a different story.' (p.290)

It is humans who make the roads, the towns and the landscape to some extent, and their nature, involving the inscrutabilities of memory, morality and imagination, is always interfering with the merely rational, functional, empirical impetuses in the physical, materially-built signifiers of society. This apprehension, which permeates *The New Road*, helps us to explicate Munro's admiration of Thomas Hardy where he sees Hardy investing 'vitality, soul and impulse' in his landscapes. In Hardy's books, 'the play of human passion does not take place in a vacuum tube... in every from of being there is an active principle, that life animates all things'. Humankind applies a vitality to all around it, both to nature and to the new-fangled synthetic objects, roads, towns etc., with which mankind foolishly seeks, to some extent, to tame nature. Mankind

175

cannot escape this constructive vitality, which is ultimately imaginatively, as well as practically, constructive. There are ghosts on the old
road and there will be ghosts on the new road. Mankind cannot
progress from its essential myth-making, imaginative road-making
capacity.

Much can be made of the pattern of Æneas Macmaster's journey
away from romantic myth in *The New Road*, as he meets Col, as he
encounters Simon Fraser, as he witnesses 'the savagery' of the
Highlands – its people and landscape, as he comes to realise that his
father did not fall gloriously in the aftermath of a battle, but has met
a much more squalid end. This, however, is not the whole story.
There is a disabusing of Æneas's mindset in relation to the myth of
modernity also, as he realises the evil of the modern Duncanson and
as he realises that myth itself – sometimes as obfuscating lie (in the
cases of the deceits practised equally by the modern Duncanson and
the antediluvian Simon Fraser) – is with us always and will not go
away. In the positing of this apprehension we see Munro the pre-
modernist, the anthropologist almost, prefiguring the fiction of the
Scottish Renaissance in the following two or three decades; the
fiction of Lewis Grassic Gibbon and Neil Gunn, with their standing
stones and houses of peace, ancient mythic symbols which speak of
'primitive' human needs which have been neglected but which are
revived by the sensibility of Gibbon's Chris Guthrie in *A Scots Quair*
(1932–4) or Gunn's Finn in *Highland River* (1937). In his encounter
with a landscape that is a palimpsest of old and new, Æneas stands
as a forerunner to such celebrated fictional characters. It might even
be argued that Munro's depiction of the mythic capacity of man
clashing with the trajectory of modern rationalism is subtler than
that of Gibbon or Gunn. For Munro there are no particular magical,
symbolic power-sources, no talismans. Ninian thinks for a time that
he is protected by Paul Macmaster's magical nut-charm but finds
that he has not actually been carrying this with him as he has
believed. Rather every object, every old and new road, every old and
new history, is prone to mankind's primitive, morally complex,
myth-shaping hand. If anything, the new road, with its technical
teething problems when it rains, is much more a symbolic talisman
for its builders (shouting 'progress') than the old drove road which
serves the people so simply and so well.

Munro speaks as a pre-modernist and as a harbinger of the
Scottish literary renaissance when, in 'The Modern Novel', he says:

It is in the combination of romance, realism, humanity, and

poetic perception that, I fancy, the future of the novel lies; it is in the search for this combination in a skilful solution that I think the highest triumphs of the modern novel have been achieved...[13]

These categories – romance, realism, humanity and poetic perception – exist in a kind of warring symbiosis in *The New Road*. They are the warp and woof of the human imagination, the human outlook, the human ordering and manipulation of the world; romance opposes and also enmeshes with reality, humanity is both poetic and savage.

In situation and character, *The New Road*'s lineage in Scott and Stevenson is fairly clear. Little commented upon, however, is perhaps the strongest specific plot-debt where this is to Scott's *Guy Mannering* (1815). There is probably a borrowing in the paired symbolism of Munro's old and new roads from the Old and New Places of Ellangowan in *Guy Mannering*. More certainly, there is a parallel where the rascally lawyer, Glossin, has cheated his way to the estate of Ellangowan in Kirkcudbrightshire with fraudulent book-keeping, just as Black Sandy Duncanson (with a similarly sibilant, serpentine villain's name and a legal training also) has fiddled the books of Paul Macmaster's Drimdorran to his own advantage.[14] Duncanson's history is related to Æneas Macmaster by Alain-Iain-Alain Og:

He had come from the Lowlands, where, for some years, he had followed the law in an obscure capacity. There were Duncansons in Inveraray; they were a Campbell sept, but long established in their own cognomen. It was thought at first that he was a relation. But there was no connection. In less than a week it was known in the town that his real name was Maclean. He belonged to the Isle of Coll – or rather to an islet 'twixt Tyree and Coll, by the name of Gunna. His father had had a croft in Grishipol in Coll, and dealt in swine. He was a man of race by all accounts, declined in fortune – a kinsman of Lochbuie. Coll, at the century's start, was a rebel and unruly island, though within a strong man's hail of the Hebridean garden called Tyree, the holding of Argyll; there was always trouble with it, and the elder Maclean, to escape a prosecution, went over the narrow strait to Gunna and settled there, befriended by the Duke. (pp.295–6)

In a recent edition of *Paragraphs*[15] Rennie McOwan has pondered over 'the puzzle of Gunna.' Why, he wonders, is Black Sandy from a small, bleak, insignificant moorland island between Tiree and Coll? My own answer to this is fairly simple. Symbolically, on the face of it, Black Sandy is a shape-changing island-demon. He is a malevolent island-spirit, a Caliban. Allow me to stretch the analogy. Black Sandy's father is, vaguely and a little ironically, a Prospero; if not the Duke himself, he is at least befriended by the Duke. Duncanson the elder has sought refuge on Gunna from a 'prosecu-tion', but settles thereafter, it seems, to a good life. Black Sandy, however, is close to being the archetypal folk and literary bastard, with all the traditional Satanic connotations of outcast evil which this fact carries, someone whose real family name, Maclean, is disowned or not transmitted by his father when he arrives on Gunna. Hence, Duncanson's later ruthlessly nefarious pursuit of the toponymic, Drimdorran. The psychological roots of Black Sandy's ambition derive, perhaps, from his upbringing in an in-between place, bearing an uncertain name, but ultimately his evil is, apart from his material lust, largely motiveless. This modern, 'psycholog-ical' uncertainty and resentment of place though is equally an ancient, primal discontent. This evil, to express it another way, comes out of nowhere (or Gunna). And the problem of evil out of nowhere is a problem for modernity as much as for earlier incarna-tions of human culture and their mythic explanation of this existence in figures such as Satan or Caliban. Duncanson cannot bear being nowhere, or having an uncertain name, just as General Wade and the Hanoverians cannot bear the Highlands, generally, being nowhere so that a well-mapped road must be driven through the north.[16]

Gunna has strong symbolic undertones as an outcast place, but like all outcast places it is deeply mysterious humanity that brings the outcast character to Gunna, rather than anything inherent in the island that makes it so. Mankind imposes the myth of nowhere. What we see is the myth-making tendency of modernity that is as primal and often as iniquitous as any more ancient myth. What I've been driving at is the way in which Munro sees past and present as equally primitive morally or as equally mythic.

I have spent a little time on the symbolic location of Duncanson as this relates, I believe, to the larger symbolic framework of Munro's novel. The master symbolic trope of the novel, embedded in General Wade's new road might seem to be progress. Throughout the novel, however, there is a much more extended metaphor of *disconnectedness*. We see this in character after character. Duncanson is clearly disconnected from his roots. Æneas Macmaster is in ignorance of his long-dead father's fate and is untroubled in being disconnected from his father's passionate Jacobite politics. (I like the historical realism of this, the way in which Æneas has no interest in Jacobitism and the way in which in this instance change is surprisingly smooth from the old Scotland to the new Scotland. That people are resilient and adaptable is one of the messages of the novel.) We see disconnectedness in Primrose Campbell married to Simon Fraser, Lord Lovat, a woman who is dislocated from her kin in the cause supposedly of greater kinship, and who is dying of melancholy in the north. Perhaps the *most* connected individual in the novel is Ninian Macgregor Campbell who, in his unflinching but down to earth courage and sense of honour, is a near relation of Scott's 'gudeman', Dandie Dinmont, in *Guy Mannering* (something we see also in Ninian's wielding of his prodigious sword, Grey Colin, like Dandie's mighty handling of his cudgel). Ninian is a scout moving with facility, though sometimes gingerly, between various parties. He traverses between the Duke of Argyll and Duncan Forbes of Culloden, on the one hand, and Lovat on the other. He is the man whose shrewd actions and thinking allow Æneas finally to know the fate of his dead father, Paul. Ninian, the understander of the old ways, slips between Gaelic and English, between the plaid and lowland clothes and between the names Macgregor and Campbell as it suits his purposes. A man of Presbyterian religion, he is, at the same time, scornful of Primrose Campbell's melancholic Calvinist reading as she pines away in the demesne of the Frasers. He can be contrasted with Duncanson whose anxiety over a lack of fixed identity precipitates his evil actions. Ninian, on the other hand is genuinely more wily and Protean. It is through Æneas's partnership with Ninian that Æneas comes to knowledge, not only in the sense of discovering that his father has been murdered and attaining the legal evidence to regain his rightful estate, but at a deeper level he gains a knowledge of the lack of fixity in things, the lack of the certainty in life in any kind of romantic stasis which humankind attempts to impose upon its version of the world.

As Brian Osborne has observed, Ninian and Æneas are a variation on Stevenson's pairing of Alan Breck Stewart and David Balfour in *Kidnapped* (1885) in being not a Lowlander and a Highlander, and instead being two Gaels on the same political side.[17] Munro is subtle here because we see shadings of difference in sensibility between two men nurtured by the same climate rather than sharp division; we see human variety in the same place. It is here, incidentally, that we see a less immediately apparent, but deeper debt to Stevenson. *The Master of Ballantrae* (1888) and *Kidnapped* are of course influences, but I think Stevenson's unfinished masterpiece, *Weir of Hermiston* (1896), is a more significant point of reference. Munro speaks in 'The Modern Novel' of the way in which Stevenson deliberately degenerates the form of historical romance developed by Scott and Dumas.[18] This is best seen in *Weir of Hermiston* where, in spite of family ties between father and son, Adam and Archie Weir, and despite kinship between the borders and Edinburgh on the larger scale, no one fits together easily. Amid this disconnectedness, romantic myths of kinship and belonging cannot be relied upon. It is in this novel that Stevenson most effectively debunks romantic myth, a technique that Munro follows in *The New Road*. Everything connects less easily than Æneas Macmaster thinks and more evilly than he could imagine.

I believe we see something almost of Neil Munro the mystic in *The New Road*. Certainly, there is a lyricism prefiguring the animate landscapes, deeply entwined with the fate of people that we find in Lewis Grassic Gibbon and Neil Gunn. Æneas and Janet commune with nature:

> They were among a concourse of hills, whose scarps were glistening in a sun that gave the air at noon a blandness, though some snow was on the bens. The river linked through crags and roared at linns; all rusty-red and gold the breckens burned about them; still came like incense from the gale-sprig perfume. They sat, those two young people, by the fire, demure and blate at first, to find themselves alone. From where they sat they could perceive down to the south the wrecks of Comyn fortresses; the Road still red and new was like a raw wound on the heather, ugly to the gaze, although it took them home. Apart from it, and higher on the slope, a drove-track ran, bright green, with here and there on it the bleached stones worn by the feet of by-past generations. They saw them both – the Old Road and the New – twine far down through the valley into Badenoch, and melt into the vapours of the noon. (p.269)

Again, then, the old and new do not stand sharply apart. They run parallel and ultimately they 'twine' and not only physically, but in the human imagination which will, with time, blend and reharmonise the two seemingly different histories which the roads represent. It is interesting that this conception of futurity stands in some contrast to that of Duncan Forbes of Culloden as he converses with Ninian:

'...Ye saw the Road? That Road's the end of us! The Romans didna manage it; Edward didna manage it; but there it is at last, through to our vitals, and it's up wi' the ell-wand, down wi' the sword! ... It may seem a queer thing for a law officer of the Crown to say, Mr. Campbell, but I never was greatly taken wi' the ell-wand, and man, I liked the sword! At least it had some glitter.' (p.200)

Forbes falls back on ancient myths of Scotland's unconquerability: the inability of the Romans to subdue the whole of the 'Caledonia' and the allegedly treacherous treatment of Scotland by Edward I. The respective military might of each of these parties is trumped by Hanoverian technology. Forbes, truly it would seem, a compassionate man (who protested against the butchery following the defeat of the Jacobites at Culloden), is here unduly pessimistic and, paradoxically, over-romantic. We see him at a moment when the myths of the Scottish people, centred on the Highlands, seem to be in doubt. That myths are remade – good myths and bad myths – and that this process is impossible to gainsay – is signalled in a number of places in the novel. Munro calls his hero Æneas for partially ironic reasons. The young Macmaster's peregrinations between Argyllshire and Invernesshire are gently mocked by the implied comparison with Virgil's epic, classically questing hero. But the irony is really only a surface-irony. As in the case of that picaresque character, Don Quixote, an inner adventure belies the seeming bathos (the debunking of romantic myth) in the outside journey. Not only this, but the actual peregrinations of Æneas Macmaster involve him in a realistically difficult and treacherous landscape in the Highlands. Mankind will not do away with romance, savagery, myth and history. These things are perpetual and played out forever in human time. Here yet again we see Munro as a pre-modernist harbinger of the fiction of the Scottish Renaissance which skims back the thin crust of civilisation, of modernity, and reveals a deeper force: that of mankind's ceaseless myth-making, plotting, building, savagery and, sometimes, goodness. *The New Road* is a bigger and more intense novel than it is often seen as being. If we can properly appreciate its real complexities in patterning and symbolism, we begin to reveal also the very substantial literary artist who was Neil Munro.

Notes

1 I am grateful to the Neil Munro Society for inviting me to give a version of this paper as the Neil Munro Lecture at its annual conference in Inveraray in May 2000. In preparing this essay I am indebted to the Society's chairman, Ronald Renton, for lending me a copy of his highly insightful unpublished University of Glasgow MPhil thesis, 'The Major Fiction of Neil Munro'. (1997)

2 The modern reprinting of J.M.Barrie's *Farewell Miss Julie Logan* edited by Alistair McCleery (Scottish Academic Press: Edinburgh, 1989) has been a very welcome development, long overdue since this publication represented only the third edition of this work

3 See the long and diffuse outlining of this case in Edwin Muir's *Scottish Journey* (1935) and *Scott and Scotland* (1936)

4 See the modern edition of John Buchan's *Witch Wood*, Oxford: World's Classics, 1993 with its penetrating introduction by J.C.G.Greig

5 Another timely piece of critical appraisal for novels of this period is to be found in Carol Anderson's sensitively introduced edition of Violet Jacob's *Flemington*, Aberdeen: Association for Scottish Literary Studies, (1994)

6 MacDiarmid, Hugh, originally published in *The Scottish Educational Journal* 3. 7.1925; reprinted as 'Neil Munro' in *Contemporary Scottish Studies*, ed. Alan Riach, Manchester: Carcanet, Manchester, 1995, pp.18–23; p.18 and p.22

7 *Ibid.* (cited by MacDiarmid), pp.19–20

8 *Ibid.*, p.23

9 Munro, Neil, 'The Modern Novel' with The Report of Stirling's and Glasgow Public Library for 1905–1906 (Glasgow, 1906). Reprinted in this volume see pp.223–32

10 *Ibid.*, p.231

11 *Ibid.*, p.229

12 All quotations are from *The New Road*, ed. Brian D. Osborne, Edinburgh: B&W Publishing, 1994

13 Munro,Neil, 'The Modern Novel' with The Report of Stirling's and Glasgow Public Library for 1905–1906, Glasgow, 1906, P.12. See p.229 of this volume

14 See Scott, Walter, *Guy Mannering*, ed. P.D.Garside, Edinburgh: Edinburgh University Press, 1999, p.353

15 *ParaGraphs* Issue 4 (Winter 1998)

16 I am grateful to Jim Alison of The Neil Munro Society for drawing my attention to an anonymous poem, 'Albania' edited by John Leyden in *Scotish* [*sic*] *Descriptive Poems* (Mundell, Edinburgh, and Longman & Rees, London, 1803). This work is dedicated to General Wade and celebrates the 'future progress' of the Highlands in the post-Jacobite period. Against this contemporary optimistic myth, the less sanguine view of the post-Jacobite situation of the Highlands from Scott to Munro represents a very different line in Scottish literature

17 See Brian D. Osborne's introduction to *The New Road*, p.vii–xi

18 Munro, Neil, 'The Modern Novel', p.231 of this volume

JOHN BUCHAN[1]

Neil Munro's New Romance
(*The New Road*)

One of the finest romances of our time

(from *Glasgow Evening News*, 10 June 1914)

It is a privilege to be allowed to express my humble admiration of
what seems to me one of the finest romances written in our time.
Mr. Neil Munro is beyond question the foremost of living Scottish
novelists, both in regard to the scope and variety of his work and its
rare quality. *The New Road* does not attain the imaginative heights
of *The Lost Pibroch* – such a pitch can scarcely be reached more than
once in a man's life; it has not the bewildering rush and glow and
poetry of *John Splendid*, or the austere inevitableness of *Doom Castle*,
or the wonderful welding of landscape and romance of *Children of
Tempest*. But in the specific qualities of fiction it seems to me the best
thing he has done, so excellent in conception and execution that I
do not know where to look for better. I may be allowed to give in a
few words the reasons for my belief.

First, as to the architecture of the book. The theme is the
confusion of Highland affairs between the '15 and the '45, when
Duke John of Argyll was ruling Scotland, and Wade was building his
new road, and Simon Lovat was casting many lines in troubled
waters. The New Road fills the same part in the story that some
features of landscape do in the novels of Mr. Hardy and Mr. Conrad.
It is at once a background and a symbol, a mute Greek chorus which
emphasises the motive. The old world of the Gael is crumbling, and
lowland ways are creeping beyond the mountains. In the atmosphere of change and blind movement, Mr. Munro's characters play
their drama of passion. A good historical novel needs a private
drama; public events may colour and twist it, but the essential
conflict should be outside the main march of history. So when
Æneas Macmaster goes north with Ninian Campbell, it is not to
discover the plot against the Road, or Lovat's gun-running, or the

misdeeds of Barisdale, but to redd out the mystery of his father's death. This aim is never for a moment lost sight of, in as fine a tangle as ever novelist contrived. Behind all the plots and elucidations the reader is conscious of a deeper mystery, and waits breathlessly on the answer. So admirable is Mr. Munro's art that the full answer is delayed until the last two words of the book.

The characters are worthy of so fine a drama. Æneas himself suffers, indeed, the fates of all young heroes; he is less interesting than his friends. But he is carefully studied, and with his decorous civilisation and romantic notions he is the first to set off the squalor of Barisdale and the blackguardism of Lovat. Ninian Campbell, once Macgregor, is the true picaresque hero, kin to Alan Breck and John Splendid, but with all the difference due to Macgregor blood, his profession of 'beachdair,' and a subtler brain. He is the Gael of the transition, with one foot in the prose of the new era and the other in the ancient world of the midnight hills. What a fellow he is to take the road with! Patient, hardy, as full of wiles as Ulysses; brave with a calculated courage, infinitely humorous, and eternally the boy. He is the true fisherman, too, and in the midst of danger has leisure to kill a salmon. He philosophises as he walks the hills, and it would be hard to find a racier or more wholesome creed. Ninian belongs to the small group of the creations of fiction whom we long to meet in the flesh. The portraits of Lovat and Duncan Forbes are the best that have been done of these notables. Lovat we see only on his gross and devilish side, as the husband of Primrose Campbell and the lord of Castle Dounie. The other aspect – his astonishing brain and his curious power of winning affection – is necessarily absent; though Forbes proclaims it. Drimdorran, the true villain of the tale, is a figure that might easily have sunk to melodrama in less skilful hands. Instead he is tragic and uncanny, and the scene where Ninian finds him in the old house with evening candle burning to ward off the terrors of darkness, reaches the very apex of romance. The two women in the book, Ninian's daughter and Lovat's ill-fated wife, are exquisitely drawn. It is hard to choose when every situation is deftly handled, but if we had to select two scenes of the highest dramatic value they would be the argument on courage between Ninian and Æneas, after the fight by Loch Laggan, and the first interview of Ninian with Lady Lovat. As for episodes which have the thrill and surprise of good romance, they are found in every chapter. None perhaps is quite equal to the wonderful scene in *John Splendid* when the fugitives come out of the storm to the lit house of Dalness; but not far behind that masterpiece I should place the flight through the corries of Glen Etive, the scene by Bunchrew Burn, and the escape from the ship 'Wayward Lass.'

The style, as in all Mr. Munro's work, is extraordinarily artful. There is none of the laborious hunting for inapposite words which mark the common 'stylist.' Rather the narrative has the ease and vigour of living speech with an undercurrent of Gaelic poetry running through it. The landscapes are so clear and sharp that they remain bitten in on the reader's mind, as Mr. Munro is an adept at catching the subtleties of atmosphere. For example, when the first touch of winter falls at Bunchrew, with Æneas missing, depression promptly sets in; we feel that the adventure has suddenly become darker and more perilous. I am inclined to think that his gift of weaving weather and landscape into the texture of human life is one of the greatest which a novelist can possess, and Mr. Munro has it in perfection. With its masterly construction, its insight into character, its drama, its complete adequacy of style, *The New Road* must take the high rank in Scottish fiction. Nowadays too many novels are masses of undigested observation, not art, but the raw material for art; but with Mr. Munro a wealth of thought and experience is wholly transmuted by the shaping spirit of imagination. Too many modern novels, again, are concerned with matters which are practically irrelevant, which someone has described as 'hairbrushing in stuffy bedrooms.' With Mr. Munro we move among the high passions and the ancient and essential drama of human hearts.

Note

1   John Buchan (1875–1940). Scottish author, journalist, barrister, politician. Conservative MP 1927–35, Governor-General of Canada 1935–40. Created Baron Tweedsmuir 1935

The Humorous Short Fiction
of Neil Munro

BRIAN D. OSBORNE

Maurice Lindsay, writing about Neil Munro's Para Handy stories in his *History of Scottish Literature* observes:

> In these stories, as in the *Daft Days* and *Ayrshire Idylls*, we are once more invited to applaud the tradition of the simple Scot as a figure of fun[1]

This judgement, by a respected critic, represents one school of thought about the nature of Munro's comic short fiction and must be given due weight, but it is surely very wide of the mark. Leaving aside the bracketing of the very different *Ayrshire Idylls* and *Daft Days* with *Para Handy* there are two essential points to be made. The first is that Para Handy is, on any fair judgement very far from being the 'simple Scot' – think of his careful management of the owner and the owner's son in 'Para Handy's Apprentice'.[2] The second point is that the essence of the Para Handy stories is that they are written from a position within the culture and environment they describe. Munro does not ask his readers to applaud a figure of fun, he does not stand outside the stories (indeed often he is in them as a narrator), above all he does not ask the reader to judge his creations. Surely what he is doing is portraying, with legitimate fictional exaggeration and embellishments, some of the characters he knew, and whom his readers might find, on Loch Fyne or the Broomielaw.

This surely ties in with all that we know of Munro's character. George Blake in his introduction to *The Brave Days* says:

> Munro at home in his native town of Inveraray assumed none of the fine airs that might have been forgiven the laureate of that delightful burgh ... His dearest friends, the friends of his boyhood – two of them helped carry him to the grave in Kilmalieu – were a shopkeeper, an innkeeper and a plumber, and he was absolutely

without any sense that his vocation might be regarded by the world as finer or more dignified than theirs.[3]

Munro, in his writing as in his life, was not given to looking down on people, or seeing them as simple figures of fun.

Para Handy first appeared in newspaper form in 1905, in book form in 1906 and has been continuously in print ever since. History has a way of being a good judge of quality – these stories have survived when most humorous fiction from that period has not.

They have always been recognised as being something special. When Munro died in 1930 the London *Times* published a long and well informed obituary. Discussing the humorous short fiction it said:

> There he let himself go with an abandon which was impossible in his more serious work, but he earned the thanks of many who found therein a constant source of fun and enjoyment.[4]

The next day an anonymous correspondent contributed a supplementary appreciation which noted:

> There is Munro's own authority for saying that the little paper-covered collection 'Erchie', sold largely for the diversion of railway travellers, brought him more money than his more ambitious stories.[5]

Be this true or not, and it is, as the correspondent said, a reflection of 'our curious literary economy', it remains an interesting sidelight on the contemporary success of these humorous short stories.

The American scholar Francis Russell Hart talks of Para Handy's 'combination of stateliness and shrewdness' which carries the Captain through his life:

> ... helping the helpless with charity and delicacy, perpetrating solemn pranks, managing minor extortions, dreaming of Hurricane Jack's gentility, boasting of the breadth of his experience and the supremacy of his boat, a humane and devious sage in whimsical mock-romance sailing on small waters.[6]

One essential point emerges from Hart's praise. It is a point which will also occur to anyone who reads the stories with due care. That point is variety. It would be too much to say that Munro never repeats himself – but he repeats himself far less than anyone would think possible – bearing in mind that he wrote about Para Handy over a period of 20 years. This freshness and variety is probably one of the explanations for the popularity and survival of the stories. Of course, many of the stories are inspired by contemporary events and preoccupations and this has contributed to the variety of the tales. Quite evidently in Para Handy, Erchie Macpherson and Jimmy Swan Munro found convenient devices he could use to comment, in a light-hearted and entertaining way, on aspects of contemporary society, politics and manners that interested and engaged him. Thus Para Handy meets women timber workers during the First World War, Erchie reflects on Royal Visits and Jimmy Swan experiences the great Glasgow Exhibitions.

Hart talks of Para helping the helpless with charity and delicacy. Perhaps he was thinking of one of the stories linked to the coming of Old Age Pensions. Undoubtedly the best known of these is 'Pension Farms' – which is wonderfully and broadly comic. Para Handy explains the concept:

> 'Up in the Islands now the folks iss givin' up their crofts and makin' a kind o' a ferm o' their aged relations. I have a cousin yonder oot in Gigha wi' a stock o' five fine healthy uncles – no' a man o' them under seventy. There's another frien' o' my own in Mull wi' thirteen heid o' chenuine old Macleans. He gaithered them aboot the islands wi' a boat whenever the rumours o' the pensions started. ... It wasna every wan he would take; they must be aal Macleans, for the Mull Macleans never die till they're centurions...'[7]

He goes on to explain the economics of the Pension Farm:

> 'He gets five shillings a heid in the week for them, and that's £169 in the year for the whole thirteen – enough to feed a regiment! Wan pensioner maybe wadna pay you, but if you have a herd like my frien' in Mull, there's money in it.'

Now this is all splendid knockabout stuff – Para Handy as the story-teller spinning a great yarn which neither the crew nor the reader is really supposed to believe but which would have considerable resonances for his readers.

Munro's versatility was such that he could take the same basic idea – the coming, in 1908, of the Lloyd George pension of 5 shillings a week to 70 years olds and, in *Christmas on the Vital Spark*, create a totally different comic picture, and one which admirably demonstrates Francis Russell Hart's quality of 'delicacy'.

Dougie brings word to the skipper of the plight of Mrs MacLachlan, a poor widow woman of Crarae, who is going to walk Lochgilphead to go into the county poorshouse. She plans to walk there because, if she took the steamer to Lochgilphead, everyone in the village would know the reason for her journey and her pride would be hurt. Para agrees to offer her passage on the *Vital Spark* as far as Ardrishaig and warns the crew that they would have to handle the widow's feelings like glass. She comes on board and the skipper puts her at her ease:

> 'We aalways have a cup o' tea at six o'clock on the *Fitaal Spark*... And an egg, sometimes two. Jum'll boil you an egg... Everything's paid for here by the owners, we're alloo'ed more tea and eggs and things than we can eat. I'll be thinkin' mysel' it's a sin the way we hev to throw them sometimes over the side' – at which astounding effort of the imagination Macphail retired among his engines... [8]

Dougie and the Captain make up a kindly story of how they owed money to her late husband and scrape up eight shillings and sixpence. They also encourage her with tales of the delights and wonders of Lochgilphead:

> '... that's the place for Life. And such nice walks; there's – there's the road to Kilmartin, and Argyll Street, full o' splendid shops, and the steamers comin' to Ardrishaig, and every night the mail goes by to Crarae and Inveraray' – here his knowledge of Lochgilphead's charms began to fail him.

The widow is somewhat consoled by the thought of seeing the mail going by to Crarae and so with yet more eggs they get into Ardrishaig. Para apologises that she will have to walk to Lochgilphead.

> 'Oh I'm not that old but I can manage the walk', she answered, 'I'm only seventy.'
> 'Seventy,' said Para Handy with genuine surprise. 'I didna think you would be anything like seventy.'
> 'I'll be seventy next Thursday,' said the widow and Para Handy whistled.

'And what in the world are you goin' to Lochgilpheid for? – the last place on God's earth, next to London. Efter Thursday next you'll can get your five shillin's a week in Crarae.'

'Five shillin's a week in Crarae!' said the widow mournfully: 'I hope I'll be as well off ass that when I get to heaven.'

'Then never mind aboot heaven the noo,' said Para Handy clapping her on the back, 'go back to Crarae wi' the *Minard* and you'll get your pension regular every week – five shillin's.'

Out of a news story, out of a piece of social legislation, Munro managed to spin two very different stories – both humorous but one which also reveals a quality of insight into the independent mind of the widow. When Para asks if nobody had told her she was entitled to a pension when they knew she was needing it the widow body bridles:

'Nobody knew I was needin' anything, I took good care o' that.'

If Munro ever does repeats himself, then it is in Para's obsessive love for the *Vital Spark*. But this isn't really repetition – it is rather the running joke, the catch phrase. It is rescued and elevated from tedium by being totally surrealistic. Munro, as narrator, tells us that he knew the *Vital Spark* as 'the most uncertain puffer that ever kept the old New Year in Upper Loch Fyne,' Alick, the temporary apprentice, stretches the skipper's tolerance by describing her as a 'coal boat', and in the stress of storm even the reliable Dougie, describes the *Vital Spark's* motion as 'pitching aboot chust like a washin-boyne'.

To Para the slow, dirty, broad-beamed, workaday *Vital Spark* is a vessel of magic and dreams. He was as proud of her as 'The Duke of Argyll, aye, or Lord Breadalbane'. She was indeed 'chust sublime' – a gold bead about her, 'four men and a derrick, and a watter-but and a pan loaf in the fo'c'sle'. With such a command he could do anything, go anywhere – across to Ireland, to the far north – to 'places that's no' even on the map'.

Of course it is one of the curses of Para Handy's life that nobody else recognises that under the coal dust and grime of the *Vital Spark* lies a crack steamer. As he said one day when the ship had just been newly tarred:

'If ye shut wan eye and glance end-on, ye would think she wass the *Grenadier*. Chust you look at the lines of her – that sweet! I'm tellin' you he wassna slack the man that made her.'[9]

It might be argued that Munro painting Para Handy as the obsessive lover of his dirty wee coal boat confirms Maurice Lindsay's comment about us being asked to applaud the tradition of the simple Scot as a figure of fun. But surely Munro's portrayal of Para and his love for the *Vital Spark* is so warm and sympathetic that we are being asked to laugh with Para not at Para – and there is a world of difference.

The hyperbole which Para engages in when describing the *Vital Spark*:

'She wass that dry she would not wet a postage stamp unless we slung it over the side in a pail'[10]

is only equalled by Munro's own flashes of poetic description – he tells us Para had 'given her funnel a coat of red as gorgeous as a Gourock sunset'.[11]

Among the sources of humour in the stories are the internal tensions within the crew, the ever shifting pattern of human relationships which provides much fertile ground for comedy. At times this leads to hard words. In 'A Night Alarm' the ship's whistle goes off in the middle of the night. Kind words, polite requests to Dougie, the sleeping Tar and Macphail all prove unavailing and the whistle continues to sound. Eventually the skipper has had enough and swears to be rid of the whole crew when he gets back to Bowling:

'Not a wan of you iss worth a spittle in the hour of dancher and trial. Look at Macphail there tryin' to snore like an enchineer with a certeeficate, and him only a fireman.'[12]

But this is extreme. Matters seldom break down to quite this extent. Dismissal is not often spoken of and while dark references are made by the crew to the mysterious and all powerful 'Board of Tred' four men in a boat, just like three men in a boat, have to rub along somehow.

The most obvious fault line in the crew, and the one productive of the most comic material is the Highland/Lowland one with Para and Dougie ('a Cowal laad') on one side and Sunny Jim and Macphail the engineer ('a Motherwell man') on the other. But just playing Highland against Lowland in ninety nine stories would be boring – so the kaleidoscope is shaken up and patterns fall in a variety of ways. Sunny Jim against everyone – the chuckie-stane soup or the exploding sausages. Everybody teasing Dougie the mate – who is 'ass timid ass a mountain hare' – by pretending that the *Vital Spark* had been commandeered by the Admiralty to block the Kiel Canal. The crew leading Para Handy into flights of fantasy about the *Vital Spark*. The crew persuading Macphail that daubing his face with golden syrup was a sure-fire way of keeping off the midges.

And there is the wonderful story 'An Ocean Tragedy' in which a cockatoo, being carried as part of a farmer's flitting, expresses criticism of Para Handy's singing and in a moment of rage the skipper throws it overboard. The crew delight in tormenting the skipper, Sunny Jim talks of Para murdering the cockatoo and when Para Handy exclaims that after all it wasn't a human being the engineer asserts:

'If it's no murder, it's manslaughter; monkeys, cockatoos and parrots a' come under the Act o' Parliament. A cockatoo's no' like a canary; it's able to speak the language and give an opeenion, and the man that wad kill a cockatoo wad kill a wean.[13]

Even the normally loyal Dougie agrees:

'... everybody kens it's manslaughter. I never saw a nicer cockatoo either, nor a better behaved bird.'

Macphail – ever the Job's comforter – advises:

'I wid plead guilty and throw mysel' on the mercy of the coort ... At the maist it'll no' be mair nor a sentence for life.'

The 'Dead Parrot' sketch, of Monty Python fame, is not actually any more surreal, or more truly alternative comedy, than Neil Munro's 'An Ocean Tragedy' and its murdered cockatoo.

It is all too easy to put the creator of Para Handy into the category of a cosy writer about couthy things happening on a funny wee boat on the Firth of Clyde. However, every now and then a story leaps out and reminds you of the true extent of Neil Munro's imagination. One of the previously uncollected war-time stories – 'The Truth about the Push'[14] is a splendid example with its surrealism and absurdity. The essence of the story is a cunning plan, by a previously unknown strategic thinker, Johnny Carmichael of Glendaruel, to bring about the collapse of the German army by frying herrings, wafting the odour over no-man's land and enticing the allegedly-starving Germans to surrender and enjoy the delights of Loch Fyne's most famous product.

We tend to divide Munro into two halves – or into Neil Munro and Hugh Foulis. We say, following George Blake, that Munro thought little of the practice of journalism. We recount how he described journalism as the 'jawbox' to which he was thirled, just as a housewife was to her sink, we remember that Para and Erchie and Jimmy Swan were published under the pen name of Hugh Foulis, and perhaps we assume because of our knowledge of these inter-esting biographical and bibliographical facts that there is first growth Munro – *The New Road, John Splendid, Doom Castle* – and then there is the *vin ordinaire* of the humorous journalism.

While accepting that there is a hierarchy of quality in any author's work are we always as fair to the Para Handy stories as we might be? If Munro had never written any of the great historical novels or the *Lost Pibroch* short stories – how would we rate him? If we were to judge him solely by Para Handy and Erchie, how would he stand up?

Surely in Para Handy and in Erchie and in Jimmy Swan Neil Munro created a body of writing which would, on its own, have ensured him a distinguished place in Scottish letters. The market place agrees – after all for a good many years it was Para Handy that kept Munro's name before the public and the novels were only to be found in the second hand shops.

But is this so surprising? It is hard to believe in a Neil Munro who switched off his artistic sensibilities when he sat down to write a Para Handy story. As Lesley Lendrum points out in her biographical article in this collection, Para Handy first appeared when Munro was at the height of his narrative powers. The Para Handy stories were not a brief phase in Munro's career from which he moved on to do other things. Para sailed into print in January 1905 and nineteen years later in 1924 he was vainly trying to learn about the mysteries of radio in *Wireless on the Vital Spark: Intercourse with the Infinite*.[15]

Professor Russell Hart writes that Para Handy:

> ... is not out of place in the romantic ironic world of *Gilian the Dreamer*, Ninian Campbell, and *John Splendid*.[16]

Nor, it can be suggested, is Para Handy out of place in other parts of Munro's world. He is just as disturbing and iconoclastic a force in the quiet world of west coast shipping and Loch Fyneside villages as Bud Lennox is in the douce household of Daniel Dyce and his sisters in *Daft Days*.

Perhaps we should be less defensive about Para Handy. Perhaps we need to stop thinking of the humorous short fiction of Neil Munro as some lesser form of writing. If Neil Munro was somewhat embarrassed by the success of his comic creations and distanced himself from them by a pen name then that was his privilege. We need not be so embarrassed. To have created Para Handy would be accomplishment enough for anyone. To create three, different, and in their own way equally accomplished series of comic characters, to sustain them with skill and variety over quarter of a century, and to have them still enjoyed and loved seventy years after your death is more than most writers can dream of. Munro's humour has passed the acid test – it has survived.

Nor is it surprising that it should do so. It has immense variety, it has its roots in the real world and skilfully intertwines this with surrealistic fantasy and it is suffused with kindliness and sympathy. The

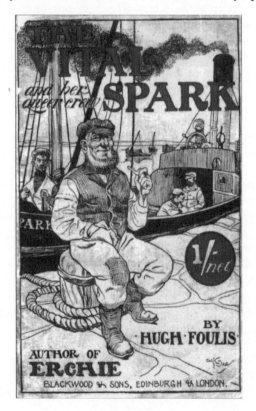

skill of the writing – a skill the more skilful for being skilfully concealed – is considerable. Take a passage from the very first Para Handy story in which the skipper describes the *Vital Spark*:

'There was never the bate of her and I have sailed in her four years over twenty with my hert in my mooth for fear of her boiler. If you never saw the *Fital Spark*, she is aal hold, with the boiler behind, four men, and a derrick, and a watter-butt, and a pan loaf in the fo'c'sle. Oh man! she was the beauty! She was chust sublime! She should be carryin' nothing but gentry for passengers, or nice genteel luggage for the shooting-lodges...'[17]

What is striking about this passage, and indeed the whole story, is that Munro has his characters and their ship fully formed and perfect. There was no trial run, no hesitancy – Para Handy came leaping off the newspaper page ready to sail the seas in a fully realised *Vital Spark*. The description of the puffer, the wonderfully controlled catalogue of its features, ending with the bathos of 'a pan loaf in the fo'c'sle' surely reminds us, if reminding we need, that Neil Munro did not keep his artistry just for his novels.

Notes

1 Lindsay, Maurice, *History of Scottish Literature*, London: Robert Hale, rev. ed. 1992, p.346
2 Munro, Neil, *Para Handy*, ed. Brian D. Osborne and Ronald Armstrong, Edinburgh: Birlinn, rev. ed. 1997, pp.46–50
3 Munro, Neil, *The Brave Days*, ed. George Blake, Edinburgh: Porpoise Press, 1931, pp.15–16
4 *The Times*, Tuesday, 23 December, 1930
5 *The Times*, Wednesday, 24 December, 1930
6 Hart, Francis Russell, *The Scottish Novel from Smollett to Spark*, Cambridge Mass.: Harvard UP, p.376
7 Munro, Neil, *Para Handy*, pp.122–5
8 *Ibid.*, pp.185–90
9 *Ibid.*, p.291
10 *Ibid.*, p.4
11 *Ibid.*, p.291
12 *Ibid.*, p.72
13 *Ibid.*, pp.153–7
14 *Ibid.*, pp.377–9
15 *Ibid.*, pp.398–401
16 Hart, *op. cit.*, p.376
17 Munro, *Para Handy*, pp.2–3

The Poetry of Neil Munro:
An Outline

BOB PRESTON

In writing his introduction to *The Brave Days* (1931), a posthumous collection of a number of Neil Munro's autobiographical sketches, George Blake identified the contrast between Neil Munro, the historical romanticist, and Hugh Foulis, the humorist and creator of Para Handy. He was, of course, referring to Munro's reluctance to acknowledge his humorous writings. Such, I believe, was also the case with his poetry.

Munro wrote poetry all his life, and shortly before his death he made a provisional selection of some thirty pieces, sufficient for a small volume As it happened, *The Poetry of Neil Munro* was not published by William Blackwood and Sons until just after his death in 1931.[1] (It was reprinted later by Spa Books Ltd. in 1987.) This selection, edited by John Buchan, spans a period in Munro's life of about forty years and seems to evoke the very spirit of *ceilidh* when 'down to the time of Burns there had survived in the mouths of the common people of Scotland a thousand ancient airs, many of them blown in Gaelic from the mountains'.[2]

However, as George Blake recalled, 'the Neil Munro of real life was the jolliest of men, friendly, simple, infinitely whimsical',[3] and not surprisingly he wrote much light-hearted, witty, and often satirical verse. Many of them were probably composed on impulse to record some passing event which either amused him or seemed to demand a response from him. Although quite happy to put his name to them, I do not believe he ever regarded them as 'real poetry', and therefore discarded them without further thought. Regrettably, many of these verses still remain hidden between the pages of long forgotten journals or in dusty boxes belonging to the archivist.

To trace the early influences in these divergent strands of poetry it is necessary to return to the Inveraray of his childhood years. Born in 1863, Munro was brought up in Inveraray, the 'capital' of Argyll, at a time when Gaelic was still spoken by the majority of its inhabitants. As a youngster he was always a voracious reader, being a regular customer at Miss Macleod's post office, where for a penny a week his first influences in literature were sampled from her circulating library. Undoubtedly, it was here that he first encountered Burns, as well as the earlier ballad makers. When not sat on the sea wall with his head in a book, Neil and his chums would have been ranging the hills surrounding Inveraray or maybe up to mischief in and around the tenement building where he lived with his mother. An amusing record of these boyhood years can be found in his poem, 'D'Ye Mind o' Auld Lang Syne?', sometimes called 'In the Gloaming'. It was first sung in public at an Inveraray shinty ball by his lifelong friend Charlie Maitland and is still on occasions sung in Inveraray to this day. Here are the first and last verses:

> *D'ye mind the days now run*
> *What rantin', roarin' fun*
> *We used to hae as callants? –*
> *Man, I think it was a sin!*
> *D'ye mind the tricks we played*
> *And the mischief that we made*
> *When the simmer days were darklin' in the gloamin'?*
> …

> *Envoi*

> *Now things have changed since then*
> *And the boys have turned to men*
> *And some are gone before us*
> *To the land beyond our ken.*
> *Some are scattered far and wide*
> *On life's rough and stormy tide*
> *Which is ruffled now and restless in the mornin'.*

Determined to become a journalist, Munro left Inveraray for Glasgow two days before his eighteenth birthday on 1 June 1881, where he took up a temporary position as a cashier with a firm of ironmongers in the Trongate. In his spare time he wrote a considerable number of short articles and verses, sending many to the *Lennox Herald* and other country newspapers. George Blake recalled how later in life Munro liked to reminisce on the first appearance of his verse in print – the publication in the *Oban Times* of a poem 'addressed in heroic terms to that hill of Dunchuach'.[4] It seems likely

that he was referring to 'Home', revealing the home-sickness
resulting from his self imposed exile;

> *'Tis ill to say it, for it's only a boyish softness,*
> *But standing at morning alone on Dunchuach high,*
> *To see all my dear place spread widely around and below me,*
> *Brings the tear that stings to the loving and greedy eye.*[5]

During the early nineties he contributed a number of short stories
to various literary journals, and in 1896 his real breakthrough into
the literary world came when these along with others were published
by Blackwoods under the collective title of *The Lost Pibroch and
Other Sheiling Stories*. John Buchan later described the opening story
of this collection 'as near poetry as prose can be without losing its
proper character.'[6] Many of them are embellished with fragments of
verse embodied in the text, a technique which he adopted for most
of his future prose writing.

Literary recognition was instant with extensive coverage in the
national literary press. The following year D.Walker Brown included
a biographical sketch of Munro in his book of *Clydeside Litterateurs*
(1897), in which can be found three of his early poems: 'The Story
Teller', a haunting tribute to Robert Louis Stevenson written shortly
after his death in 1894 which praises him in these terms:

> *O fine were these tales that he narrated,*
> *But there were others that he had in store;*
> *Ours was the gain had he a little waited,*
> *But now our ears are vain for evermore;*

'Flora in Urbe', a frivolous, and for the poet Munro, a rare
glimpse of Glasgow; and 'The Nettle', which he later altered slightly
for use in his book *The Clyde*, (1907), to illustrate how 'the Clyde
has drained these glens, not of water only, but of men, and melancholy broods among the shadows of Benmore as if it, too,
remembered lonelily the unreturning generations';[7]

> *In yon valley I had friends once;*
> *There I have friends no more,*
> *For lonely lies the rafter,*
> *And the lintel of the door.*
> *The friends are all departed,*
> *The hearthstone's black and cold,*

And sturdy grows the nettle
On the place I loved of old.

On 9 January 1897, at a meeting of The Glasgow Ballad Club held at the North British Station Hotel in Glasgow, Henry Johnston, the Club Secretary, proposed Neil Munro as a member. Other members at this time included William Freeland, George Eyre-Todd, Robert Ford, James Hedderwick, and Hamish Hendry; and in Munro's life-time would later include J.J. Bell, W.D.Cocker, Violet Jacob, and Charles Murray, to name but a few. Of the latter two names, Munro later observed how their Doric was an 'affectation', and although 'quite inoffensive', did 'not spring from the earth born spirit'. He considered 'the truest artistic expression of Scottish sentiment' to come 'from people unknown to fame,'[8] and would have empathised with a large number of the Club's members who were drawn from the local artisan classes. No doubt he reviewed and published the verses of many of these would-be poets in the pages of the *Evening News*. Munro remained a member of the Club until his death thirty-four years later, during which time no fewer than nine of his poems were published in the *Second* (1898), *Third* (1908), and *Fourth Series* (1924) of the Club's *Ballads and Poems*. 'Home' was included in the *Second Series*, as well as 'The Heather', previously printed in *Blackwood's Magazine* in November, 1896, and 'John o' Lorn', the lament of a Jacobite exile, which was also thought by John Buchan to be worthy of inclusion in his celebrated *The Northern Muse – An Anthology of Scots Vernacular Poetry* (1924).

'The Sergeant of Pikes', is a salutary reminder that mercenaries existed in the mid-seventeenth century, and can be found in Munro's first full length historical novel, *John Splendid* (1898), a tale of the Little Wars of Lorn, set in the locality of Inveraray.[9] It is a poem which moves with sure metrical control and is full of darkness and blood as well as zest and swagger:

The ram to the gate-way, the torch to the tower,
We rifled the kist, and the cattle we maimed;
Our dirks stabbed at guess through the leaves o' the bower,
*   And crimes we committed that needna be named:*
Moonlight or dawning grey, Lammas or Lady-day,
*   Donald maun dabble his plaid in the gore;*
He maun hough and maun harry, or should he miscarry,
*   The Hielan's, the Hielan's will own him no more!*

It was reprinted in the Ballad Club's *Third Series* (1908), together with 'The Only Son' and 'To Exiles'. The latter was sent to Blackwood on 3 January 1899 for inclusion in the February issue with the accompanying sentiment that '*Maga* must have many Scottish readers in India, Africa, etc, who will think fondly of this stormy, rain-swept land of their nativity, so I indite the verses 'To Exiles''. It is a piece of powerfully evocative writing as its third stanza illustrates:

> *Wild cries the Winter, and we walk song-haunted*
> *Over the hills and by the thundering falls,*
> *Or where the dirge of a brave past is chaunted*
> *In dolorous dusks by immemorial walls.*
> *Though hails may beat us and the green mists blind us,*
> *And lightning rend the pine-tree on the hill,*
> *Yet are we strong, yet shall the morning find us,*
> *Children of tempest all unshaken still!*[10]

In between writing further historical novels, Munro toured Canada in 1903 with a Parliamentary group as guests of the Canadian Government. They travelled across Canada by the Canadian Pacific Railway, which brought Munro into contact with George Ham, the Company's public relations representative, and the two struck up an immediate and lasting friendship. His warm and spontaneous tribute to George Ham in his poem 'How Laughter Came to Canada', was typical of Munro:

> *So wherever the C.P.R. lines run*
> *From Montreal to the setting sun,*
> *If there be folk who are tired and sad*
> *They will welcome George, the perennial lad,*
> *Georgius Rex – true King of Smiles*
> *Who carries laughter ten thousand miles.*[11]

George Ham later visited Munro and his family at their home in Helensburgh.

Munro's ties with his home town never slackened. He made frequent visits to keep old friendships alive and was still very much a part of Inveraray life, having a holiday home there for many years. As 'bard' of the St. John's Masonic Lodge of Inveraray it befell him to commemorate the diamond wedding anniversary in 1904 of Alexander Guthrie, 'Father' of the Lodge. The fact that Guthrie was tee-total was evidently not lost on Munro in the following quotation from 'The Old Master'. The reference to Altan-aluin is to the town's water supply.

> *I cannot dance, nor tell a tale,*
> *The master approves not of drinking ale.*
> *Gladly would I drink to his health,*
> *And his content, which is more than wealth,*
> *But if there be no ale or wine,*
> *How can I toast him for 'Auld Lang Syne?'*
> *The brothers laughed, and cried 'come fall in,*
> *And give your heart in Altan-aluin.*[12]

Munro's interest in poetry extended beyond writing it. He regularly reviewed the work of others, publishing much of it in the *Glasgow Evening News*. He also wrote introductions to *Selected Poems of Robert Burns* (1906), and *Scottish University Verses 1918–1923* (1923), as well as writing an appreciation of Dr.W.H.Drummond's *Complete Poems* (1926). The principal interest of these introductions lies in the insight they give us into his own work. Take for example his introduction to *The Old Highlands, being papers read before The Gaelic Society of Glasgow*, 1895–1906, wherein 'we have called our volume *The Old Highlands*, not, perhaps, so much because the greater part of its contents deals with bye-gone conditions in the glens and on the hills of our inheritance, as because the spirit which the following essays disengage is one of pride in the past and affection for surviving ancient things. The Highlands and the Highland heart are very old; they find expression in the oldest and most valuable monument that exists in this Country – that Gaelic tongue....' Although attracting a wider audience than writing in Gaelic would permit, the atmosphere of Munro's poetry invites the reader to experience the spirit from those ancient Gaelic songs of his forefathers.

In a letter addressed to Walter Jerrold, dated 14 October 1907, to whom he is returning proofs, probably in connection with Jerrold's subsequent *The Book of Living Poets*, Munro refers to a tempting salary being offered to him to become General Editor of all of Cassell's publications: 'Herewith proofs with a few corrections. The verses, with their insistent note of "Scotland for Ever!" hit me rather curiously today, when I am gingerly contemplating a very tempting proposal to pick up my tent-pegs and flit to London!' Munro turned down the post. But with what gusto does he react to a number of like-minded journalists, who in February 1911 turned their backs on Scotland for Fleet Street. 'The Lost Legion – Dedicated to our Deserters', is the light-hearted Munro at his best:

> *Just for a wheen English bawbees they left us,*
> *Jinked a' their creditors, took the Sooth train,*
> *A' their bit works and repute in a hankey,*
> *Never to venture near Scotland again.*
> *Well, here's to Hell w'them –* **we're** *daein' brawly,*
> *Sae lang's there's the heather, the hill, and the burn,*
> *(Wi' just a wee drap o' Auld Kirk to put intill't)*
> *We'll no break oor he'rts if they never return!*[13]

In his *Ayrshire Idylls* (1912), a sumptuously illustrated book of literary sketches, Munro moves away from the Highlands to paint some unconventional portraits of, amongst others, Burns, John Galt, Samuel Johnson and James Boswell. His last, and perhaps his greatest historical novel, *The New Road*, was published in 1914, a few months before the outbreak of the First World War, an event which inspired some of his most emotionally responsive poetry.

Until this time, the writing of poetry had for Munro been at best a sporadic occurrence. However, during the next four years he wrote some twenty or more poems of which sixteen were published serially in *Blackwood's Magazine* from April to August 1917 under the collective title of *Bagpipe Ballads*. Sometimes these are simple, sometimes they are written on a grander scale. Of the sixteen *Ballads*, nine are war poems, and record a number of contemporary events from these turbulent years, often based on his own personal experiences. Significantly, and as their name suggests, they owe much to the bagpipe airs with which Munro was so familiar: 'whether we are Highland or Lowland, the pipes – the only instrument of music carried through the battle charges of a world at war – speak to us out of our past, stir in us, whether we live in glens or cities, feelings strange and deep, ancestral ecstasies.'[14] His first poem of the war was the patriotic, but not jingoistic, 'Evening Prayer of a People (Sunday, 9 August 1914)', first printed in the *Glasgow Evening News*, and later reprinted on a postcard with the proceeds from the sale going to the Prince of Wales National Relief Fund:

> *Lord, from this storm-awakened isle,*
> *At this dark hour on land and sea,*
> *'Twixt bugle-call and Sabbath bell*

Go up our prayers to Thee.[15]

During October 1914 he visited France for the first time as a war correspondent and shortly after took over the reins of the *Evening News* as acting-editor from James Murray Smith 'whose nerves cracked up with the stress of these times'. In 1915 he was to experience the traumatic loss of his eldest son Hugh, who was killed in France on 22 September 1915 whist serving in the Argyll and Sutherland Highlanders. There seems little doubt that 'Macleod's Lament', a haunting, elegiac poem, written during 1916, owes its poignant verses not just to a fallen hero at the battle of Loos, but more particularly to Hugh's death:

When in that strange French country-side war-battered,
Far from the creeks of home and hills of heath,
A boy, he kept the old tryst of his people
With the dark girl Death.[16]

Munro revisited France during May and June 1917, and the impression made on his mind can be glimpsed in 'Hey! Jock, Are Ye Glad Ye Listed?'[17], and 'Pipes in Arras'.[18] The latter commemorates the British offensive during April 1917 during which the battle of Arras was fought, a battle with a strong Highland presence, on which he reflects after his own visit to the town a month later:

So played the pipes in Arras
Their Gaelic symphony,
Filled with old wisdom gathered
In isles of the Highland sea,
And eastward towards Cambrai
Roared the artillery.

His remaining war poems, which include 'Fingal's Weeping', 'Romance', 'The Brattie', 'Wild Rover Lads', and 'Lochaber No More!' are all included in *Book III* of *The Poetry of Neil Munro*, along with 'The Bells o' Banff', a simple love song with all the ingredients of a minor Greek tragedy, which seems to owe more to Culloden than to the Great War:

O God! My heart was like to break,
Hearing her guileless strain,
For pipes screamed through the Highland hills,

And swords were forth again.[19]

Other ballads included in this collection are 'The Tocherless Lass', 'Bannocks o' Barley', 'Monaltree', 'Wild Geese', and 'The Kilt's My Delight'. Whether pastoral or elegiac, songs of love or songs of labour, they confirm Munro's profound sensibility in remaining true in style and form to the songs of his cultural past.

However, his poetry of the war years was not confined to his *Bagpipe Ballads*. In 1917 he wrote 'Captain Clyde' which has more in common with J.J.Bell's *Clyde Songs* than the *Ballads*.[20] It gives some indication of the pressure of the times, having been hurriedly written whilst in a train travelling between his home in Gourock and the Glasgow office. As he acknowledges to George Neilson in a letter dated 8 August 1917, the verses 'are not quite satisfactory, as was to be expected from a hurried hack cudgelling them out of his head in the Gourock railway train at the last moment....' And for a rich example of Doric there is 'Rations – An Echo of War', probably written during the Spring of 1918 when rationing was introduced:

Nae meat on market-day for kintry folk!
They're shairly cairryin' war beyond a joke.
We micht hae tholed the want o' fancy breid,
Puddin's, and pastry – but the auld sheep's heid!
For forty years, ilk Wednesday, I've left hame
And come to Gleska wi' expectant wame,
For naethin' else but for a sheep's-heid dinner,
And noo it's aff the caird, as I'm a sinner!
No ashet brimming bounteous and bonny,
But organ-grinder stuff – their macaroni![21]

After the war Blackwoods continued to press Munro for more *Ballads*, but unsuccessfully, in spite of his many assurances, including that of 19 March 1923 that 'I am brimful of Bagpipe Ballad stuff, and realise a noble volume to knock all other Scottish bards since Burns out of time! The cursed thing is that editing a daily paper makes any consistent and steady preoccupation with Literature impossible'. However, there is evidence from his subsequent correspondence with Blackwoods that a few more ballads had been written, probably including 'Colin's Cattle', which contains the traditional superstitions of an ancient fairy song.[22]

Much of his work has been anthologised, perhaps most notably in C.M.Grieve's (Hugh MacDiarmid) *First Series* of *Northern*

Numbers published in 1920, which was 'dedicated with affection and pride to Neil Munro'. Significantly, Munro is excluded from the *Second Series* although perhaps not surprisingly, given Grieve's later comments in his autobiography, *Lucky Poet*: 'whatever use I had for the work of Neil Munro and others, I speedily lost as I got 'further ben' in my chosen task!'[23] The 'others' included John Buchan, Violet Jacob, and Charles Murray, who were of course, like Munro, not at the cutting-edge of the 'Scottish Renaissance'! However, Munro anticipated Grieve's rejection in his article of 4 September, 1919 in the *Views and Reviews* column of the *Evening News*: 'It is the modern fashion to ignore old songs or even scorn them openly: a suicidal fashion. It is cursing the breed of which one is born.'

And unquestionably, Munro was true to his birth and remained for most of his life, like so much of his poetry, a Highlander in exile. Therein lies the strength of his poetry and not its weakness. Whether in the narrative muse of the Gael, or in the satirical verse of the shrewd observer of life, to know his poetry is to know Munro, and it is well worth more than a second glance.

Lives of great men often remind us
We can make our lives sublime,
And, departing, leave behind us
Footprints on the sands of time.[24]

Notes

1 *The Poetry of Neil Munro*, ed. John Buchan, Edinburgh & London: William Blackwood and Sons, 1931. Page references to this edition are designated PNM

2 Munro, Neil, Introduction to *Selected Poems of Robert Burns*: Red Letter Library, 1906

3 Munro, Neil, *The Brave Days*, ed. George Blake, Edinburgh: The Porpoise Press, 1931, p.23

4 *Ibid.*, p.18. Subsequent research has shown that the first poem published in *The Oban Times* was in fact a narrative piece called 'The Phantom Smack'. It appeared on 3 February 1883, under the pen name Bealloch-an-Uaran. See *ParaGraphs* No 11, pp. 18–19

5 PNM p.18 This poem was originally published in the Glasgow Ballad Club's *Ballads and Poems* (Second Series, 1898) where the first line of this quotation reads: ''Tis ill to say it, for it's only a foolish softness.'

6 Preface to *The Poetry of Neil Munro*, 1931. p.8

7 Munro, Neil, *The Clyde: River and Firth,* London: Adam and Charles Black, 1907, p.138. Also see PNM, p.23 for a slightly different version

8 *Scottish Minstrelsy*, from the *Views and Reviews* column in the *Glasgow Evening News*, 4 September 1919

9   Munro, Neil, *John Splendid*, Edinburgh: B&W Publishing, 1994, pp.149–50

10 See PNM p.28 for a slightly different version

11 National Library of Scotland, MS. 26926 H42V–3R

12 See *ParaGraphs* No.9, 2001, p.5

13 See *ParaGraphs* No.4, 1998, pp.11–12

14 *Call of the Pipes to Scotland*, from *Country Life*, 9 December 1916

15 See *ParaGraphs* No.6, 1999, p.15

16 PNM p.52, where the title has been changed to 'Lament for MacLeod of Raasay.' See also *ParaGraphs* No.11, 2002, pp.5–9

17 PNM p.59

18 PNM p.54

19 PNM p.72

20 See *ParaGraphs* No.4, 1998, p.17

21 See *ParaGraphs*, No.7, 2000, p.11

22 PNM p.81

23 MacDiarmid, Hugh, *Lucky Poet*, 1943

24 Munro, Neil, *The Daft Days*, Colonsay, Argyll: House of Lochar, 2002, p.34

Thanks are due to Lesley Lendrum, Brian Osborne, Rae MacGregor, and also to staff at the Mitchell Library in Glasgow, and the National Library of Scotland for helping to locate a number of Munro's 'fugitive' poems

A Review of Neil Munro's
Late Journalism

BEATA KOHLBEK

After Neil Munro's death in December 1930, his younger protégé, George Blake, selected a number of Munro's newspaper articles and published them in two volumes: *The Brave Days* (1931) and *The Looker-On* (1933). Blake was the first and, until now, the only critic to review Munro as both writer and journalist. Since Blake's treatment in the 1930s, most scholars have concentrated on the historical novels and short stories, creating a rather one-sided image of the author and avoiding a confrontation with the Neil Munro who emerges from the newspaper pages. William Power who wrote a history of Scottish literature in 1935, shortly after Munro had died, still mentioned him as 'the most interesting journalist of his time',[1] but already in Kurt Wittig's literary history from 1958 no acknowledgement of Munro's journalism is made.[2] Also, more recent works[3] describe Munro solely as a novelist and often put him in the category of Kailyard literature alongside with J.M. Barrie and S.R. Crockett, the genre Munro did not wish to be associated with. Such treatment obscures the real picture of Neil Munro and requires re-examination. Indeed it is through the reading of Munro's journalistic work that our understanding of his attitude to Scotland, its cultural and social development, can be enhanced; furthermore, it allows us to see Neil Munro as he was seen by his contemporaries: as one of the central figures in Glasgow, surrounded by artists, writers and always at the heart of contemporary affairs. Munro was a well-known figure in Glasgow's literary and artistic circles and his newspaper reviews gave first-hand information about the cultural scene in Scotland around the turn of the nineteenth and twentieth centuries. His reviews and articles appeared on the pages of various British newspapers and magazines for nearly fifty years between 1884 and 1930. The readers of his columns were rewarded with Munro's never-fading enthusiasm for his country, as well as his crisp sense of humour and considerable journalistic skill.

In this essay I will concentrate on the series of articles written towards the end of Munro's life, for the *Daily Record and Mail*, under the pseudonym of 'Mr Incognito'.[4] These articles, some of which were selected by Blake for *The Brave Days* and *The Looker-On*, lay out Munro's views on art, literature, scientific progress and on his own life, and can be regarded as representational for his journalistic career. He began writing the column 'Random Recollections by Mr.Incognito' on 6 November 1928. The articles appeared every Tuesday and Thursday, although from May till June 1930 there was only one article per week due to Munro's fading health, as his doctor's advice was to reduce or give up writing. These would be Munro's final writings.

The first five articles appeared with the following subtitle:

Mr. Incognito, whose pseudonym hides the identity of a well-known Scottish writer, has for over forty years intently observed and noted with wonder, resignation, or philosophic amusement the ever-changing aspects of social life in Scotland. In a series 'Recollections' specially written for the *Daily Record* he reviews our foibles, fashions, and amusements in a spirit of gaiety.[5]

What the subtitle promised, 'Mr Incognito' delivered with great skill. It ought to be mentioned that the column was not an entirely new project for Neil Munro. He was the editor of a similar column, 'Random Reminiscences', for the *Glasgow Evening News* from 1919 to 1924, and in 1926–7 he wrote a series 'Something I Want to Say' for the *Daily Record & Daily Mail*; not to mention the 'Looker-On' and 'Views and Reviews' which Munro wrote for the *Glasgow Evening News* in earlier years. His articles in the *Daily Record* had been so popular that the newspaper approached him again with a commission for a new series. From Blake's introduction to *The Brave Days* we know that, despite the use of a pseudonym: 'The identity of 'Mr. Incognito' was never a secret to his readers.'[6] It is surprising that Munro chose to use a pseudonym for this column at all. Before he started to write as 'Mr Incognito', he wrote the column 'Something I Want to Say' and signed it with his real name. The reader of the column would have quickly identified the author of 'Random Recollections' as that of 'Something I Want to Say' as, again on the authority of Blake, Munro's style was so characteristic, that fellow journalists used to talk of 'the Munro touch'.

From the one hundred and forty four articles collected and deposited in the Mitchell Library in Glasgow, about one third were published in Blake's *The Brave Days* and in the *Looker-On*. The other articles have not been critically assessed as yet and no attempt has been made to publish another volume of Munro's journalism. One remarkable feature of these articles is Munro's versatile use of style. While fluent and crisp in its humour in some articles, it can become solemn and poignant in others, depending on the author's emotional involvement or personal interest. The humour surfaces best in recollections of his own childhood adventures and in the events he witnessed as a young journalist in Glasgow. However, when the subject of the importance of Gaelic or Scots is mentioned, Munro takes on a different tone, producing articles which could be easily viewed as serious essays on the languages of Scotland and their history. For example, in the article 'Simplified Gaelic?' from 20 August 1929 Murno's defence of Gaelic betrays his personal interest.: 'From 1515 down to our own time, the foolish idea, arising from educational basis, that English is phonetically spelled and that Gaelic is not, and that Gaelic spelling ought to be reformed on the basis of English orthography has lingered in many minds and has been a serious deterrent to progress in Gaelic literature.' Although not involved in the Literary Renaissance led by Hugh MacDiarmid which encouraged the use of the vernacular, with his defence of Gaelic, Munro comes close to the ideas of this movement.

Another subject interwoven in 'Mr Incognito's' recollections is the First World War. Neil Munro was a war correspondent in France and visited the country in 1914 and 1917. The portrayal of what he witnessed proves how deep an effect this experience had on the sensitive and humanitarian character of Munro. Again, the tone changes; it is not only serious, it is restricted as if trying not to give away the true concern of the author. The sentences are short and the words carefully chosen. About his stay in France in 1914 Munro says: 'A single hour in Boulogne made it clear to us that here was not a single thing to write about that would pass the censor, even had we the heart to write it.'[7] This sentence implies that the author of the article is also its first censor. Munro wrote little about his experiences in France and what he put on paper reflects his strong aversion to the events he had witnessed. There was also another side to his attitude to World War I. In 1915, Munro's eldest son, Hugh, then twenty two years old, had died in France at the front. Munro dedicated his very first novel, *John Splendid*, to Hugh. The dedication reflects the father's affection for his son:

...when (by the favour of God) you grow older and more reflec-

tive, seeking perhaps for more in these pages than they meant to
give, you may wonder that the streets, the lanes, the tenements
herein set forth so much resemble those we know to-day.... I give
you this book, dear *Hugh*, not for History, though a true tale – a
sad old tale – is behind it, but for a picture of times and manners,
of a country that is dear to us in every rock and valley, of a people
we know whose blood is ours. And that you may grow in wisdom
as in years, and gain the riches of affection, and escape the giants
of life as Connal did the giants of Erin O, in our winter tale, is my
fervent prayer.

This dedication was written into *John Splendid* in 1896 when Hugh
was only three years old. How bitter his father must have felt when
the son did not escape 'the giants of life' and fell in a foreign country.
He visited the grave of his son in 1917 during his stay in France.

In about a dozen of his 'Random Recollections' 'Mr Incognito'
returns to his childhood and the places in which he grew up. These
articles are light and entertaining and show a carefree childhood and
adolescence. Most of them were selected by George Blake and
appeared either in *The Brave Days* or in *The Looker-On*. The characteristic feature of these articles is that they often start with a loose
recollection about something which then leads Munro back in time
and back to his home town of Inveraray. One such article appeared
in the Thursday column of 'Mr Incognito', on 10 January 1929
when he wrote about skating and the coldest winters he remembered.[8] Starting with a humorous criticism of modern skaters,
Munro goes back to the days when he was young. In 1880/81 there
was a severe winter in Scotland and he remembers: 'How long the
frost held then I cannot remember, but I know that for weeks I
skated day and night, and felt I could gladly keep it up for ever.'

In the article entitled 'Our first 'Phones'' from 17 January 1929,
written only a week after his story about skating, Munro returns in
his recollections to Inveraray, this time to write about the telephones
he and his life-long friend, Charlie Maitland installed 'at least some
months before Graham Bell's invention was seen in Glasgow.'[9] We
recognise here Munro's fascination with technical devices and
inventions. In similar spirit, another article can be quoted. On 4 June
1929 we could follow Munro to the Inveraray election in 1878 when
the fifteen-year-old in his youthful spirit of adventure helped to tear
down the flags from the George Hotel which was the Tory party
headquarters. He justifies this action in a following way: 'In the
county town of the great MacCailein we were, of course, Liberals

and Colin's men almost to a man. Our headquarters was the Argyll Arms Hotel. The George Hotel, as Tory headquarters, however, got most of our attention.'[10] The last words appear like a hidden smile playing on Munro's lips and is a typical example of his sense of humour. In addition, we learn about Munro's dislike of his first job in the lawyer's office in Inveraray and of his first impressions of a prison which he visited as a child, probably in company of his mother.

Apart from these purely biographic references, the stories about his early years give an account of his first introduction to literature. In 'A Circulating Library' from 14 November 1929 Munro remembers a shop in Inveraray which was his first source for books: 'For threepence you could buy the yellow-covered 'bloods' of the Red House Library Series...' The real thrill came with the opening by the same shop-keeper of a 'circulating library': 'By this time I was almost fourteen ... I became the first subscriber to Miss Macleod's new Circulating Library, and the two books I carried off with me that evening were those classic hair-raising Gothic romances, *The Monk* and *The Castle of Otranto*.'[11] From his works of fiction, especially the novel *Doom Castle* (1901), we know how much the Gothic novels had impressed the author. He chose later to parody the Gothic elements which stayed on his mind from those early years in Inveraray. Another source of books in the small town was the house of the Darrochs[12] in which Munro's aunt used to be a housekeeper. The old lady of the house, Miss Lavinia, kept books in the attic library: 'When she discovered I had a taste for reading she would send me up to the library I have mentioned for such books as *Danesbury House*, *The Mysteries of Udolpho*, or *Pickwick Abroad*, which she guaranteed as 'much more amusing than Dickens'.'[13] Other books he read there were *Roderick Random* and *David Copperfield* which introduced Munro to eighteenth century Scottish literature and to the Victorian novel.

In 'Random Recollections' Munro used every opportunity to mention the development of Scottish literature, and, as already pointed out, he was very serious in his defence of Scotland's unique languages. These articles have an altogether different tone from those describing social life or entertainment. On 1 April 1930 Munro describes the literary scene in Scotland as follows:

For the greater part of a century [nineteenth century] fatality has attended nearly every attempt to exploit Scottish imaginative literature, otherwise than by leaving it to speak for itself.... In the last forty years sheer patriotic or parochial and critical indiscrimination have loudly proclaimed the superlative merits of scores of new Scottish novels and books of verse which already are quite forgotten. Most of them died at birth.[14]

His criticism is often aimed at the Kailyard and Celtic Twilight literature which was immensely popular at the turn of the century. Munro was always very forthright in his disapproval of Kailyard and the novels of 'Fiona Macleod' (William Sharp), as other articles and his correspondence with William Blackwood, the main publisher of Munro's works, can confirm.[15]

Besides the early introduction to literature there was another important influence in Inveraray, Munro's school teacher, Henry Dunn Smith[16]. It was not only his school lessons which left an impression on Neil Munro, far more effective was his love of the mountains and the Highland countryside. Munro later commented: 'I bless my stars that my first school teacher was a sportsman poacher!'[17] The dominie taught his apt student how to enjoy and protect the wild country and injected him with his own passion for Gaeldom: 'he loved the wilds like an altar and would keep them spotless'. Munro's diary mentions numerous trips to the mountains and lakes he undertook when already living and working in Glasgow. The Highlands offered a welcome escape from the busy city life. He never missed an opportunity of going out of the city and it was his deep wish to live in the country. One of the entries in the diary expresses the wish of 'relinquishing journalism wholly & writing stories for living altogether in the country, preferably somewhere on Lochfyne [sic].'[18] In his novels Munro often depicts the beauty of the Highlands and sets it in contrast with human nature. In one of his best novels, *The New Road* (1914), the 'proud petty chiefs' are undeserving of the landscape they live in and young Æneas Macmaster is disgusted with their readiness for money-making at the expense of Highland landscape.

One of 'Mr Incognito's' best articles was not reprinted in Blake's selections. It is a description of the four-day journey across Scotland which Munro undertook as a journalist for *Glasgow Evening News* and recollected in article No. 58 of 20 June 1929. In June 1906 he was invited to join the 674.5 mile 'Reliability Trial' which was also his first car journey ever. The article reveals Munro's journalistic craft. It is exciting, humorous and provides an interesting insight into the Scotland of the time. The journey took Munro from Glasgow through Edinburgh and Stirling, to Perth and up north to the Devil's Elbow, through Tomintoul to Grantown-on-Spey, then south to Pitlochry, Killiecrankie, Inveraray, through the 'Rest-and-be-Thankful' pass and back to Glasgow on the fourth day. Munro was amazed to be able to see so much of Scotland in such a brief period of time. His article written twenty three years later shows how fresh his memory was and what an impact the ride had on his imagination:

> Scotland, whose geography had been a torture to my innocent youth, was for the first time revealed as something compact and comprehensible; speeding over it on air, we seemed to see it as the wild bird sees it when it flies in the empyrean, over valley, mountain, lake, and forest.
>
> Now we knew what made our country's history – it was those alluring and fertile straths; it was those broad rivers; it was those high passes between mountain wilds. And now we knew the deeper meaning of The Road; we saw The Road for the first time not as a variety of fortuitous and brief bands of macadam, rambling from one place to another, but as the land's arterial system, a vital thing and endless, the greatest thing in our inheritance, to be loved and nourished.[19]

One can see how this car journey across Scotland found reflection in *The New Road*, written eight years later and focusing on the building of the road through the heart of Scotland. The young hero of the novel, Æneas Macmaster, travels across the country and discovers it very much like the author of the novel discovered it in 1906.

Despite his great interest in progress and development, Munro never forgot their potential to spoil nature. His preferences were always with the latter. When talking about the building of new roads in order to make the Highlands accessible to buses and cars, Munro recognises the danger of cutting through mountains and valleys which are the natural environment of deer and other wildlife. In the article from 23 May 1929 Munro comments on the new road over 'Rest-and-be-Thankful', the picturesque pass between Glen Croe and Glen Kinglas on the way from Glasgow to Inveraray. He outlines the history of that particular track and describes how famous writers travelled along it. Samuel Johnson and James Boswell rode on horseback in 1773 as did Robert Burns and, later, Wordsworth. To Munro the building of a modern road and the new means of travel had robbed the landscape of its romantic, dangerous aspect. A similar regret was discovered by Munro in an older account of the Highlands.

In the article entitled 'Over the Rest' from 23 May 1929 and in 'Rural Preservation' from 22 October 1929 Munro refers to the nineteenth century *Circuit Journeys* by Lord Cockburn[20]. He shares many of Cockburn's views, such as opposing building of railways and canals through Scotland because of their negative effect on the land. Munro quotes Cockburn: 'In 1838 he [Cockburn] was already at the stage of revolt against such innovations as 'railways, and canals, and steamers, and all those devices for sinking hills, and raising valleys, and destroying solitude and nature', and rejoiced to think that the view from Rest-and-Be-Thankful, Glen Croe, would never be vulgarised by any of those intrusions.' And he adds with a dose of cynicism: 'I used to feel like that, myself, about Glencroe, little guessing that neither railway, steamer nor canal was to be feared, but the highway itself, over which Cockburn, with his grand carriage, outriders, trumpeters, macer, and Court staff from Edinburgh, ambled so agreeably.'[21] Munro builds on Cockburn's fear of new technical developments destroying the rural landscape of Scotland. In the 1920s, he experienced the new threat of motor cars and road building through the most secluded parts of the Highlands. It is only from today's perspective, that we can recognise how prophetic and justified indeed this early fear of Munro's was.

The love of the countryside, of lakes and mountains amongst which he spent his life, is a *leitmotif* in Munro's writings. From this interest rises another, namely his careful approach to new developments. It is not sentimentalism speaking through Neil Munro when he defends the unspoilt Highlands from the intrusion of roads, cars and all they bring with them. On the contrary, Munro speaks as a modern and forward-looking man. Munro is a fore-runner of today's environmentalists. Such should be the interpretation of the following comment Munro made in 'Rural Preservation': 'He [Cockburn] could not anticipate an age when the shores of Loch Lomond should be frightfully soiled by the litter left by the multitude frequenting it in search of natural beauty, nor the intrusion – doubtless transient – of outrageously inelegant advertisement hoardings and petrol pumps on lovely rural scenes.'[22]

As much as he was a lover of the Scottish countryside, Munro was also a city man. Abandoning the theme of Inveraray and the Highlands, a later section of articles takes us to Glasgow. The city known to Munro like no other had no secrets from him. As 'Mr Incognito' he reviews the events and people from the time when he arrived in Glasgow in 1881 to the days when the articles were written. To the readership of the *Daily Record and Mail* these would have been the most entertaining and interesting of the articles in the series. Today, they are important documents in the history of Glasgow. Out of the one hundred and forty four articles by 'Mr Incognito' about one third are either about the city or set there. The tone in which the author writes about Glasgow expresses his pride and admiration of it, not forgetting to criticise it when the occasion arises. It is typical for Munro to criticise what he loved best, although his criticism is always benevolent.

The opening article in the series of 'Random Recollections' of 6 November 1928 goes back to the last years of the nineteenth century when the world was witnessing the introduction of the Röntgen or X-rays and of the first gramophones. Munro mentions his friend Dr John MacIntyre who, like Munro himself, was very keen on inventions and made his own gramophone records as well as having an X-ray machine at home. There is a delightful scene where Munro describes an evening in MacIntyre's house in Glasgow in company of the famous novelist Joseph Conrad:

> Following dinner at 179 Bath Street one night in September, 1898, Joseph Conrad was entertained till one a.m. in a fashion which the novelist gleefully recounted in a letter to his friend Edward Garnett a few days later. All the best 'celebrity' records in the doctor's private repertoire, all the wizardry of Röntgen rays were turned on. I stood in front of a fluorescent screen behind which Conrad and the Doctor contemplated my ribs and backbone, the more opaque portions of my viscera, my Waterbury watch and what coins were in my pocket.[23]

This article is characteristic of 'Mr Incognito's' recollections of an earlier Glasgow. It not only mentions events, but also the people and places he visited, giving the whole article a distinctive air of the old days. It also describes Munro's first meeting with Joseph Conrad. Conrad was already a renowned writer while Munro had only just published *The Lost Pibroch* (1896) and *John Splendid* (1898). This did not prevent the two writers developing a friendly relationship and enjoying each other's society so much that, on Conrad's next visit to Glasgow where he was boarding the ship to America, they were photographed together.[24]

Next to the entertaining articles like the above, which betray Munro's readiness to experiment with new devices or techniques, there are those dealing with the art scene of Glasgow towards the end of the nineteenth and in the early twentieth century. Again, Munro was at the very heart of the artistic scene; personally acquainted with painters, attending exhibitions and assessing new trends. He was a member of the Glasgow Art Club and a regular visitor to galleries and museums. He sat for his portrait to William Strang and wrote about many contemporary Scottish artists, for example Sir Muirhead Bone, of whom Munro thought very highly, but also about the growing popularity of Whistler and Edward Hornel. In one article especially his deep interest in contemporary art is presented to us. On 18 April 1929 an article about the 'Glasgow School' of painting appeared in the *Daily Record* in which 'Mr Incognito' described the beginnings and development of this artistic movement formed in Glasgow in the 1880s. Munro describes one episode from this time: 'One day in 1889 or 1890, the 'regular art man' on a Glasgow paper came to me shortly before the exhibition season, somewhat distressed about two young fellows whose studio he had been visiting to see what they intended to send to the Institute.'[25] Did his colleague see in Munro some kind of authority in the question of art? He was still a very young journalist at the age of 26 or 27, but already a member of the Glasgow Art Club. The two young painters who, according to Munro, belonged to the new school of painting were George Henry and Edward Hornel. He further describes the growing interest of foreign art critics in the new movement, betraying his pride in the popularity of Scottish painting in London and on the continent. In another article[26] further painters are mentioned; personal friends of Neil Munro: James Stuart Park and David Gauld, were both associated with the 'Glasgow School'. Gauld was also a friend of Charles Rennie Mackintosh.

An even more obvious area of interest to Neil Munro was the world of newspapers and journalism. He illustrates the situation of Glasgow's journalism:

A little less than a century ago, social and personal intelligence, humour, satire, poetry, signed or pseudonymous special articles, short stories or serial fiction – any kind of writing at all deliberately unconventional, amusing, artistic, or instructive, was rarely to be found in daily newspapers, either morning or evening. In Scotland, particularly, the daily newspaper was compiled exclusively for middle-aged gentlemen with square hats and 'a stake in the country.'[27]

From this opening of his article we can see what sparked Munro's own interest in journalism. He was not interested in writing dry factual accounts about politics, commerce and legal cases, addressing only a narrow readership; on the contrary, what Munro always wanted to achieve, was to entertain, to write with humour and satire, to be poetic when the theme allowed it and to offer a wide range of articles in which every reader could find something. This type of journalism did not emerge until the 1890s and Munro was one of the first journalists to grasp the opportunity. Writing about the 'new journalism' in 1929, he mentioned the names of some short-lived periodicals offering young journalists a chance to try out their talents. Names such as *The Bailie, The Chiel* and *Quiz* are mentioned and it is very probable that Neil Munro contributed to all of them. He describes the journalists who wrote for these periodicals: 'They were, in the main, on the staffs of Glasgow daily journals – young men delighted to find such an opening for freelance work more merrily to be undertaken, more conductive to imagination and originality than the routine work by which they earned very modest salaries.'[28] This was also his situation. In 1887 Munro resumed his work for the *Evening News* after a short spell of writing for the *Falkirk Herald*. The columns he had to write at the beginning were sports and cultural events. In 1888 he was appointed Chief Reporter of the *Evening News* and started writing a 'leader per day' as his diary informs us. Even as a Chief Reporter he had to write about current events and did not have the freedom to write what he chose to. Naturally, Munro welcomed the opportunity to contribute to other papers with more unconventional articles or short stories. Also in his diary, we find a note from August 1891 mentioning his publications in *Quiz* – one of the new type of magazines. There is no mention of *The Bailie* or *The Chiel* and we cannot be entirely sure whether Munro wrote for them or not. The articles of young journalists were published anonymously which leaves room for some speculation whether they contain some written by our author.

St. Mungo, the last periodical mentioned in this article creates a new challenge for a Munro scholar. It is said to have appeared for only a year and it was edited 'somewhat too casually by the late Hugh Foulis'. A question emerges, whether Neil Munro alias 'Mr Incognito' refers to himself. This would mean that he had ventured into an entirely new project by trying to run a new periodical. When reading about the launch of *St. Mungo* one cannot resist thinking that it was a launch to Neil Munro's taste: 'About the hour of noon, which was appointed for this cheap publicity, two formidable six inch calibre mortars were hoisted to the roof by block and primed by three of Barlow's pyrotechnic experts.... The first discharge from one of the mortars shook the whole central division of the city'. He also mentions the editor of *St. Mungo* again, probably himself: 'As for the police... they were placated in Gaelic by the editor and presented with the first free copies of the first Glasgow humorous journal'[29]; Munro was also a Gaelic speaker, which again seems to indicate that it was he who had to cope with the police at the unusual launch.

From the Glasgow articles we gain a fuller picture of their author. We find him visiting a Gaelic church in Glasgow which would have reminded him of the community in Inveraray where he grew up and helped him to keep in touch with the language. We see him drinking tea in the first tea-houses of the city such as Miss Cranston's Tea Rooms and going out with painters and other artists. He remembers the Scottish Repertory Theatre with which he was associated at the time.[30] The Scottish Repertory Theatre was launched in 1909 and closed at the outbreak of war in 1914 and Munro wrote his only finished play for performance by this company. The play was successfully performed in 1909 but never published. Called *Macpherson*, it is a romantic comedy set mainly in Glasgow. Experiments with literary genres were not new to Munro and *Macpherson* was not his only attempt at drama. He started drama-tising his novel, *The Daft Days* (1907), and the manuscript of this project is available in the National Library of Scotland. However, it was not always his own material he worked with. 'Mr Incognito' tells us about another project in which he was asked by the director of the Grand Theatre in Glasgow to rewrite Fred Lock's *The Babes in the Wood*, with the following result: 'When I was finished cobbling *The Babes* there was not an original line of Lock's surviving, and the plot, as disclosed at the opening of December 15, at the Grand, would seem to him a daring innovation.'[31]

Journalism was certainly a natural milieu for Neil Munro. He knew how to keep a reader entertained, interested and how to touch deeper emotions. The column of 'Random Recollections by Mr Incognito' deals exclusively with the late nineteenth and early twentieth centuries and the articles often illustrate local events and characters of no immediate relevance to a reader at the beginning of the twenty first century, yet the charm of their author's humour and style makes them irresistible. Today's readers profit from his jour-nalism in two ways: it helps to picture the time and place in which the writer Neil Munro lived and it is a unique source of information regarding the sources of his inspiration and ideas. The reader of 'Mr Incognito's' recollections is rewarded with stories which were clearly re-used by Munro in his fiction writing. One such inspiration was his journey to the Outer Hebrides. In August 1901 Neil Munro was invited to accompany a school inspector on his journey to the Outer Hebrides. This journey inspired an immediate and powerful response in his fiction writing. The accounts given by 'Mr Incognito' of this journey are a revelation to a reader of Munro's novel *Children of Tempest*.[32] The novel was published in 1903 and is clearly based on Munro's experience on the islands. Especially important was Munro's acquaintance with Father Allan McDonald from Eriskay who is the prototype of Father Ludovick in the novel. Other articles will show how Munro got his ideas for creating such characters as the famous Para Handy, or John Latimer, the Glasgow engineer in *Macpherson*.

For a student of literature the articles containing comments on and recollections of Munro's contemporary writers are of great importance. He knew famous literary figures such as Joseph Conrad, Cunninghame Graham and the younger writers: Hugh MacDiarmid, John Buchan, George Douglas Brown and John Macdougall Hay. The last dedicated his novel, *Gillespie*, to Munro and even Hugh MacDiarmid who was to criticise Munro in later years, dedicated his collection *Northern Numbers* to Munro and included poems by Munro as one of the leading Scottish writers. Munro highly admired the work of some of his colleagues and praised (in an article from 1 April 1930) *The House with the Green Shutters* as a work of a prodigious writer. He never felt that Scottish literature needed a 'Renaissance' because the tradition of Scottish writing was of a permanent quality. However, Munro could also be critical. He did not approve of the 'Celtic Renaissance' movement initiated by Prof. Patrick Geddes and laughed at the pretentious Gaelic heritage of 'Fiona MacLeod':

> Every successive book of 'Fiona' had made it more obvious to him [Munro] that the author's inspiration came almost entirely from Irish and Scandinavian sources; that the topographical knowledge displayed in the stories was merely as much as could be got from a few trips on the *Claymore* or *Clansman*; and that a Gaelic dictionary and a 'Guide to Gaelic Conversation' were responsible for all the Gaelic phrases with which the books were recklessly inter-larded to maintain the illusion that here was the voice of the veritable Gael.[33]

Munro's vantage-point as novelist and journalist reviewing numerous new Scottish works allowed him to view the scene of Scottish literature with a unique insight. From his early correspondence with the publisher of Munro's first short stories and novels, William Blackwood, we know that he used that position to separate himself from the Kailyard school of writing and also from Fiona MacLeod's 'Celtic Twilight'.

'Mr Incognito's' column appeared regularly twice a week, every Tuesday and Thursday for about a year and a half. From May 1930 the Thursday articles are often missing, a sign of Munro's declining health. Lesley Lendrum, Neil Munro's granddaughter, has kindly supplied a copy of Munro's letter to a friend, dated 14 June 1930, in which the writer describes his health condition and the doctor's advice to reduce his writing: 'For the past year I have been reducing my writing to one article a week, but even that is now forbidden me as well as one business meeting a week which took me to Glasgow.' Munro was writing more than one article per week until May 1930. However, in June his condition must have worsened and the author followed his doctor's advice strictly. On the 24 June 1930 the last article by 'Mr Incognito' appeared on the pages of the *Daily Record and Mail*. The article was entitled 'Pomp' and the choice of theme is quite remarkable. Munro writes about a funeral he watched twenty years earlier during his visit to Italy. This Catholic funeral must have moved him very much, as he could still recall every detail of it in 1930. The burial of a young Italian girl who was loved and admired for her respectability and devoutness was the last recollection Munro shared with his readers in the 'Mr Incognito' column. This was his farewell to the newspaper world. Neil Munro died in December 1930.

'Random Recollections of Mr Incognito' are not only delightful articles to read even today; they also form an important part of the available materials for those interested in Neil Munro. The recollections back to his first eighteen years in Inveraray show a young boy full of ideas, hungry for knowledge and open to new directions. Whether it is the installation of a simple telephone device with his friend Charlie Maitland, or taking part in the organising of local elections, he is always passionate about his task. The hunger for knowledge finds its nourishment in books, any books which he can lay his hands on, until he finds a better choice of classic works by leading Scottish, English and foreign authors. The author we encounter in 'Random Recollections' is a man of many interests and passions, a friend of writers and other artists, a man with forward-looking views on environment and progress. Neil Munro was an inspired person and gifted journalist and novelist. The examination of his journalistic work creates a valuable contribution to the understanding and interpretation of his fictional works and it is time to bring these two parts of his work together in order to gain a full picture of his part in Scottish literature.

Notes

1   Power, William, *Literature and Oatmeal*, London 1935. p.167.f
2   *Cf.* Wittig, Kurt, *The Scottish Tradition in Literature*, Edinburgh, London 1958. p.270ff.
3   *Cf.* Bold, Alan, *Modern Scottish Literature*, London, New York 1983, p.171ff and Beth Dickson, 'Foundations of the Modern Scottish Novel' in: *The History of Scottish Literature*, Vol. 4. Ed. Cairns Craig. Aberdeen 1987. pp.49–60.
4   The Mitchell Library owns two volumes with cuttings of all 'Mr Incognito's' articles which was presented to the library anonymously. The reference number for both volumes is GC f 920 MUN
5   'Mr Incognito's' article no. 1, 'Glasgow's First Talking Machines', 6 November 1928, in: *Daily Record and Mail*
6   Munro, Neil, *The Brave Days*, Edinburgh: The Porpoise Press, 1931. 'Introduction' by George Blake, pp.7–24. Quoted from p.7
7   'Mr Incognito's' article no. 28, 'Battlefield Buttinsky's', 26 February 1929
8   For this article see *The Brave Days*, pp.54–8
9   See *The Brave Days*, p.96
10 *Ibid.*, p.51
11 *Ibid.*, p.37
12 The names Munro used in his article ('Darroch' and a 'Miss Lavinia Darroch') are fictitious
13 Munro, Neil, *The Looker-On*, Edinburgh: The Porpoise Press, 1933. p.35
14 *Ibid.*, p.278
15 A good source for Munro's correspondence is: Völkel, Hermann, *Das literarische Werk Neil Munros*. Frankfurt *et al.* 1996
16 Munro does not give the name of his teacher in the article quoted below, but since Henry Dunn Smith was his main teacher in Inveraray, it may be assumed that he was meant here. Lesley Lendrum pointed this out to me
17 *The Looker-On*, p.58
18 From Neil Munro's diary kept in the National Library of Scotland, MS 26925, entry from 18 June 1891
19 No. 58, 'An Old Reliability Trial', 20 June 1929
20 Lord Cockburn (1779–1854) was an advocate and judge. Educated in Edinburgh, Cockburn travelled in Scotland during the 1830s and described his journey in *Circuit Journeys*, published posthumously in 1888. Other publications include: *The Life of Lord Jeffrey* (Edinburgh, 1852); *Memorials of His Time* (Edinburgh, 1856); *Journal*, 2 volumes (Edinburgh, 1874). As a Whig Cockburn welcomed reform, but his writings also show his sentimental regret for aspects of the past and a deep concern with the loss of Scottish cultural

identity
21 Both quotations are taken from No. 88, 'Rural Preservation', 22 October 1929
22 *Ibid.*
23 *The Brave Days*, p.113
24 The photograph can be found in the National Library of Scotland in Neil Munro's files
25 *The Brave* Days, p.234
26 No. 91, 'First Steps to Horsemanship', 31 October 1929
27 *The Brave Days*, p.137
28 *Ibid.*, p.138
29 *Ibid.*, p.143
30 In an introduction to the latest anthology of modern Scottish drama, Cairns Craig and Randall Stevenson list the Scottish Repertory Theatre as an example of an early attempt to revive Scottish drama and theatre: 'Until the Second World War, serious theatre in Scotland remained almost entirely a matter of short-lived professional organisations and long-running amateur groups. The example of the Abbey Theatre in Dublin encouraged both the Scottish Repertory Theatre in Glasgow in the years before the First World War – an early inspiration for James Bridie – and the establishment in the 1920s of the Scottish National Players, who organised regular seasons in Glasgow and tours of the Scottish regions.' Cairns Craig, Randall Stevenson (ed.), *Twentieth-Century Scottish Drama. An Anthology.* Edinburgh: Canongate, 2001. Introduction, pp.vii–xiv. Quoted from p.viii
31 No. 3, 'Forty Years Syne', 13 November 1928
32 *Cf.* article no. 52 of 28 May 1929 'The Outer Isles' (this article can also be found in *The Looker-On*, pp.85–9) and no. 99 of 3 December 1929 'Father Allan, Eriskay' (this can be also found in *The Brave Days*, pp.302–8)
33 *The Brave Days*, p.296

The Modern Novel

NEIL MUNRO

*Text of a lecture given at Stirling's and Glasgow Public Library
on 10 April 1906*

You have had, of recent years, men of such academic training and
distinction address you at these annual meetings, that I, who have
neither, am somewhat surprised at my own temerity in consenting
to be here at all. I am the more diffident in asking for a little of your
time and attention to-day because, unlike most of my predecessors
here, I have no striking information to impart, and no counsel to
offer, and have chosen for the subject of my desultory remarks, a
theme for which it has become the custom to be rather apologetic.
It is only since I have learned on what weighty topics you have been
addressed by previous speakers at these annual meetings that I
recognise how bold I have been in assuming that the Modern Novel
is really worth speaking about to the members of a serious and
dignified institution like the Stirling Library. No doubt I ought to
have selected some more recondite and momentous topic for
consideration – the Greek drama (if I happened to know anything
about it), or the future of English poetry, for instance – but
momentous issues are, unhappily, not in my line, and I venture to
assume that no inconsiderable proportion of you may be almost as
much interested in the novel as I am. Of course we are interested in
other forms of literature too – it is never necessary to be apologetic
about them – but I think I may safely calculate that even among a
peculiarly bookish body of men and women like the members of the
Stirling Library, fiction, for most of them, occupies more of their
leisure than poetry, biography, history or any other single department of letters. At least I find it is so even among some of my
studious and earnest friends who assure me they have no time for
reading novels. When put to the question, I find that they go through
a great many more novels in the year than they think they do.

The fascination of fiction ought to be more remarkable when we
consider that the professional critical attitude towards the modern
novel in the abstract is one mainly contemptuous. There are few

periodicals you can take up in which you will not discover from time to time some righteous indictment of the public taste for what used to be termed light literature. Worthy men, for the most part anonymous, and generally suspected of having, themselves, written novels which nobody would publish, deplore the patent fact that the vast bulk of reading of the public takes the form of fiction, and they never weary of telling us either directly or inferentially, that the production of decent fiction worth reading practically ceased half-a-century ago. They themselves, it is to be supposed, barricaded themselves up behind full tree-calf editions of Scott and Thackeray, and George Eliot, and have never succumbed, even momentarily, to the economic attractions of the sixpenny reprint. Perhaps, if we made inquiry we should find that this expressed contempt for the modern novel, when it is not the result of old age and its prejudices – the result of that ossification of the human interest which we ought to stave off as long as we can – is sheer cant.

Singularly enough, in the very same periodicals, and as I sometimes suspect, from the very same pens, you will find many new novels praised in such superlative terms that you must wonder what adjectives would be at their command if a new Scott or a new Dickens appeared on the scene. As it happens, however, professional criticism has very little influence on the preferences of a people as a whole, and the world at large pays no attention. It goes on deliberately reading novels for the simple reason that it likes reading novels. In a measure it cannot help itself. For the novel, in some form or other, is the first, the oldest of the arts that appeal to the imagination, destined to eternal popularity because all men like and will like a story, and because the world has learned and will go on learning its morality by means of the fable, apologue, allegory or parable. What other printed matter to-day is better calculated to influence human character? Poetry meanwhile marks time, our poets all apparently deriving their inspiration from books and not from life; the study of history has become so purely objective a business, that there are no unalloyed heroes and no thorough scoundrels left to us, and so history has fallen so hopelessly into the hands of the Dryasdusts, that new histories merely bore the public. The drama, even if it were not in so pathetic a condition as its devotees say it is, is by its very nature restricted in its influence, for we go to the theatre only now and then, but we are reading every day. It is in the novel then that the majority of reading mankind learn most that they know of life and manners, of philosophy, of art, even of religion and science. It inculcates a higher morality than is found in the actual world. It is the only book which the great mass of reading mankind ever read, or enables them to learn what other men and women are like: it is an unfailing source of delight to millions. 'So much novel-reading cannot leave the young men and maidens untouched,' wrote Emerson, 'and doubtless it gives some ideal dignity to the day. The young study noble behaviour, and, as the player in 'Consuelo' insists that he and his colleagues on the board have taught princes the fine etiquette and strokes of grace and dignity which they practise with so much effect in their villas and among their dependents, so I often see traces of the Scotch or the French novel in the courtesy and brilliancy of young mid-shipmen, collegians, and clerks. Indeed, when one observes how ill and ugly people make their loves and quarrels, 'tis a pity they should not read novels more, to import the fine generosities, and the clear, firm conduct, which are as becoming in the unions and separations which love effects under shingle roofs as in palaces, and among illustrious personages.'

These words of Emerson were written a good many years ago, but they still apply, and the increasing popularity of the novel need cause no distress. That common assumption of the scholar, that every devotee of fiction is a possible lover of poetry and the classics spoiled, has no warrant in human nature. Fiction-reading never yet monopolised wholly the time of anyone naturally equipped for study in other departments of literature; on the contrary it has been and will be the means of introducing many into fields of literature that but for fiction they would never have wandered into.

But, ladies and gentlemen, I am not going to set up, here and now, any unnecessary defence of novel-reading, which, of course may be overdone like any other kind of reading. That is a point on which I feel sure you may be left to your own convictions. I feel more inclined to consider whether there is reason for the frequent wholesale denunciation of the art of the modern novel on the part of the professional critics I have alluded to, whether the novel has seen its best days, whether it is capable of improvement, and whether there is any certainty of its further development. Here, I suppose, I must part company with the critics and the curmudgeons who labour under the extraordinary delusion that the full capabilities of an art, which took its present form only about 150 years ago, were exhausted in less than a hundred years. I have a few friends who say, 'I find Scott and Dumas sufficient for me as far as fiction goes,' which is a frame of mind quite defensible. But when, with an exasperating air of self-complacence they go on to let me know their conviction that there never will be any more new novels worth reading, and plume themselves on the fact that they are always better engaged than to waste their time on modern fiction, they suggest pitifully that type of art amateur who never goes to picture galleries except in Italy, and has given up all hope of painting now that Raphael's dead. With that kind of critic we have nothing to do; he is impossible. The other type who *does* sample modern fiction, and declares it pretty poor stuff on the whole, is entitled to more consideration. They are certainly able to prove that the great majority of new novels in circulation fall far short of perfection. It would be a surprising art and a surprising age indeed in which there were more masterpieces than mediocrities.

I am unable to say at the moment exactly how many novels are published each year in the British Islands. It is certainly an extraordinarily large number. Fortunately you never see more than a small proportion of them even in circulating libraries, for a great many are published at the expense of the authors, and the publisher's costs and commission having been paid, and a certain number of copies having been sent by him to the newspapers, there his interest ceases. There are hundreds of novels issued each year which you never see, which you never hear of – that painful necessity rests wholly with the burdened book-reviewer who is accustomed to sum them up perfunctorily in a phrase like 'the plot is very ingenious, and once taken up the book will not be readily put down again,' or 'the story is a sweet and tender love-idyl, with many delightful, descriptive passages.' No doubt when Stirling's Library readers see a book reviewed in that spirit they understand at once it is exactly the sort of book they can dispense with.

Why should there be so many people – most of them without any natural equipment for it – writing novels? To answer that question I must take you back 150 years – to the year 1750. It was the period of Richardson, Fielding and Smollett. The population of the three kingdoms then was ten millions; the working classes, speaking generally, could not read at all, and it has been estimated by the late Sir Walter Beasant that at that time the total number of persons interested in new books numbered no more than 30,000. Seventy-six years ago, the population was twenty-four millions, but the great bulk of the people were not yet readers; there was practically no demand for books in our Colonies or in America, and the buyers of English books are estimated by the same authority to have numbered less than 50,000, not that so many would, or could buy them, but that there were so many readers at the outside. It was towards the close of the Scott period. The publication of a new novel was almost as momentous as the launch of a ship. Scott indeed came upon the scene at a time when people did not buy novels at all, though they 'formed libraries' as the phrase went, for fiction had been steadily declining until it had become a literature of crime, insanity, and nightmare. He opened the flood-gates of fiction on Britain and the English-speaking world; indeed, he turned the whole civilised world into readers of novels. The fact that his novels cost a guinea each – and doubtless they were worth it – did not affect their sale to any great extent, for his books were bought by all the people who had the taste for books and who could afford to buy them.

Now we will turn to the present day. What is the area open to the book market? The population of the British Isles which was ten millions 150 years ago and twenty-four millions 75 years ago is now swollen to over forty millions, and in this country, the colonies and in America there are 150 millions of possible readers as compared with 50,000 sixty years ago. Everybody can read and everybody reads – novels. It is such a temptingly expansive field that is thus presented for the commercial enterprise of the race that it is no wonder so many writers try to make some money out of it. And here enters another influence unknown sixty years ago, for we not only can all read nowadays, but we can all write; at least we all think we can. The inclination to story-telling – like the spirit of song – is latent in all of us; what could be more natural, therefore, than that we should all be tempted to put our stories on paper? There seems, to the superficial eye, little difficulty about writing a story. Everyone proverbially has within himself the material of at least one novel; everyone, almost, can write passable grammar; all that is required is plenty of paper, pen and ink. No other art in existence can be invaded so cheaply, and we are being trained as novelists from the first day we make pot-hooks. But up till twenty years ago, while the three-volume novel still persisted, the cost of production kept the amateur out of the market and the output of novels within reasonable bounds. The introduction of the six shilling novel, with all that it involved, and the extraordinary reduction in the cost of paper as well as the no less remarkable reduction in the cost of printing, due to the Linotype composing machine, were the immediate causes of our position to-day. It led to the start of many cheap publishers and to the bewildering multitude of cheap authors. The ambitious amateur can now have his work set out upon the book-stalls if he is willing to pay a sum equivalent to the price of a pianola, while the publisher can venture upon the floating of any new novel without the risk of any loss whatever, so it is no wonder he should be flooding the market with all kinds of fiction, good, bad. or indifferent.

For, coming now to the really important matter, there is, of course, good fiction being produced as well as indifferent. We must not take the professional critics too seriously when they bewail the barrenness of the land. When they take up that position it is either for the purely personal reasons I have delicately suggested or for the sake of rhetorical effect. There is no publishing season in which there is not produced one or two novels which in their human interest and artistic structure are immensely superior to a good many others that come down to us with all the weight of classical names. I am very tempted to air some of my own heresies here, but you have no time for that, and even if you had I have no time to defend them afterwards as I should probably have to do. But while I discreetly let sleeping dogs lie, I am, I hope, at liberty to say that the taste of the discriminating readers, who must always be a mere minority of readers generally, is steadily improving, and the art of the novel, where it is practised not as a matter of purely commercial exploitation but with ardour and love, is no less steadily advancing.

There would be no use of my making these assertions unless I could back them up with example. Take the claim I make for cultured readers that they are more discriminating readers of novels than their fathers or grandfathers were, and I appeal to the experience of George Meredith. His novels, many of which were contemporary with those of George Eliot, Thackeray, or Dickens, were far too subtle for our fathers; they demanded more brains for their comprehension than an age could give them which looked upon the novel as something concerned with costume and gesture primarily, and having nothing legitimately to do with the mysteries of the mind of man. Meredith, a psychologist as much as a tale-teller – though a noble tale-teller, too, in spite of what I humbly think his too common abuse of the English language – has poetry, romance, wit, and humour in as great a degree as any of his great predecessors, but he has realised more profoundly than any of them the mighty resources of the novel as a revelation of life. It is the age that welters in novels – as the saying goes – which has understood him, or could understand him; up till twenty years ago or less, he was as caviare to his age as if he had been wholly – as he is only in part – a poet in verse. To-day we appreciate Meredith without surrendering in the least degree our admiration for the Titan elemental genius of Scott; we have extended the bounds of our pleasure, and I fancy a wholesome new delight that does not destroy our old ones is a great gain.

So much for the reader's progress. And coming to the writer of novels, I believe that in the present generation he has, like Meredith, though in different ways, greatly broadened the scope of his art, and made it the vehicle of emotions and aesthetic messages undeveloped at any earlier period. I think he is unfortunately lacking in discernment who would deny that Thomas Hardy is worthy of a place in the hierarchy of English imaginative writers. To many of us his stories, especially his earlier stories, are a perpetual delight, because they open up regions of thought and feeling untouched by any who came before him. He has made the earth speak as no other writer of prose in the last century did. Plains, valleys, cliffs and towers, dawn, darkness, weather, and the stars are not, in his books, mere flatly-painted back-cloths, as the stage calls it, but have vitality, soul and impulse. His beautiful prose invests nature with moods as certainly as the poetry of Wordsworth does, though it may not leave behind the same comfort and elation that are in the Ode on Intimations of Immortality. He has realised for us that the play of human passion does not take place in a vacuum tube, that in every form of being there is an active principle, that life animates all things. The stars of midnight have been dear to him, and he has leaned his ear in many a secret place. And from many minor novelists you will find that they have learned something from Hardy, in this intimacy with the soul of all created things, an intimacy peculiar to the modern novel, and carried to exquisite lengths in the work of W.H.Hudson, whose books, though as yet little known I fear, are likely to please the discerning long after we have discovered the emptiness of the detective story, the tale of smart society life, and the outworn fable of intrigue.

It is in the combination of romance, realism, humanity, and poetic perception that, I fancy, the future of the novel lies; it is in the search for this combination in a skilful solution that I think the highest triumphs of the modern novel have been achieved, and if you want to realise how much more profound, how much more moving, how much finer in every way the new man with loftier ideals and deeper insight can treat old themes than they were treated by the pioneers therein, I would refer you to the sea stories of Joseph Conrad and invite you to compare them with the stories in which Smollett for the first time brought the real sea into novels and gave his characters the veritable odour of tar. We scarcely knew the actual sea, which is our heritage, till Joseph Conrad, a foreigner by birth, at least a man whose mother tongue is not English, gave us stories of the sea that are perfect in their diction and invest the salt and plangent world with sweet new terrors for the imagination; that show

how much was still to be done, how far the novel of the sea was still
to be carried beyond the point at which Marryat, Fenimore Cooper,
or Clark Russell brought it.

Just as the world expands – that is to say, just as our knowledge of
the habitable globe increases, and philosophy and science open up
new vistas, and the apparent meaning of our brief sojourn here
becomes clearer, there will always be men who will adapt the old
fable to our new conceptions. There can be no standing still. I do
not know what your opinion may be of Mr. Kipling, but even if you
may think his imperial lust not the noblest kind of inspiration, you
must be prepared to sink your political repugnances for the moment
and admit that he had directly or indirectly for some time the most
powerful influence of any man of his generation on the thought of
his fellow-countrymen. More than any other he illustrates my
contention that the novel must march abreast with the race. He
discovered aspects of the world to which we had hitherto been blind.
The clanging, somewhat brassy note of imperialism is by no means
the most universally esteemed of his characteristics, what is really
valuable in him is his appreciation of the teeming interests, the
human activities of to-day. Man the artificer, 'the disease of the
agglutinate dust, lifting alternate feet,' he has seen in the light of
comprehensive humanity and brotherhood. Ships thrashing the
seas, armies combating fever, heathendom and death, railways
roaring over continents, pioneers, outposts of progress, marine
engines and motor cars – all these things have made a new earth
whose emotional meanings few people realised till Kipling taught
them. He taught us:

'For to admire and to see
For to behold this world so wide.'

He wrested new meanings from our sinful lives. He rescued the
novel from the hands of preachers, propagandists, and bookish
people – the worst people in the world to tell us stories and show us
what things mean. Just when the material of conventional fiction and
poetry had become spread out thin almost to invisibility and the
problem novel was sending us all to the contemplation of our own
insides, he brought us back to a world where people, as in the days
of Scott, were eternally doing things and not simply whining at
existence. In other words, he gave the novel a fresh start, as Scott
did, as Meredith did, as Hardy did. And literature in prose or poetry
is saved periodically from eternal perdition by fresh starts.

Perhaps some of you may be surprised that I have not sooner introduced the name of Robert Louis Stevenson. There is no modern novelist I like better, but I think Stevenson's work, beautiful though it is, was not a fresh start, and so he does not quite come within the scope of my argument. He simply carried on the romantic traditions of Scott and Dumas, and brought them to that pitch of refinement where it is almost impossible to go further, and refinement is the last stage that precedes decay. And yet Stevenson, working in a convention nearly outworn, contributed his own share to the progressive elements of fiction; he took his characters off stilts in their talk, a posture they had somewhat too often even in Scott. The fresh start is more apparent in the work of Mr. Barrie. *The Window in Thrums*, and its successors are constructed with more art than the stories of John Galt; their humour is more refined than Galt's, though he has nothing like the sheer physique of Galt, who worked at his trade like a blacksmith. The charm of his work lies in his having tried to forget all stock situations and stereotyped characters and gone back to the native kailyard with *naivete* and fresh vision. His contributions to the modern novel are not like the work of some of his compatriots, contemporaries, and imitators, merely of passing interest, they are more than documents for the future study of the philologist and the local historian; they rise in their treatment of things from the particular to the general and everlasting truths of human consciousness and conduct; they will, some of them, become classics like *Cranford*.

There are, then, as I started out to say, at least a few novelists living who have proved the vitality of their art by considerably developing it from the art they got from Scott, the father of them all. The men I have named have given the novel psychological subtilty (*sic*) (not so dreadful as it sounds once you have got used to it), mystical insight, closer observation of detail than it had before. You may say that it is all very well, but that most of these men did their best work years ago, and that half-a-dozen men who write well do not make up for the vast and nameless corps who write novels, if not all badly, at least too often without distinction, without any apparent call from a native genius. But, personally, I think we ought to be content if we only get a first rater or two in a generation; it is probably as much as was ever got in any art in any age among any people. And of the great mass of minor new novels, it can be said that on the whole the average is higher than it ever was before. It is with the extraordinary cleverness and interest of novels by men and women who are not considered of the first class, that one is very often most impressed.

That they are not recognised as greatly superior to the bulk of the old classic second-raters is doubtless due to some extent to the multitude of them. At least their ideals are right; they feel, the best of them, that they work in a fascinating medium which is still under-going modification in structure and content, and they feel that the greatest novels are still to be written.

Neil Munro as a young man

Bibliography

JAMES BEATON

1. The Short Story Collections and Monograph writings of Neil Munro

The Lost Pibroch and Other Sheiling Stories
Edinburgh : William Blackwood, 1896.
[6], 285p.
Gaelic glossary on pages 283–5.
This edition does not contain the story 'Jus Primae Noctis'. This was first included in the Inveraray edition of 1935, in which 'The Lost Pibroch...' was published along with 'Ayrshire Idylls' and 'Jaunty Jock'.

Translations
The Lost Pibroch and Other Sheiling Stories / translated into Gaelic by Archd. MacDonald
Inverness : Northern Chronicle Office, 1913.
56p.

Am Port Mór a Bha air Chall agus Sgeulachdan Eile na h-Àiridh / eadarthangaichte bho an Bheurla Sassunaich gu Gàidhlig Albannaich leis an Urramach G. MacDhomhnuill.
Inbhirnis : Comunn Foillseachaidh na h-Airde Tuath, [1934].
[8], 100, [1]p.

John Splendid : The Tale of a Poor Gentleman and The Little Wars of Lorne.
Edinburgh : William Blackwood, 1898.
viii, 363p.
Coloured Frontispiece, entitled 'The Land of the Little Wars' and 'A Part of the Shire of Argile by Neill Bane in Kenmore', with the journeys of John Splendid and Elrigmore delineated in red.

Transatlantic Editions
New York : Dodd, Mead and Company, 1898
475p.

Toronto : Copp, Clark, 1898
475p.

Translation
Iain Áluinn / aithinnsint Gaedhilge a rinn Seán Tóibín ar 'John Splendid' do scríobh Dr Neil Munro.
Baile Atha Cliath : Oifig Díolta Foillseacháin Rialtais, 1931.
345p.
Includes map entitled 'Alba Gaedhal'
A second impression (dara cur-amach) of this work appeared in 1936.

Gilian the Dreamer : His Fancy His Love and Adventure.
London : Isbister and Company, 1899
400p.

Transatlantic edition
Toronto : Copps Clark Company 1898.
400p.

Translation
Gaoileán na n-aisling / Donn Piatt a rinne an leagán Gaedhilge.
Baile Atha Cliath : Oifig an t-Sólathair, 1940
499p.

Doom Castle : a Romance
Edinburgh : William Blackwood and Sons, 1901
vi, 322p.

Transatlantic editions
New York : Doubleday, Page and Company, 1901
vi, 385p. [1] leaf of plates : illustrated.

Toronto : Copps Clark Company ; Edinburgh : William Blackwood and Sons, 1901
vi, 322p.
This appears to be the U.K printing of the book, distributed in Canada by Copps Clark. In a letter dated 1 August 1900 to G W Blackwood, the author notes, 'The arrangement you intimate with the Copps Clark

Comp. for the Canadian rights is quite satisfactory and you may conclude with them accordingly.' (National Library of Scotland, MS 4705, f28)

The Shoes of Fortune : How They Brought to Manhood Love Adventure and Content as Also Into Divers Perils on Land and Sea in Foreign Parts and in an Alien Army Paul Greig of the Hazel Den in Scotland One Time Pursuer of 'The Seven Sisters' Brigantine of Hull and Late Lieutenant in the Regiment D'Auvergne All as Writ by Him and Now for the First Time Set Forth.
Illustrated by A. S. Boyd.
London : Isbister and Company, 1901.
403p., [8] leaves of plates. : illustrated.

Transatlantic Editions
New York : Dodd, Mead, 1901.
vii, 344p.

Children of Tempest : a Tale of the Outer Isles.
Edinburgh : William Blackwood and Sons, 1903.
298p.

Translation
Muinntir Inis Anaithe / aith-insinnt i nGaedhilg a rinn Seán Tóibin, M.A. ar 'Children of Tempest' do scríobh Neil Munro.
Baile Atha Cliath : Oifig Díolta Foillseacháin Rialtais, 1933.
vii, 346p.

Erchie : my Droll Friend / by Hugh Foulis (The Looker-On)
Edinburgh : William Blackwood and Sons, 1904.
viii, 191p., [4] leaves of plates : illustrated.

The Vital Spark
Edinburgh : William Blackwood and Sons, 1906.
[6], 183,[1]p. : illustrated.

The Clyde : River and Firth
London : Adam and Charles Black ; Glasgow : printed at the

James Beaton

University Press by Robert Maclehose and Co. Ltd., 1907.
x, [i], 205, [1] p., [68] leaves of plates, 1 of which is folded.
The folded leaf is a map entitled 'A Sketch Map of the Clyde'

The Daft Days.
Edinburgh : William Blackwood, 1907.
[4], 281p.

Translation
Nuppu : romaani / englanninkielestä suom. Värnö Jaakola
Helsinki : Kirja, 1923.
232p.

Transatlantic edition
Bud : a novel.
New York : Harper and Brothers, 1907.
[4], 314, [1]p., 1 leaf of plates : illustrated.
The illustration is a frontispiece signed 'W. Strang'.

Fancy Farm
Edinburgh : William Blackwood and Sons, 1910
[4], 318p.

In Highland Harbours with Para Handy S.S. 'Vital Spark' / by Hugh
Foulis
Edinburgh : William Blackwood and Sons, 1911.
[4], 204p.

Ayrshire Idylls.
Illustrated by George Houston.
London : Adam and Charles Black ; Edinburgh : printed by R & R
Clark, Limited, 1912
x, 139p., 20 leaves of plates : illustrated, some colour.

The New Road.
Edinburgh : William Blackwood and Sons, 1914
vi, 374p.

Transatlantic edition
Toronto : Musson Book Co, [1914?]
vi, 374p.
The pagination suggests that this is the UK edition distributed in
Canada by Musson.

Jimmy Swan the Joy Traveller
Edinburgh : William Blackwood, 1917.
vi, 312p.

Jaunty Jock and Other Stories
Edinburgh : William Blackwood and Sons, 1918.
[6], 304p.

Hurricane Jack of the Vital Spark.
Edinburgh : William Blackwood, 1923.
vi, 142p.

The History of the Royal Bank of Scotland 1727–1927.
Edinburgh : Privately Printed by R & R Clark, Limited, 1928.
xviii, 416, [1] p., [20] leaves of plates : illustrated.

The Brave Days : A Chronicle from the North.
With an Introduction by George Blake.
Edinburgh : The Porpoise Press, 1931
334p.

> *Transatlantic edition*
> The Scotland I Remember : a Chronicle of the Brave Days in the
> North
> Toronto : McClelland and Stewart Limited., [1931?]
> 334p.
> *This title and imprint are found on the dust jacket, but the book is
> otherwise that published by the Porpoise Press.*

The Poetry of Neil Munro / with Preface by John Buchan.
Edinburgh : William Blackwood, 1931.
87p.

The Looker-On / with an Introduction by George Blake
Edinburgh : The Porpoise Press, 1933.
307p.

Modern Scholarly editions

John Splendid : the Tale of a Poor Gentleman and the Little Wars
of Lorn / Introduced by Brian D. Osborne.
Edinburgh : B&W Publishing, 1994
xvi, 334p., map.

The New Road / Introduction by Brian D. Osborne
Edinburgh : B&W Publishing, 1994
xi, 345p., map.

The Lost Pibroch and Other Sheiling Stories / with an Introduction
by Ronnie Renton. Notes by Rennie McOwan and Rae MacGregor.
Colonsay : House of Lochar, 1996
xii, 116p.

Jaunty Jock and Other Stories / with an Introduction and Notes by
Ronnie Renton and Lesley Bratton.
Colonsay : House of Lochar, 1999
xv, 104p.

Gilian the Dreamer / Introduced by Douglas Gifford
Edinburgh : B&W Publishing, 2000
xxiii, 295p.

Para Handy : the Collected Stories from 'The Vital Spark', 'In
Highland Harbours with Para Handy' and 'Hurricane Jack of the
Vital Spark' : with Nineteen Previously Uncollected Stories /
Introduced and Annotated by Brian D. Osborne and Ronald
Armstrong.
Edinburgh : Birlinn, 2002
xiv, 435p. : ill.

Erchie, My Droll Friend; with One Hundred and Thirteen Uncollected Stories. Introduced and Annotated by Brian D. Osborne and Ronald Armstrong.
Edinburgh : Birlinn, 2002
xxviii, 629p

Jimmy Swan, the Joy Traveller; with Seven Uncollected Stories. Introduced and Annotated by Brian D. Osborne and Ronald Armstrong.
Edinburgh, Birlinn, 2002
xxvii, 176p.

That Vital Spark; A Neil Munro Anthology. Edited and introduced by Brian D Osborne and Ronald Armstrong.
Edinburgh, Birlinn, 2002
vii, 320p.

2. Select Critical Bibliography

Bold, Alan, *Modern Scottish Literature,* London and New York: Longman, 1983
Burgess, Moira, *Imagine a City: Glasgow in Fiction,* Glendaruel: Argyll Publishing, 1998
Campbell, Ian, *Kailyard,* Edinburgh: Ramsay Head Press, Edinburgh, 1981
Craig, Cairns (Ed), *The History of Scottish Literature: Vol 4 Twentieth Century*: Aberdeen: Aberdeen University Press, 1987
Dickson, Beth, 'Foundations of the Modern Scottish Novel' in Craig 1987 (pp49–60)
Gifford, Douglas (Ed), *The History of Scottish Literature: Vol 3 Nineteenth Century*: Aberdeen University Press, 1988
Gifford, Douglas, Dunnigan Sarah, MacGillivray, Alan (Eds), *Scottish Literature,* Edinburgh: Edinburgh University Press, 2002
Grierson, H.J.C., *Edinburgh Essays on Scots Literature,* Edinburgh: Oliver & Boyd, 1933
Grieve, Christopher, Murray, 'Neil Munro', *Contemporary Scottish Studies,* Edinburgh: The Scottish Educational Journal, 1925
Hart, Francis Russell, *The Scottish Novel: A Critical Survey,* London: John Murray, 1978
Lindsay, Maurice, *History of Scottish Literature,* London: Robert Hale, 1977

Macdonald, Angus, 'Modern Scots Novelists' in Grierson 1933 (pp144–76)

Mackechnie, Donald, *The Inveraray of Neil Munro*, 1936

Mackechnie, Donald, *Inveraray Notes*, Oban: The Oban Time, 1986

Mackechnie, Donald, *Inveraray Tales and Traditions*, 1990

Power, William, Literature and Oatmeal: What Literature Has Meant to Scotland, London: George Routledge and Sons, 1935

Renton, Ronald W., *The Major Fiction of Neil Munro:A Revaluation*, Unpublished M Phil Thesis, University of Glasgow, 1997

Reid, James, *Modern Scottish Literature*, Edinburgh: Oliver & Boyd, 1945

Völkel, Hermann, *Das literarische Werk Neil Munros*, Frankfurt: Peter Lang, 1996

Watson, Roderick, The Literature of Scotland, London: Macmillan, 1984

Wernitz, Herbert, Neil Munro und die nationale Kulturbewegung im modernen Schottland, Berlin: Junker und Dünnhaupt, 1937

Wittig, Kurt, *The Scottish Tradition in Literature*, Edinburgh: Oliver & Boyd, 1958

Inveraray Castle

240

Contributors

Ronald Armstrong
Born in 1940 in Dumbarton and spent all of his professional life in education. In a late career shift, however, he left the chalkface in 1989 to work with the advisory body for the curriculum in Scotland on the 5-14 Programme. Since retiral, he has been involved in consultative work with several national agencies. Professionally and privately, he has a particular interest in Scottish history, culture and literature and is co-author of a number of books and plays on Scottish subjects. Stage fright struck some years ago and he no longer treads the boards, but retains an enthusiasm for AmDram.

James Beaton
James Beaton is a native of Inveraray. Educated in Argyll, and at Edinburgh University, The Robert Gordon University and the University of Wales at Aberystwyth, he has held a number of library posts in London and Glasgow. Since 1995 he has been Librarian of the Royal College of Physicians and Surgeons of Glasgow. He has longstanding interests in the history of medicine and the languages, history and culture of Scotland.

Gerard Carruthers
Gerard Carruthers holds a PhD in Scottish Literary Criticism. He lectures in the Department of Scottish Literature at the University of Glasgow. He has published essays on Robert Burns, various aspects of eighteenth century Scottish culture, Muriel Spark and James Kelman. He is co-editor of the forthcoming *English Romanticism and the Celtic World* (Cambridge University Press, 2002).

Edward J. Cowan
Ted Cowan is Professor of Scottish History at the University of Glasgow, having previously taught at the universities of Edinburgh and Guelph, Ontario. He has written numerous books and articles on various aspects of Scottish History. He is frequently called upon as a keynote speaker in the USA and Canada, and has been on lecture tours of Australia and New Zealand as well as various

European countries. Recent publications include *The Ballad in Scottish History* (2000), *Scottish Fairy Belief: A History*, with Lizanne Henderson, (2001), *Scottish History: The Power of the Past*, with Richard Finlay, (2002) and *For Freedom Alone: The Declaration of Arbroath 1320* (2002).

Beth Dickson
Beth Dickson, a graduate of the universities of St Andrews and Strathclyde, teaches English at St Aloysius' College, Glasgow. Stemming from her postgraduate research on late nineteenth and early twentieth century Scottish fiction, she has published a number of articles on writers such as William MacIlvanney, Annie S. Swan, Willa Muir and A.L.Kennedy. She is a council member of the Association for Scottish Literary Studies and editor of its biannual news sheet *Scotlit*.

Douglas Gifford
Douglas Gifford holds the Chair of Scottish Literature at the University of Glasgow. Until recently he was Head of the Department of Scottish Literature, the world's only autonomous department in the subject. He has written and edited many books on Scottish literature, from studies of James Hogg, Lewis Grassic Gibbon and Neil Gunn to *The History of Scottish Literature: Volume3, Nineteenth Century* (1988) and (with Dorothy MacMillan) *A History of Scottish Women's Writing* (1997). With Professor Ted Cowan he edited *The Polar Twins: Scottish History and Scottish Literature* (1999). His latest production (with Sarah Dunnigan and Alan MacGillivray) is *Scottish Literature* (Edinburgh University Press, 2002), a mammoth reader's guide. He is a Fellow of the Royal Society of Edinburgh, Honorary Librarian of Walter Scott's Library at Abbotsford and Director of the Abbotsford Library Research Project.

Beata Kohlbek
Beata Kohlbek was born in 1969 in Poland. She took her MA degree at the Heinrich-Heine-University in Düsseldorf. In 1995 she was awarded the Hedwig and Waldemar Hort scholarship to research Scottish Renaissance Literature in Edinburgh which resulted in the completion of her MA thesis *Gunn & Gibbon and the Religion of the Unconscious* in 1997. Her studies in Scottish literature have since continued at the University of Glasgow, where she is completing her doctoral thesis. This examines the work of Neil Munro, reassessing

his contribution to the history of Scottish letters. Since 1998 Beata Kohlbek has taken part in the teaching programme of the Department of Scottish Literature in Glasgow. She is also involved in language tuition at Edinburgh University.

Published article: Der Reformgedanke in Thomas Mores *Utopia* und David Lindsays *Ane Satyre of the Thrie Estaitis*. In: Christoph M. Peters, Friedrich-K. Unterweg (eds.), *Thomas More and More. Freundesgabe für/Liber Amicorum for Hubertus Schulte Herbrüggen*. Frankurt a.M. et al.: Peter Lang, 2002.

Lesley Lendrum
Lesley Lendrum, one of Neil Munro's grandchildren, was born in Glasgow. Going to schools there and in Inveraray and Helensburgh meant she was familiar with Munro's world before starting to write her forthcoming biography. She studied modern languages at St Andrews and has had translations of German poetry published e.g. in *Bertolt Brecht: Poems 1913–1956* (Eyre Methuen, 1976). She is a founder member of The Neil Munro Society and co-editor of *Jaunty Jock and Other Stories* (House of Lochar,1999).

Rae MacGregor
Rae was born and raised in the Parish of Glenarary and Inveraray. She is descended from the MacLaren family who have worked on the Argyll Estate since 1845. Married to Peter MacGregor, she was a shepherd's wife in Glenshira. In 1980, thanks to the late Donald MacKechnie, she developed an interest in local history, and has since amassed a vast store of data about the town and parish. A member of the local History Society and a Fellow of the Society of Antiquaries (Scotland), she produced *Inveraray, A Pictorial History* in 1997, and is at present working with Brian Wilkinson on gathering information for a proposed history of Inveraray Shinty Club. She has long been interested in Neil Munro and is a founder member of The Neil Munro Society.

Rennie McOwan
A writer, broadcaster and lecturer who specialises in environmental and outdoor topics, Scottish culture and religion. He is a founder member of The Neil Munro Society. In addition to books on outdoor themes and newspaper and magazine articles, he writes children's novels which are used in Scottish schools. In 1996 he was given an honorary doctorate by Stirling University for his contribution to Scottish writing and culture. The following year he received

the Golden Eagle award from the Outdoor Writers Guild for access campaigning and writing on Scottish subjects. In 1998 he was given a Stirling Council's Provost's Civic Award. He describes himself as semi-retired and lives in Stirling with his wife Agnes.

Brian D. Osborne
Brian D. Osborne, BA, MCLIP, worked in libraries in Dumbarton and Midlothian ending up as Chief Officer: Libraries and Museums in Strathkelvin from 1989 to 1995, when he retired to concentrate on writing. Publications include *The Ingenious Mr Bell, Braxfield, the Hanging Judge?, The Last of the Chiefs* and *The Clyde at War* (the last with Ronald Armstrong). Other collaborations with Ronald Armstrong include the standard editions of Neil Munro's Para Handy, Erchie and Jimmy Swan stories and a series of Scottish literary anthologies. He has been Secretary of The Neil Munro Society since 1996.

Bob Preston
Born in Bournemouth in 1949, Bob moved to Somerset with his wife and 2 sons in 1985, where he works as a Building Surveyor. They live in a small village nestling between the Quantock and Brendon Hills, and when not enjoying his garden Bob likes to walk the hills with the family dog. He believes his interest in Scottish literature and poetry stems from his days at Bournemouth Grammar School where he was taught by an ardent 'Scot in exile'. He is currently compiling a complete collection of Neil Munro's poetry as well as working on an overview and history of the Glasgow Ballad Club and its Members.

Ronald W. Renton
Ronald W. Renton is Deputy Head Master of St Aloysius' College, Glasgow. He is currently Convener of the Schools and FE Committee of the Association for Scottish Literary Studies and Chairman of The Neil Munro Society. He was awarded the degree of M.Phil by Glasgow University for his thesis on *The Major Fiction of Neil Munro* in 1997. He has co-edited a pocket Gaelic dictionary and two collections of the short stories of Neil Munro.

Brian Wilkinson
Although born in Edinburgh, Brian was raised in Perthshire, Angus and Aberdeenshire, and has family roots in Mid Argyll. He is an Honours Geography and Divinity graduate of Edinburgh University

and at present Parish Minister of Glenaray and Inveraray. He is deeply involved in the life of the local community and has an interest in Highland and Irish, as well as local, history and culture. A committee member of Inveraray Shinty Club and a keen supporter of the game, he is involved with Rae MacGregor in gathering information for a proposed shinty history of Inveraray. He is also a founder member and Honorary President of The Neil Munro Society.

Neil Munro about ten years before his death